THE UNIVERSITY OF CHICAGO
SCIENCE SERIES

THE UNIVERSITY OF CHICAGO SCIENCE SERIES, established by the Trustees of the University, owes its origin to a belief that there should be a medium of publication occupying a position between the technical journals with their short articles and the elaborate treatises which attempt to cover several or all aspects of a wide field. The volumes of the series differ from the discussions generally appearing in technical journals in that they present the complete results of an experiment or series of investigations which previously have appeared only in scattered articles, if published at all. On the other hand, they differ from detailed treatises by confining themselves to specific problems of current interest, and in presenting the subject in as summary a manner and with as little technical detail as is consistent with sound method. They are written not only for the specialist but for the educated layman.

THE TWO SOLAR FAMILIES

THE SUN'S CHILDREN

THE UNIVERSITY OF CHICAGO PRESS
CHICAGO, ILLINOIS

THE BAKER & TAYLOR COMPANY
NEW YORK

THE MACMILLAN COMPANY OF CANADA, LIMITED
TORONTO

THE CAMBRIDGE UNIVERSITY PRESS
LONDON

THE MARUZEN-KABUSHIKI-KAISHA
TOKYO, OSAKA, KYOTO, FUKUOKA, SENDAI

THE COMMERCIAL PRESS, LIMITED
SHANGHAI

THE TWO SOLAR FAMILIES

THE SUN'S CHILDREN

By

THOMAS CHROWDER CHAMBERLIN

Professor Emeritus of Geology and Paleontology in the University of Chicago, and Research Associate in the Carnegie Institution of Washington

THE UNIVERSITY OF CHICAGO PRESS
CHICAGO · ILLINOIS

Published September 1928

Composed and Printed By
The University of Chicago Press
Chicago, Illinois, U.S.A.

PREFACE

Geological revolutions are slow to come, and they stay long. Revolutions of geological doctrine come faster and go sooner. When I was in college, catastrophic deluges were set forth as the critical events of the earth's history. Now and then "the fountains of the great deep" were broken up, and the heavens poured out their floods and destroyed all living things. Jupiter Pluvius and Neptune joined hands in displaying their power. The Diluvial theory was standard doctrine—"held by the most eminent authorities." And as eminence goes, these "authorities" stood forth as few later leaders have done. The text I studied was written by one of the foremost of American geologists. It taught specifically that at the close of the great eras all life was swept away; creations followed—each more advanced than the preceding—creative evolution in the most explicit sense. In particular, we were told, and with emphasis, that "not a single living species passed from the Paleozoic to the Mesozoic."

It may seem strange that views now held to be so untenable could have been standard belief so recently. But in reality is it any stranger than the history that is now repeating itself? Views dominant in the middle of the last century had their grounds of appeal and their seemingly natural interpretations. Marine fossils were found in beds high in the mountains and in strata spread over the middle of the continents. There were thick terranes that bore no fossils. There were great gaps in the fossil record.

But the theory of universally destructive deluges soon died—died of progressive studies in the very line to which it most appealed, the fossil record. The gaps that had indeed been great where they were first studied were gradually filled by later studies in other places. The closing of these gaps proved the continuity of life.

After Jupiter Pluvius and Neptune had failed to show full mastery, came Pluto; after the acceptance of the Diluvian concept, came the acceptance of the Hadean concept. This came easily and naturally, for the way had been prepared for it. For ages before this men of the Mediterranean region had seen Vesuvius, Aetna, Stromboli, Santonin, and other volcanoes pour out their lavas, now and then; and these outpours had led to imaginary "lakes of fire" below. The Greeks had given the concept classic expression and a name; the Romans had taken it over and handed it on. Dante and Milton had given it modern poetic settings; classical dictionaries, the old-fashioned preacher, and the low-fashioned profane had spread it among the people. No thought was taken by these as to what it might mean in a scientific sense; but none the less they prepared the soil, and the Plutonian view took root and flourished like a green bay tree. The poets were followed—or distanced—by the rounding out of the concept into a holo-molten earth descendant from a gaseous nebulous state. As the holo-molten earth cooled, it crusted over; and this crust was pictured as floating on its mobile bed. It was Pluto's turn to show his might. How has this later doctrine fared?

It seemed at first logical to look for outcrops of the original crust where it bulged outward and had been worn down to supply material to form beds elsewhere. We thought we found it. We found igneous granites on which lay beds carrying fossils of the oldest types then known. The geologists of other countries found similar relations. But later field work showed that in all these cases the granite had been pushed into or through beds formed on the surface and could not therefore be parts of the original crust. Continued field work revealed still older terranes one below another down to depths of several miles, as geologists reckon depth, without disclosing the original crust, but only an ever-deepening jacket of surface-formed terranes riveted by igneous intrusions.

The theory of a once molten state was thus forced to fall back for its evidence upon the outpours of lava. But progressive study is showing that these are fed from mere pockets of melting rocks. And, moreover, these are quite independent of one another below. If the lava pockets had any connection with a molten interior or a common substratum of liquid rock below, the lavas would obey hydrostatic laws and find exit on the bottoms of the deep basins.

It appears also that volcanoes are most common on mountain ridges. Lavas often pour out many thousand feet above the bottoms of adjacent basins. This fits the pocket principle well enough but drives home the conclusion that these lavas have no connection with a common liquid substratum below.

And so, just as the progressive study of fossils put the deluge theory on the shelf, so the outpours of lava seem to be putting the theory of a molten earth on the shelf beside it.

From three quite independent sources, concurrent evidences that the earth is an elastic solid have been coming fast in recent years. One source is the "wabbling" of the pole; one is the body tide; and one is the deep penetration of the interior by transverse seismic waves. Taken together, these have practically demonstrated that the outer seven-eighths of the earth is solid, in the elastic-rigid sense; the rest is yet to be determined. By this growing evidence of present solidity, the concept of a molten state is forced back into past history, if it has any place in earth history at all.

Still another cloud is gathering over the theory, but the storm is not yet on. This is the growing conviction that no crust resting on a mobile substratum is competent to offer the resistances implied by the stages of base-leveling, sea transgression, and parallel deposition which have followed one another from Archean times onward. It is further felt that no such crust, or thin shell of any kind, could accumulate the great elastic strains and stresses implied by the slow rhythmical readjustments and rejuvenations of the continents which have intervened between the eras of base-leveling. The challenge on this line has been quietly made; the issue belongs to the future.

The foregoing succession of concepts and trends of thought serves perhaps better than anything else to show the place and meaning of the studies that form this little book. They are its best preface. Its themes do not stand by themselves; they are essential parts of a great history. They center on the earth, to be sure, as the one accessible planet, for the earth is our only available contact-source of knowledge of this kind. It is the one source of those material vestiges of events and these hereditary traits by which we trace history concretely backward and forecast the future.

In the preparation of the book, Professors Forest Ray Moulton, William Duncan MacMillan, Rollin Thomas Chamberlin, and Walter Bartky have read all or at least parts of the manuscript and have made comments and criticisms of great value, for which the reader will join me in thankfulness. This aid, however, does not make them responsible for all the views expressed. To Drs. Moulton and MacMillan I have been under profound obligations throughout the whole study, which runs back to the closing of the last century. They have been especially helpful in the technical phases of the subject; indeed, their help has made the study possible to one who approached the subject from the geologic point of view and who has relied on the interpretation of vestiges and hereditary traits rather than celestial mechanics. Because of this vital aid, more than for any other reason, I shall make free use of the editorial "we" as best suited to a joint product; but now and then my colleagues will be freed from responsibility by the use of the first personal pronoun.

I am under very special obligations to Drs. Walter Bartky and Rollin T. Chamberlin for reading the proof.

For illustrative material, my cordial thanks are due to Director E. B. Frost and Dr. S. B. Barrett of Yerkes Observatory; to Director W. S. Adams and Mr. Ferdinand Ellerman of Mount Wilson Observatory; to Associate Director R. G. Aitken of Lick Observatory; to Director George Otis Smith and Senior Geologist M. R. Campbell of the U.S. Geological Survey; to Dr. George P. Merrill of the National Museum; to Dr. O. C. Farrington of the Field Museum; to Dr. J. P. Goode; and to Henry Holt and Company, as specifically noted in the text.

T. C. C.

TABLE OF CONTENTS

PART I

HISTORICAL AND CRITICAL

PART II. THE GENESIS OF THE PLANETARY FAMILY

PART III. THE GENESIS OF THE COMETARY FAMILY

INTRODUCTION

In any attempt to analyze the kinships of the attendants of the sun, two classes of bodies at once disclose themselves, one embracing the planets, planetoids, and satellites, the other embracing the comets, chondrulites, and meteorites. In a study of the genesis of these, it is appropriate to regard them as families, for their parentages are a matter of the first importance. Phrased in terms of kinship, they constitute the *Planetary Family* and the *Cometary Family—the two solar families.*

Certain of their traits and relations clearly imply that both these families are the offspring of the sun. Certain other traits and relations imply with equal clearness that each had another parentage. It is natural that they should owe their differences chiefly to this second parentage. We may thus catch at once an important key to the interpretation of their genetic traits. Both branches belong to the bi-parental order of genesis. One parent was common to both; the other was the chief differentiating factor.

There is no ground to doubt that both families had a common parentage from the sun. It is then logical to look to this common parentage for their similarities. It is equally logical to look to their diverse parentages for their dissimilarities and their incongruities.

To the planetary group we assign a passing star as the second parent; to the cometary group we assign a feebler co-operation on the part of the starry host outside the solar system. The offspring of the sun, itself a star, are thus assigned other stellar parentages also. The star-play of this other stellar part is the Hamlet of our drama.

In the genesis of the planetary family the contribution of the passing star was definite and pronounced. The traits of the family that arose from it were distinctive and vital, and gave character to the family. The contributions of the starry host to the cometary family were less definite and less concordant. They manifest themselves today in erratic behavior and moribund tendencies.

These are mere preliminary characterizations. We must wade through a wilderness of details before we reach these finalities, but a few glimpses of their ultimate emergence may serve as beacon lights on the horizon to cheer us as we struggle through the swamps and jungles of the cosmogonic wilderness. It should be especially cheering to us to foresee, at the outset, what the planetary children inherited from their stellar father, and how it has influenced all their subsequent careers—for we ourselves come of the planetary lineage.

The parental star in passing called forth larger masses of sun-substance than the sun was accustomed to give forth at other times, either before or after the star's visitation. Thus the planetary offspring were given relatively robust constitutions. But this was of less import than the dynamic endowment conferred by the star, a vital part of its own kinetic endowment, the kinetic energy of revolution. But for this endowment, the matter ejected from the sun would have turned back to it promptly and the episode would have ended as a trival eruptive event. The parental star not only gave the solar ejecta subcircular revolutions about the parental sun, but drew all the ejecta into a narrow disk oriented by its own motion. As a result, the whole planetary family has revolved ever since in a single concurrent direction in concentric orbits, forming a celestial whirl.

The planets thus became by inheritance *an orderly family of the most declared type*. There are few mechanisms in the known cosmos more orderly than the planetary system, and yet it is formed of very individual and independent members. This order, combined with individuality, has given opportunity to each planet to grow up in its own way in friendly and concurrent relations with the rest of the family. This has made not only for security but also for stability, and for prospective longevity.

No such unity and harmony was inherited by the cometary family. It fell heir to too much of the turbulence and the fiery antagonisms of the sun, and to too little of the revolutionary energies of the starry host outside, and that *little* was too inconstant and too diverse from episode to episode. Instead of being born to keep in a narrow disk and to follow the steady habits of the planetary family, the cometary group took to notoriously erratic ways. Instead of all going the same way, or all keeping in a narrow tract their courses were all-wayward. And yet their erraticisms are accompanied with spectacular brilliancy, as is often the case. The planets, planetoids, and satellites are plain plodding children compared with the comets, the meteors, and the meteorites. But the lives of the latter seem to be as notably short as they are spectacular and reckless in the wastage of their energies, while the lives of the former seem likely to be as long as they are modest, steady, and exemplary in the husbanding of their energies.

There should be no surprise that the diverse heredities of these two families found expression so far back among the events of the cosmos, if we are true derivationists, for if what *is* has evolved from *what has been*, then that which now actuates paternity and mentality should have lain concealed somewhere and somehow in the most distant sources from which the present has come. True evolution is supremely a doctrine of heredities, and heredities should follow as sure lines when things were simpler, as they do now when things have grown complex. The climax of evolution, as we see it, should not logically have come from that which was naught, or was an illusion, but from a genuine working reality.

Under genuine derivation, the chain of parentages should run back indefinitely, however hidden and elusive. Our story is merely that of an endeavor to trace the chain of parentages of our planet and its kin, as well as its wayward relatives, back to their stellar parentages.

PART I

HISTORICAL AND CRITICAL

It is essential to a clear understanding of the recent endeavors to disclose the genesis of our planet and its kin to know the main lines of previous endeavor and the chief hypotheses that were entertained during the last century, together with the reasons that led to their rejection. Part I of this book is therefore chiefly historical and critical, and a notable part of it is not new. Certain portions are taken over bodily from an earlier work by the author, *The Origin of the Earth*.

However, chapters ii, iii, and v depart notably from the previous treatment of the subjects to which they relate, while chapter iv is entirely new and relates to principles and generalizations of wide applicability.

The first chapter of this part gives a brief statement of the unusual and almost incidental way in which the author was drawn from studies in glacial geology to inquiries into the genesis of the earth. It is followed by general considerations growing out of the development of the kinetic theory of gases as this is related to the origin of the earth, but the part consists chiefly of destructive criticism of the earlier theories of the origin of the earth and the related bodies of the solar system.

CHAPTER I

PERSONAL ENTANGLEMENT

If it shall seem strange to anyone that a student of the story of the rocks should turn aside from a field so solid and congenial to venture wantonly into the nebulous wilds of cosmogony, I can only plead in defense the urgent necessities of the scientific chase. It came to be clear that only by close pursuit along the trail that led into the cosmogonic fens and fogs was there any hope of overhauling the quarry that had awakened my instincts of pursuit—a pack of sophistical sprites that had long been wont to vex a pet climatic enigma on whose solution I had set fond hopes. It may be some little further extenuation of my temerity to plead that, at the outset, the trail was picked up and the chase begun almost as far away as possible from the pass that led into the bogs and mists, and that at the start the trail was as cold as a glacier.

My early geologic work happened to fall in a tract that was overlain by a thick mantle of glacial drift and underlain by the sheeted sediments of the Paleozoic seas. Above, there was little but the products of the strange ice invasion; below, there was little within reach but the products of the ancient seas. Coral reefs and crinoid fields contested with moraines and drumlins the place of first affection. Early bias favored the sea life, but the glacial beds were uppermost in the field and soon came to be foremost in the zest of inquiry. How ice sheets could have crept so far south upon the low plains in the heart of our continent grew to be a more and more insistent puzzle as the verity of the invasion grew more and more incontestable. There were indeed inherited theories, but when these were brought to test by the precise realities of the record as it was met from day to day in the field, they seemed to limp under the burden of explanation they had taken upon themselves, and so, one after another, they were turned out to pasture as lame horses no longer fit to be ridden. New theories were sought in their place and ridden as far as they would go. Among the rest, an old suggestion of Tyndall's was saddled up and mounted with little thought of the outcome. This proved to be the mount that was to carry me into the fens and fogs of cosmogony.

Tyndall had found, in the course of his physical researches, that carbon dioxide was an efficient absorber of heat, and so he had entertained the suggestion that a deficiency of this gas in the atmosphere might be the cause of the low temperatures that gave rise to the ice sheets. The suggestion had been made so long before my day that it had been well-nigh forgotten. The probabilities seemed all against its tenability. Tyndall had neglected to point out any natural process by which such a former deficiency in carbon dioxide could have arisen, and had thus left the theory without a working basis; still, as a physicist, merely throwing out a suggestion incidental to the main line of his study, he had done all that could fairly be required of him. The history of the atmosphere, as then currently interpreted, looked quite the other way. It was generally held, in accordance with Laplace's beautiful theory of the origin of the solar system, that the earth was at first all gas—all atmosphere, as Laplace put it—and that all the carbon later locked up in the coals, the oils, the carbonaceous shales, the limestones, and the other carbonates was then free gas and diffused throughout this great gaseous globe. It was held that later, when cooling had made some progress, the refractory matter that was soon to form the rocks gathered into a white-hot globe of lava, but that still all the oxides of carbon and all the water remained in the hot atmosphere and gave it enormous extent and density. It was reasoned that later, as cooling proceeded, the waters must have been gathered gradually to the earth, but that the carbon dioxide still persisted in the atmosphere until slowly, as the ages went on, it entered into union with the rock crust to form carbonates, or was extracted from the air by plants to form coals and other carbonaceous deposits. And so, each earlier age was thought to have held more carbon dioxide in its atmosphere than the succeeding ones. If this were true, it seemed idle to go backward in time to find deficiency in carbon dioxide.

Besides this infelicity, there seemed to be in this very fact of a great decline from the very hot to the cold a basis for a plausible hypothesis of glaciation—the simple, natural trend of a moribund earth toward a cold senility. The sun was growing cooler and less heat came to the earth; the earth-body was growing colder and was shrinking and cracking and drinking in the water on its surface; the carbon dioxide, oxygen, and other elements of the air were being drawn in also and were uniting with the rocks, and so they blanketed the earth less and less effectually; less moisture rose into this thinned, cold atmosphere and so there was less blanketing by vapor, and even when it rose, the vapor was more promptly condensed to cloud or floating frost, and in this form cut off and reflected away the sunlight. So it was said that the earth was cooling off and drying up, that glaciers and deserts were increasing, and that a final desiccation and a final winter were coming events of the near geologic future. We were told how the moon had lost its seas (behold the Maria) and how its atmosphere had been absorbed; and then the moon was brought into court as a witness to the impending fate of the earth. Our recent icy stage was but an October frost; December was yet to come. Such was the picture, and, granting the cosmogonic views then current, such was the logical drama foreshadowed by the earth's great decline from a hot beginning toward a cold end. "The final winter," "the universal desert," "the last man," were moving themes, and there was much fine writing—albeit of a gruesome sort—by those who delight in such things.

But this theory of a simple decline from a fiery origin to a frigid end, from a thick blanket of warm air to a thin sheet of cold nitrogen, consonant with the current cosmogony as it was, logical under the premises postulated, pessimistically attractive in its gruesome forecast, already in possession of the stage, with a good prospect of holding it—this theory of a stupendous descensus none the less encountered some ugly facts as inquiry went on. It seemed to accord well enough with an ice age, *if* the ice age came *only* in the later stages of the earth's history, but it was ill suited to explain an ice age in the earlier geologic eras.

Unfortunately for it, there began to appear signs of ice ages far back in time, and, besides, some of these had their seats much nearer the equator and, in other respects, were even stranger than the latest great glaciation. The evidence of these earlier and stranger glaciations was at first quite naturally received with incredulity; but the proof grew steadily stronger with every new test, and the range of the evidence was found wider and clearer as exploration advanced. While all this should have weakened, and did weaken, the fundamental concept of great warmth and a rich atmosphere in the earlier ages, while it should have roused skepticism as to the verity of the cosmogony on which it was based, and perhaps did so, still the old thermal concept and the old cosmogony continued to hamper all attempts at a radical revision of glacial theories. The old ideas served as a handicap to the suggestion of Tyndall perhaps more than most other attempts at an explanation of an ice age.

None the less, it seemed to me worth while to inquire what might be the possible climatic effects of secular variations in the constituents of the atmosphere, not merely such changes in the carbon dioxide as Tyndall had suggested, but whatever changes had taken place in any of the constituents, not the least among these the variations in water-vapor, the factor that comes and goes with a peculiar freedom of its own. Back of this search for variations, it was of course important to inquire what agencies could cause such variations.

It was not long before a plausible reason for variation in carbon dioxide was found. In a study of the deformations of the crust of the earth, attention was soon centered on the evidence that stresses had arisen within the body of the earth as time went on and had gathered in force so long as the crust had been able to withstand them, but that, when resistance was no longer possible, the crust had yielded, and had become crumpled and folded into mountains, or bowed up into great swells or warped up into plateaus. There was naturally much riving, fissuring, and crushing of the rock in the course of these processes. Back of these there seemed also to be grander movements by which areas of continental magnitude were lifted, while areas of oceanic extent were depressed. The waters were thus drawn more deeply into the great basins while the continents stood more boldly forth. In these various ways, wider and fresher contacts of the air with the rocks arose after each of these episodes of readjustment, and the active constituents of the air entered into combination with the rocks at accelerated rates.

But when the stresses of the crust had been eased by these episodes of warping, folding, and faulting, a long epoch of crustal quiet ensued, awaiting another such growth of stresses into strength enough to force a new episode of disruption. During such long epochs of quiescence, the rugosites of the surface were worn down by the elements, in a greater or less measure, and the débris was carried into the oceans where it displaced an equal volume of water and, by so much, lifted the sea-level. So, too, all this time the sea was gnawing steadily at the borders of the land and creeping out upon it. In doing this, it was aided by the lifting of the breaker zone—its cutting edge—by the deposit of sediments on its bottom. A study of the stratigraphic record showed that, at times, a third or half of the continental platforms were covered by the overlapping of the sea and that the action of the air upon the rocks was thus shut off. At the same time, the lands that were not thus covered by the sea had been brought low, in some large measure, by erosion, and became covered by a deep mantle of soil and residual clay, and hence suffered a notably lessened effect from the action of the air. Such epochs of base leveling were therefore clearly times of very slow depletion of the atmosphere.

Here, then, was a natural process of a large order by virtue of which the air was robbed of its active elements in one set of stages at a relatively fast rate, while in the other set of stages at only a relatively slow rate. The cause of the fast action was, if a technical term may be pardoned, diastrophism; the cause of the slow action was planation. Each stage occupied a long time but the periods of planation were much longer than the episodes of diastrophism.

The recognition of this alternation of rapid atmospheric depletion with slow atmospheric depletion gave a pulsatory aspect to the atmospheric history. When, in addition to this, it was recognized that the earth through its volcanoes had all along been *feeding* the atmosphere as well as feeding upon it, and that this feeding was also pulsatory, the case took on troublesome complications; and a more severe scrutiny of the stratigraphic record, and of the relics of life imbedded in it, became imperative. In the course of this, still further departures from the generalizations of the inherited view came to notice. Desiccation products were found to be scarcely less abundant and characteristic in the early strata than in the later, and no steady progress from humidity to aridity seemed to mark the progress of time; nor were there found any conclusive evidences of even an oscillatory progress from predominant humidity to predominant aridity. If the record favored any generalization, it seemed to be that the severest and most prevalent period of aridity fell near the middle of the stratigraphic record.

When the testimony of life was similarly rescrutinized, with as much freedom from inherited presumptions as possible, it failed to show clear evidence that the early atmosphere was in any essential respect different from the atmosphere of the later ages, particularly when the units of comparison embraced an adequate lapse of time to cover the cycles of variation. Even when the inquiry was pushed back to the very earliest strata that carried a good record of the life of the times, not only was the inherited view found wanting in clear support, but adverse evidence accumulated rather than disappeared.

When the inquiry was pressed still farther back, and support for the postulate of a molten globe was sought in the crust itself, it was not forthcoming. With strange perversity the supposed granite *foundations* proved to be granitic *intrusions*. Thus in a literal sense the very foundations of the old view proved illusive.

It was thus that the trail was followed back, with a weakening faith in the inherited theory, till the borders of the primitive stage were reached. But one further step remained—to examine the cosmogonic postulates themselves. Could the earth ever have had the vast hot atmosphere postulated? Was the earth's gravity sufficient to hold so vast and vaporous an envelope at such high temperatures and in such an intense state of molecular activity as the old mode of genesis assigned? Was the gaseo-molten genesis a reality? Thus I was already across the pass that leads from the land of rocks into the realm of cosmogonic bogs and fens. Its mists were already gathering over the path ahead. Strangely enough, the cold trail of the ice invasion had led by this long and devious path into the nebulous field of genesis.

CHAPTER II

THE OVERTURN IN THE THEORY OF GASES

At the time these studies were begun—near the turn from the last to the present century—the planets were commonly held to have taken their origin from a gaseous or quasi-gaseous nebula. The most definite and symmetrical of the views then current was the nebular hypothesis of Laplace. This had been given currency perhaps as much by the fame of its distinguished author as by its own intrinsic attractiveness. To some large extent this hypothesis was combined with the earlier Kantian view. Laplace did not postulate any real creation or any real beginning. He merely started with a nebula. Kant, on the other hand, postulated a creation *ex nihilo* and held that the original state immediately after creation was chaotic and that order was evolved out of this chaos. The Kantian and Laplacian hypotheses were therefore often merged to give completeness and for other reasons. In the latter part of the last century the concept of a quasi-gaseous assemblage of meteorites was offered by Lockyer and supported by George Darwin. This was regarded more as a modification of view as to the state of the parental nebula than as a new theory of planetary origin.

The chief working-feature of all these early hypotheses was the view that small masses, suitable for forming planets, were separated from the parent nebular mass by centrifugal force. Now, since the act of such separation was the immediate event that gave the planets their individual existence, it is a critical point to be scrutinized, and, as it is best set forth in the beautiful Laplacian hypothesis, it will be convenient as well as generous to treat that hypothesis as representative of the whole centrifugal group. It will also be safest to begin with things best known. "Nebula" is but the Latin term for cloud. As seen by the early astronomers, the nebulae of the heavens were merely cloudlike spots.

Our most intimate knowledge of natural cloudy states or nebular states comes from our contact with the atmosphere, and especially with its fogs. It was, perhaps, a happy accident that started our own studies with a scrutiny of our atmosphere for reasons quite unrelated to the origin of the earth. It was in the natural order of these other purposes that our inquiry should seek correct fundamental views of the modes of action of the natural gases that enveloped the earth. This led to the consideration of dispersed matter that acts more or less as gases do. Such an inquiry happened to be all the more important at that time because the scientific concept of gases was undergoing a profound revolution. It is only fair to Laplace and the Laplacian followers to state explicitly at once that this revolution in the concept of gases only began a half-century after he had advanced his theory and it had found general acceptance. It is not material here to consider what concepts Laplace and his followers entertained, further than to note that they were not inconsistent with the view that a small planet might gather a gaseous envelope about itself and that this might become as great as its source of supply was capable of furnishing. There even seemed, at that time, to be no bar to supposing that any little bunch of free molecules might assemble and hold themselves together and build up a large gaseous cloud or nebula, if the material was available.

THE ADVENT OF THE KINETIC THEORY OF GASES

About a half-century after the Laplacian hypothesis had come into favor, the concept of gases entered upon a profound revolution. It is to be regretted that this revolution is not yet altogether complete. Although the kinetic theory is held to be fully established, its intimate applications are not yet adequately recognized even so far as its demonstrations have gone. As is well known, in a *general* way, the kinetic theory pictures a gas as an assemblage of free molecules constantly colliding and rebounding from one another in all sorts of ways and at all sorts of speeds. A gas is thus intrinsically dispersive. The molecules are driven apart indefinitely by their rebounds except as these are restrained by the self-gravity of the assemblage itself or by the attraction of the mass about which the gas is gathered.

It is at this point, the alternative of being held or of escaping, that our inquiry naturally begins. Was the gravitative restraint of the assumed masses adequate to control them? Or were the embryos of the planets and comets held together on some other than the gaseous principle? Specifically, was the gravitative control adequate in the actual cases presented by the planetary and cometary families?

It will appear, as we go on, that small assemblages of free molecules, under the conditions that affect our part of the planetary system, ordinarily lack self-gravity enough to hold themselves together. Even small, solid, rather dense bodies, such as the planetoids, lack gravity enough to gather appreciable atmospheres about themselves. When we turn from the earth, and the few big planets that so commonly monopolize our thoughts, and scrutinize the whole range of the planetary and cometary families, the outcome is really quite awakening. Neither the moon, nor most of the other satellites, nor any of the planetoids, hold an observable atmosphere. Less than 1 per cent of the planetary bodies, and none of the known cometary bodies at all, seem to have gravitative power enough to gather about themselves and to hold atmospheres like that of the earth.

It is no wonder then that the new theory of gases which revealed such an array of deficiencies should have put under serious stress the theories of planetary genesis entertained before the dispersive nature of gases was recognized.

It is not unnatural that the bearings of the new concept of gases on the gaseous and quasi-gaseous theories of planetary genesis were not at once realized. A little after the kinetic theory began to be entertained, about the middle of the last century, Johnstone Stoney urged that the atmospheres of the planets must be restricted whenever the planetary masses were small, because their gravity was insufficient to hold rebounding molecules of the gases under control. If the temperatures were once higher than they are now, the collisions and rebounds would have been more rapid than now and the velocities greater. Special studies of gases had shown that certain small percentages of the molecules would acquire specially high velocities by the cumulative effects of a succession of favorable encounters.

Stoney attempted at first to determine the limitations of the planetary atmospheres by mathematical computations based on statistical laws, but with poor success, because, as it transpired later, he assumed that the "critical velocity of escape" of the free molecules from the control of a planet was the "parabolic velocity," or "the velocity of fall from infinity," or the velocity of projection required to send a molecule to infinity. Finding his computed results unsatisfactory, and yet confident that the principles on which he was working were correct, Stoney turned to the atmospheres of the planets themselves and tried naturalistic methods of interpretation. He found the observed facts in fair accord with his contention that the atmospheres of the planets are restricted in proportion to the planetary masses.

Stoney made a further contribution by analyzing the actions of atmospheric molecules under the kinetic theory. He reasoned that though the collisions and rebounds of the molecules near the surface of the planet—the earth, for example—might be extremely frequent, and hence their paths between collisions too short for the earth's gravity to affect them sensibly, yet in the upper thin atmosphere, where the mean free paths between collisions were greatly increased, gravity would curve the paths. He reasoned further that when the attenuation became sufficient, many a molecule rebounding outwardly would fail to encounter another molecule before it was turned about by gravity and pulled back toward the earth. He thus pictured the outer atmosphere as a zone of vaulting molecules that gave to the whole a fountain-like aspect. Stoney thus made two contributions of high value toward a true concept of the planetary atmospheres.

None the less, his views encountered sharp opposition mainly based on computations which assumed that the parabolic velocity was the "critical velocity of escape." Had not Stoney made the same unfortunate assumption, he might easily have demolished these criticisms and cut short the controversy.

THE TRUE CRITICAL VELOCITY OF ESCAPE

It should be obvious to anyone who gives the subject critical thought that it is not necessary for a molecule to acquire a velocity capable of carrying it to infinity to enable it to escape from the control of the earth or the control of any other planet. The spheres of control of all the planets are limited in size and are enveloped by the sphere of control of the sun. This in turn is limited by the spheres of control of neighboring stars, or by the conjoint sphere of control of the star-cluster to which the sun belongs, and this is enveloped by the sphere of control of the stellar galaxy, and so on. How far the series goes no man knows. (Laplace worked out "the spheres of activity" [essentially the same as "spheres of control"] for the planets. Herein, however, we shall use the results of Moulton's computations as these are based on later data, but the slight differences have no value in a general discussion of this kind. A table of both sets of results will be given in chapter iv with some general considerations bearing on the subject.) "Sphere" is here used in much the same sense as "sphere of influence" in international affairs. Geometrically, it is a spheroid, or may even have a polyhedral form. Moulton finds the sphere of control of the earth to be an ellipsoid whose shortest radius is 620,000 miles (1,000,000 kilometers) and its longest radius 930,000 miles (1,500,000 kilometers). Molecules rebounding from collisions in the outer atmosphere, and at velocities sufficient to carry them to these distances, *escape into the enveloping sphere of control of the sun* and become factors in the sun's ultra-atmosphere. A million or a million and a half of kilometers is considerably short of infinity.

ULTRA-ATMOSPHERES AND ALTERNATIVE MODES OF ESCAPE

Great as was the contribution of Stoney, it was not complete. The vaulting molecules of Stoney's fountain-like super-atmosphere were liable to collide with one another in the course of their vaulting flights; indeed, they were sure to do so in a certain proportion of cases. The rebounds from these collisions were liable to take directions tangential to the earth's surface; indeed, they were sure to do so in a certain proportion of cases. When the molecules in these cases had velocity enough—as some of them would inevitably have—they would take *orbital courses about the earth and continue to follow them indefinitely until they encountered other molecules*. Thus the *gaseous type of mechanics would be displaced for a time by orbital mechanics*. A body in an orbit about a controlling center forms a self-sustaining mechanism that normally maintains itself until disturbed. In this respect it is quite different from a molecule which merely vaults, for that falls back to the collisional atmosphere.

Under the kinetic theory of gases, certain proportions of the molecules acquire higher and higher velocities up to a theoretical infinite velocity. This law applies to the collisions of the vaulting molecules—hence a part of their collisions with one another would have velocities high enough to give them orbital courses about the earth. This gives rise to a type of atmosphere that is not gaseous —in the strict collisional sense—but orbital. Neither are the vaulting molecules in the strict to-and-fro collisional gaseous state. It seems best, therefore, to distinguish these outer very attenuated envelopes as ultra-atmospheres, the krenal (fountain-like) ultra-atmosphere and the orbital ultra-atmosphere.

AN ORBITAL MODE OF ESCAPE

In the outer part of the earth's sphere of control the sparseness of the molecules is so great that many revolutions would take place before an encounter would occur such as would throw an orbital molecule back into the collisional atmosphere. It has been computed that at a height of 200 miles above the earth's surface the mean free path of an atmospheric molecule, subject merely to ordinary collisional action, would be 60,000 miles. This should give each molecule, on the average, two revolutions before it made its next encounter. Two hundred miles is only one three-thousandth of the height of the limit of the sphere of control. There is thus ample room for an extremely tenuous distribution of molecules in the outer part of the earth's sphere of control, and hence ample room for the development of both the krenal and the orbital ultra-atmospheres.

The accumulation of an orbital ultra-atmosphere, however, has its limitations, by reason of its own automatic checking-system. As the number of molecules in orbits increases, their encounters with one another increase, as also their encounters with the vaulting molecules of the krenal atmosphere which may cross their orbits. A part of these encounters would throw the orbital molecules back into the collisional atmosphere, and a part would throw them into new orbits, some of which would be smaller and some larger. A sufficient succession of enlargements *would carry the molecules outside the sphere of the earth's control;* and this, under the laws of chance, would inevitably occur.

THE SUPERIORITY OF THE ORBITAL MODE OF ESCAPE

Thus, by carrying the logic of the vaulting atmosphere onward to the formation of an orbital atmosphere, a mode of molecular escape from the control of the earth, step by step, is reached. This is almost in contrast to escape by a single leap from the surface of the collisional atmosphere. One cannot jump from the street to his apartments in the seventh story, but he can reach them by the stairs, especially if there is ample provision for rests on the way.

The objections urged against the strict application of

the kinetic theory of gases to the limitation of planetary atmospheres were based on two errors: the first, and most indefensible, the use of the velocity from infinity for "the critical velocity of escape"; the second, based on the more excusable neglect of a strictly logical analysis of the outward development of an atmosphere under the kinetic theory of gases, back of which lay concealed a more gradual mode of molecular escape.

How inferior, quantitatively, escape by parabolic leaps is to the climbing of the orbital stairs, step by step, may be gathered from the mechanical law that the velocity in a circular orbit is to the corresponding parabolic velocity as $1 : \sqrt{2}$, or as $1 : 1.41+$; in other words if the velocity in the circular orbit be increased so that escape will take place, the corresponding parabolic velocity will be 40 per cent greater.

INTERCHANGE OF ATMOSPHERES

Another important result follows the recognition of the orbital ultra-atmospheres. Molecules are being systematically pushed by stages out of the spheres of control of the planets into the sphere of control of the sun. By an analogous process an ultra-atmosphere is formed within the sphere of control of the sun and this feeds into the planetary atmospheres just as the planetary atmospheres feed into it. In the very nature of this reciprocal process, it tends to establish an equilibrium between the solar and the planetary atmospheres. The richer atmosphere inevitably feeds more into the leaner atmosphere than the leaner feeds back.

SUMMARY OF ATMOSPHERIC FUNDAMENTALS

The approach to the problem of planetary genesis along atmospheric lines revealed very serious obstacles in the way of all efforts to build up small planetary bodies by gaseous processes. The logical application of the kinetic theory of gases, pushed to its ulterior consequences, leaves little or no ground for any gaseous explanation of the origin of 99+ per cent of the bodies that constitute the planetary and cometary families.

The positive results of the inquiry were (1) full support of the doctrine of Stoney that the atmospheres of the planets are restricted in proportion to their masses; (2) support of Stoney's view of vaulting molecules and his fountain-like (krenal) ultra-atmosphere; (3) the recognition of the inevitable passage of the vaulting molecules into orbital molecules, forming an orbital ultra-atmosphere; (4) the detection of the serious error of using the parabolic velocity as the critical velocity of escape of molecules from a planetary atmosphere; and (5) the recognition of a progressive mode of escape by transfer from one orbit to another orbit, giving rise to escape with smaller increments of energy and at lower velocities.

But the simple application of the kinetic theory of gases does not cover the whole case. Atmospheres, like other bodies undergoing evolution, are subject to influences coming from their environment. We must consider, in the next chapter, what influences coming from their environments affected the planetary atmospheres, especially the atmosphere of the earth.

REFERENCES

1. G. Johnstone Stoney, "On the Cause of the Absence of Hydrogen from the Earth's Surface and of Air and Water from the Moon," *Transactions of the Royal Dublin Society*, 1892; "On Atmospheres upon Planets and Satellites," *ibid.*, 1897; *ibid.*, 1898, p. 305; "On the Presence of Helium in the Earth's Atmosphere and Its Relation to the Kinetic Theory of Gases," *Astrophysical Journal*, VIII (1898), 316.

2. S. R. Cook, "On the Escape of Gases from Planetary Atmospheres According to the Kinetic Theory," *Astrophysical Journal*, XI (1900), 36; G. Johnstone Stoney, "On the Escape of Gases from Planetary Atmospheres According to the Kinetic Theory," No. I, *ibid.*, XI (1900), 151; No. II, *ibid.*, XI (1900), 325; "Note on Inquiries as to the Escape of Gases from Atmospheres," *ibid.*, XII (1900), 201.

3. T. C. Chamberlin, "On the Bearing of Molecular Activity on the Spontaneous Fission of Gaseous Spheroids," *Carnegie Institution of Washington, Publication 107* (1909), pp. 161–67.

4. T. C. Chamberlin, "A Group of Hypotheses Bearing on Climatic Changes," *Journal of Geology*, V (1897), 653.

5. F. R. Moulton, *ibid.*, p. 659.

6. A. W. Whitney, *ibid.*, p. 661.

7. T. C. Chamberlin, *The Origin of the Earth* (1916), chap. i.

CHAPTER III

AGENCIES CO-OPERATING IN ATMOSPHERIC CONTROL

The evolution of the krenal and orbital ultra-atmospheres from the denser collisional atmospheres that immediately envelop the planets has been sketched as a logical deduction from the kinetic theory of gases. It leads to an ideal tripartite atmosphere, filling, in its sparse way, the entire spheres of control of the planets. But this ideal atmosphere is subject to serious modifications by the effects of certain repellent agencies emanating from the sun, which also take part in the formation, restriction, and maintenance of the planetary atmospheres. These co-operative agencies were in part tributary to the atmospheres and in part depletional. They include (1) the projectile effects of solar eruptions; (2) radiation pressure (of which light-pressure is the phase best known) (3) the repellent influences of electric and magnetic charges; and (4) the propulsatory effects of electrons and protons emanating from the sun. The naturalistic evidence seems to imply that these commonly act in combination and that the degree of their co-operation with one another is liable to vary more or less with each propulsatory effort. It is sufficient for our purpose to deal with them simply as a group of allied agencies acting in a radial, repellent way. For simplicity, we may take our own atmosphere as representative. Later in the story there will be occasion to tell something more of the nature and power of these agencies of repulsion. Just here we are only specially interested in the modifying effects these have on the ideal tripartite atmospheres which were deduced, in the last chapter, from the kinetic theory of gases.

Until the full evidence is forthcoming, let it be assumed that this group of solar repellencies is able jointly to project and propel, far out into planetary space, not only solar molecules of different kinds, but trituration and perhaps other dust, and possibly even some of the smallest orders of accretions, though not the larger orders of accretions. The evidences of this will gradually appear as our story goes on. However, lest doubts dull the points we wish to urge here, perhaps it may be best to turn aside at once long enough to call certain spectacular witnesses to the stand, the tails of comets, in particular. As every one knows, comets' heads sweep close about the sun under the laws of gravity; while tail-stuff, including molecules of considerable specific gravity, carbon monoxide, cyanogen, sodium, and iron, as well as particles large enough to reflect light, is driven out from them at all stages in their approaches, their turns, and their retreats. This mixed material is propelled at high velocities to unknown distances into the outer reaches of the solar domain, and perhaps beyond. Some hundreds of comets have swept the inner planetary field in various directions since scientific observation began, and have thus demonstrated that a very declared repellency is felt throughout the whole immediate environment of the sun. It is, to be sure, only a selection of matter that is thus vigorously repelled, but the selection includes material substantial enough to have once terrified mankind, though it may not have been any more substantial than trituration dust.

With this impressive testimony we may safely assume that the sun is a center of repellency as well as attraction, and that materials as heavy as those which make up most of the earth's atmosphere are driven from the sun and may strike into our atmosphere. How far does this modify the ideal tripartite atmosphere deduced solely from the kinetic theory?

MODIFICATION OF THE IDEAL ATMOSPHERES

No more than a rough approximation to the specific degree of such modification is possible in the present state of uncertainty relative to the repellent group. The auroras and occasional "magnetic storms" appear to be special manifestations of this radial group, but they have not yet been reduced to scientific terms available for deciding whether they tend to enhance or to deplete the atmosphere.

A more serious uncertainty arises from the recent discovery that the atmosphere is habitually charged in one sense while the earth's surface is charged in the opposite sense, and that there is an active tendency toward equilibrium of sufficient value to equalize these charges in a small fraction of an hour.

While we must wait, with such patience as we can command, for the advance of knowledge in these lines and for a valuation of their bearings on atmospheric supply and maintenance, it is both wholesome and helpful to consider them tentatively.

Let us recall the three factors of the ideal atmosphere subject to modifications: (1) the relatively dense collisional atmosphere that closely hugs the earth's surface, extending outwardly only a mere fraction of the way to the border of the earth's sphere of control; (2) the zone of vaulting molecules grading up from the collisional zone into extreme tenuity; and (3) the very sparse zone of orbital molecules—the last two occupying, in their scant way, the remainder of the earth's gravitative domain above the collisional atmosphere.

In so far as atmospheric material is shot from the sun into the lower zone, it is quite certainly captured and is a source of feeding. In so far as the outshot particles drive into the zones of the sparser krenal and orbital ultra-atmospheres, they must almost as certainly drive some of the vaulting and orbital constituents out of the earth's control, but almost as certainly will sometimes be themselves thrown into orbits, or into the collisional atmospheres below. It thus becomes uncertain how much of solar emanation would be caught and held, and how much of the sparse atmospheric material would be driven out of control.

Some of the details are worth noting. There can be no question that molecules shot from the sun and penetrating the outer part of the earth's sphere of control would tend to drive molecules into orbital courses, for their impacts would be specially effective when most nearly tangential to the earth. This would increase above the normal rate the passing of vaulting molecules into orbital courses. At the same time, molecules already in orbital courses would be liable to be given new orbital motions with new centrifugal components, and some of these would be quite certain to be too great to be controlled by the earth's gravity.

It does not seem possible to evaluate these diverse influences at present, but, on the whole, it appears probable that there would be loss in the higher levels to be set over against gain in the lower levels. The total effect would probably be a keener contest for control and a sharper restriction of the atmosphere to the immediate vicinity of the earth's body. There would quite surely be more activity in both supply and depletion, a more sustained mixture of solar and terrestrial derivations, and probably a depletion of the ultra-atmospheres.

Even if a molecule shot from the sun does not encounter a molecule of the ultra-atmosphere in passing through the earth's sphere of control, it must be deflected toward the axis joining the center of the earth and the center of the sun. It would thus already have an inward curvature before encountering an atmospheric constituent, and the two molecules after encounter would have components of motion tending to give them elliptical courses with a major axis in the general direction of the axis joining the sun and the earth. This is the direction of greatest elongation of the sphere of control; and so the new orbits of the colliding constituents would tend to elongate the ultra-atmosphere along its greater axis.

CHAPTER IV

CELESTIAL CONTROLS

Although the verity of the kinetic theory of gases is fully established, current scientific thought has only partially undergone the full conceptual revolution that is due to follow. There is a regrettable lag in realizing the secondary applications of the theory. Even in pretentious scientific literature just off the press (1927), we not infrequently stumble upon lingering inheritances from untenable gaseous concepts. We read of "former atmospheres" of the moon, of mathematical analyses of the earth's upper atmosphere computed on the basis of assumptions long ago discredited by meteor trains, and of similar secondary residues of obsolete gaseous concepts. These are natural enough, but their departures should be hastened.

Still more tardy is an adequate acceptation of the principles of celestial government. There is a notable lack of adequate appreciation of the gravitative spheres of control that attend all appreciable masses. This tardiness is the more notable because the specific spheres of planetary control were made known more than a century ago by Laplace.

The general subject of celestial government is not in place here, but some phases of it are so vital to what follows that they are briefly considered at this point in the hope that this may be helpful in the later discussions.

ORDERS OF CELESTIAL CONTROL

Instead of simple, direct control, celestial government is effected chiefly by means of intermediate subcontrols, these lesser controls being usually subordinate to and embraced within higher orders of control. Essentially the same principle obtains in the better class of human governments in which municipal government is subordinate to and yet embraced within state government; state government is subordinate to and embraced within national government; while national government is yet to

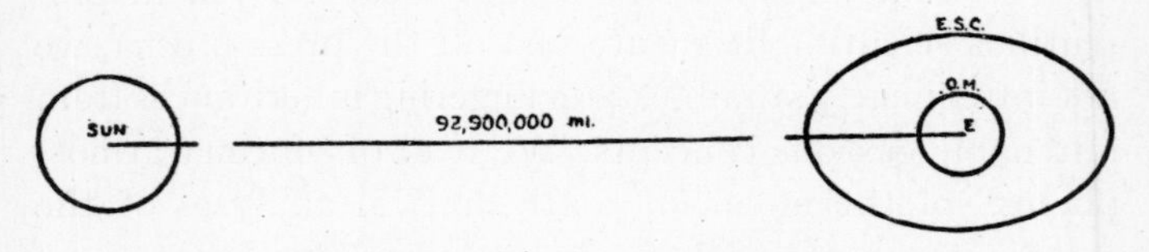

FIG. 1.—Diagram illustrating general relations of sphere of control of earth to sun. E., earth; O. M., orbit of moon; E. S. C., earth's sphere of control. Scale of sun and E. S. C. the same.

yield to international government. Both the celestial and the terrestrial systems rest on the principle of *prior obedience to immediate forces.* The satellites have little domains within the domains of the planets; the planets have larger domains within the domain of the sun; the sun has a domain within the star assemblages. Each lower rank has its own special functions subject to obedience to a higher control. The method employs the economy of immediate action in immediate relations, secondary action in more remote relations, and so on. It avoids action by large masses when action by small masses will suffice.

PARADOXES

The occasion for control arises from the prevalence of motion which seems to be universal, and hence becomes highly complicated. In cosmologic studies it is essential to distinguish between motions that are opposed to one another and motions that are concurrent with one another. The former favor escape from control; the latter yield readily to control and favor construction. Equilibrium between the two commonly takes the form of revolutional motion. Stationary states are unknown in the heavens, but they swarm in our concepts and give rise to paradoxes. For example, the revolutional motions of the earth and of the moon are highly concurrent. Both orbits are concave toward the sun and the centrifugal components of their motions relative to the sun nearly balance one another. The centrifugal components of their motions offset the larger part of the sun's attraction, leaving them free to respond to their own mutual attractions. This gives the earth greater control over the moon than it would have without this neutralization of the sun's attraction. The position of "equal gravity" between the sun and earth (when misconceived as stationary bodies) lies *well inside the orbit of the moon*, but still the earth controls the moon. The outer border of the earth's "sphere of control" over the moon in their actual state of motion is far outside this "equal gravity," as plotted in Figure 2. At the time when the moon is eclipsing the sun, it seems, on the face of things, very strange that the point of equal pull between the earth and the sun (considered as stationary bodies) should be *between the earth and the moon*.

CONTROL, IN A QUALIFIED SENSE ONLY

"Spheres of activity" or "spheres of control" relate to the ability of a body to control the motions of another body *under the conditions of motion that actually obtain.*

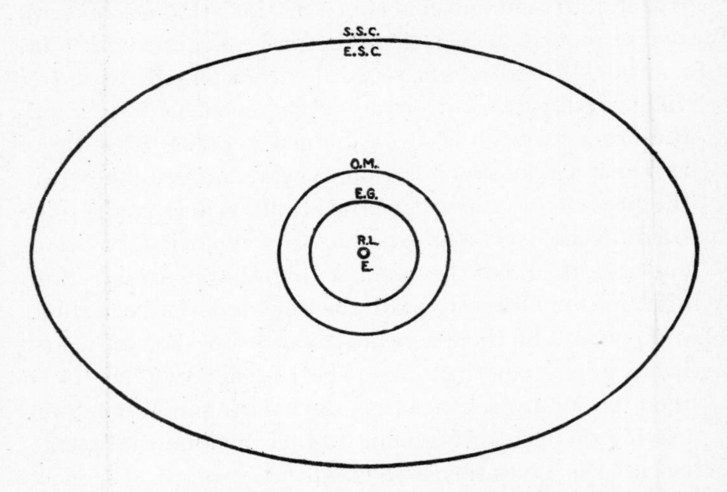

FIG. 2.—Diagram illustrating sphere of control of earth on larger scale. E., earth; R. L., Roche limit; E. G., limit of equal gravity between earth and sun; O. M., orbit of moon; E. S. C., earth's sphere of control; S. S. C., inner earthward border of sun's sphere of control, which extends outwardly several hundred astronomical units. Shortest radius of earth's sphere of control, 620,000 miles (1,000,000 kilometers); longest, 930,000 miles (1,500,000 kilometers).

This is always to be understood when not otherwise specified. We shall frequently encounter combinations of this kind in the motions of satellites relative to their planets and in motions of the constituents of atmospheres relative to the planets they surround.

ENVELOPMENT

To form a good working concept of each lower sphere of control, it should be pictured as enveloped by the sphere of control of the next higher order. If a molecule, particle, or other body, escapes from a given sphere of control, it immediately enters the surrounding sphere of control. Whatever escapes from the control of the moon immediately enters the sphere of control of the earth; whatever escapes from the sphere of control of the earth, immediately enters the enveloping sphere of control of the sun; and so on. It may thus be seen that in the very nature of such a system of control within control (each factor being in constant motion), a simple "fall from infinity" is merely an abstract unrealizable idea, liable to be misleading because it is so far from the realities of the case. The use of the "parabolic velocity" or "the velocity of fall from infinity" as a "critical velocity of escape" is to be classed among "denatured" concepts, and its use scrupulously eschewed.

REALISTIC PICTURES

To rightly picture falls to the earth due to the earth's attraction, these falls should be regarded as starting at the border of the earth's sphere of control, the true limit of the earth's domain. It is just inside this surface that the attraction of the earth, in competition with the attraction of the sun, first realizes the advantage of prior obedience, though secondary and higher obedience is still yielded to the sun. While the earth's attraction may be pictured as reaching on indefinitely, it is submerged beneath the greater gravity of the sun, and so disappears as a tangible effect. The limit of the sphere of control as thus defined, is the true border of the earth as a dynamic organization. This is where geology yields wholly to astronomy, though geology at best is only the domestic chapter of astronomy, and astronomy the foreign department of geology. Falls to the sun, due to the sun's attraction, start at the border of the sun's sphere of control. Motions coming from beyond the sun's sphere of control, due to influences in the environment, are alien to the solar domain and may well be pictured simply as inherited motions. Bodies that enter the several domains with motions acquired from any source outside may, of course, traverse them at various velocities by virtue of acquired inertia. In passing through the specific domains, they are, of course, subject to the attractions of the bodies within them.

PLANETARY SPHERES OF CONTROL

Table I gives the "spheres of activity" of the planets, as worked out by Laplace, and the spheres within which satellites may be controlled, as worked out by Moulton. The latter will be used in the following chapters, but the differences are of no importance in this general discussion. The computations of Laplace are given as a recognition of his early contribution to this indispensable factor in cosmologic studies. The "spheres" are not strictly spherical; commonly they are spheroids of three unequal dimensions. The minimum radii are given in the table.

GRAVITATIVE DOMAINS OF THE SUN AND STARS

When we rise to the higher order of gravitative control, such as star against star, or star against its enveloping star-cluster, or star-cluster against the enveloping galaxy, we must be content with defective determinations, for as yet adequate data for anything better are lacking. But even such approximations are valuable as working-steps toward something better. It does not seem probable that the stars as individual centers of control divide the

TABLE I

SPHERES OF GRAVITATIVE CONTROL OF THE PLANETS AS AGAINST THE SUN

Planets	Laplace		Moulton	
	"Spheres of Activity"		Sphere of Satellite Control	
	Miles	Kilometers	Miles	Kilometers
Mercury	55,700	129,000	87,000	139,200
Venus	325,000	520,000	419,000	670,400
Earth	501,000	801,680	620,000	992,000
Mars	316,000	505,600	449,000	718,000
Jupiter	26,000,000	40,000,000	22,000,000	35,200,000
Saturn	29,000,000	46,400,000	27,000,000	43,200,000
Uranus	28,000,000	44,800,000	29,000,000	46,400,000
Neptune	47,000,000	75,200,000	48,000,000	76,800,000

whole of instellar space between themselves, because of their wide separation, their great numbers, and their limited differences in mass. It seems more probable that their individual gravities are combined in a common field of gravity such as the grouped gravity of a star-cluster or of the galaxy.

THE SUN'S SPHERE OF CONTROL

An approximate estimate of the sun's sphere of control —sufficiently near the truth for this general discussion—

may be derived from the decline of the curve of gravity outwardly from the great planets, projected graphically or mathematically. Such a curve, however, soon becomes almost asymptotic to the solar radius, and its limit is very uncertain. It will serve our general purpose to place the limit of the sun's gravitative dominance, as against that of the competing outside attractions, roundly at a hundred billion kilometers, which, however, is much less than that indicated by the extrapolation. At any rate, the outer reaches of the sun's domain cover a vast enveloping space. The degree of control in the larger part of it is, however, very slight, and of course it graduates slowly down to zero at its outer limit.

To fill out the picture—at least for the known part of the cosmos—let similar spheroids of gravity be pictured as moving in their respective paths through the common composite field of stellar gravity. The control close about each star is very strong, but it lessens very rapidly with distance and then grades more slowly away to zero at the limits of each domain.

Such a concept gives a fairly definite background on which to picture the encounters of the spheres of gravity of the stars as they move among one another. Such an encounter is a concept of radical importance in cosmology. It will be urged later that such an encounter was the first step in the genesis of our planetary system. The stars of our galaxy are moving in diverse directions, and their spheres of attraction are certain sooner or later to impinge upon one another in greater or less degree. On so simple an event as the close approach of a star to our sun, without bodily collision, but with deep penetration of one another's normal spheres of control, we shall build our interpretation of the genesis of our earth and its kin.

SPHERES OF EFFECTIVE LIGHT-PRESSURE

Stellar light, like stellar gravity, takes its origin from concentrated points. As a rule, the points of strong radiation of light are the same as the great concentrations of gravity. It is common opinion that the light springs from the gravity. As indicated in the last chapter, there often goes with light and light-pressure the repellent effects of electric and magnetic charges, as also the propulsion of electrons and protons. Since these co-operate with light in so many ways and degrees that they cannot be separated at present, it serves our purpose to treat them as a group of repellent agencies, with light pressure as their representative. It is possible that in many cases the co-operating influences may be even more effective than light-pressure, but light-pressure lends itself more readily to visualization and brief discussion.

Light, like gravity, dies away with the square of the distance. As solar light spreads far out toward interstellar space, it encounters light from the surrounding stars, just as gravity meets countergravity from the same stars. And so, like solar gravity, light-pressure reaches at length a zero limit where the counterpush of light-pressure from the stars matches it. Beyond this the counterpush is the stronger, becoming increasingly so with distance.

At a relatively small distance from its origin, the light from each star becomes feeble; and so the larger part of interstellar space is relatively dark, perhaps about as dark as a moonless but starry night.

THE RELATIVE STRENGTHS OF THE PULL OF GRAVITY AND THE PUSH OF LIGHT

Keeping in mind that light-pressure stands for the whole group of radial repellent pressures emanating from the sun, and that this group stands over against gravity and the whole attractive group (including the electrical and magnetic attractions of opposite charges and the concentrative push of electrons and protons), let us try to form as fair a picture as we may of the relative values of these antagonistic forces.

In the main, of course, the gravity group preponderates, otherwise the stars would disperse themselves. In all normal cases, it is taken for granted that gravity is present and dominant; but it is necessary to note that the ratio of surface to cubic content gives rise to an exception to this. The surfaces of spheres vary as the squares of their diameters, while their cubic contents, and hence their masses, vary as the cubes of their diameters. Light-pressure acts on the surface, while gravity varies with the mass. It follows that very small bodies may be controlled by light-pressure, while larger bodies of the same substance may be controlled by gravity. Some other factors enter into the case, but we need not consider them in this merely general sketch. It is this fact that minute material is sometimes controlled by solar-repellency that requires us to compare the spheres of light-pressure with those of gravity.

The stars vary much less in mass than in light, and so their gravitative spheres of control vary much less than the spheres of their light-pressure. As the space to be apportioned to gravitative spheres, on the one hand, and to light dominance, on the other, is the same, it follows that the very bright stars have relatively large spheres of dominant light-pressure, while the dull stars have proportionately small spheres of dominant pressure.

Now the sun is a relatively dull, yellow star, and its sphere of dominance of light-pressure, as against the brighter class of stars, must be relatively small. The sun's density, on the other hand, is relatively higher. Hence we conclude that its sphere of gravitative control is greater than its sphere of light-pressure. If so, the limit of its sphere of effective light-pressure is reached sooner than the limit of its gravity control.

This conclusion is abetted by the fact that all outlying matter in the solar domain obstructs, absorbs, or otherwise interferes with radiation, while this same matter increases the gravitation. Even if the sphere of light-pressure would otherwise have been as great as the sphere of gravitative control, the intervening matter would have reduced the former and enlarged the latter. This would have opened a zone between the outer borders of the two spheres.

The bearing of these considerations will appear if we now try to form a concrete picture of the dynamic zones of the solar domain.

THE DYNAMIC ZONES OF THE SOLAR DOMAIN

Considered in respect to the contest between attractive and repellent influences, the solar domain takes on four deep concentric zones.

I. The first constitutes the inner environment of the sun. It embraces the orbits of the small, naked or slightly clothed planets, Mercury, Venus, Earth, Mars, and the planetoids. The repellent agencies effectually drive out of this zone free molecules and fine dust, except as they are held by the superior attractions of Venus, Earth, and Mars. Comet's heads suffer wastage and depletion while traversing this zone. Tail-stuff is developed from comet heads and driven out of the zone with great velocity. At the same time, it seems to have been possible for small planets, planetoids, and satellites to assemble, to survive their "perils of infancy," to grow to their present states, and to give promise of living on to unknown lengths in spite of all solar repellency. These planetary bodies even seem to have thrived under conditions that were hostile to the comets.

II. Outside this inner environment of the sun lies the zone of the great gaseous planets, Jupiter, Saturn, Uranus, and Neptune. In this zone the selective solar repellency seems to be much abated. There seems to be greater tolerance of gases, and there certainly was greater gaseous growth.

III. The third zone lies between this belt of great gaseous planets and the limit of the sphere of the sun's light-pressure. As previously noted, its outer limit is the surface at which solar light-pressure is matched by the counterpush of light-pressure from the starry host outside.

IV. A fourth, and outermost, zone is thus left between this boundary of the sphere of light-pressure and the still more remote boundary of the sphere of gravitative control. In this outermost zone the counterpush of outside light-pressure joins forces with gravity in preventing, to the extent of their combined power, the final escape of the minute matter that had previously been subject to light-pressure. This is thus *a zone of special conservation of minute matter which otherwise might escape because of radial repellency.*

CLARIFICATION OF THE HEAVENS

If recent estimates of the enormous distances to which the light of stars penetrates space without absorption or dispersion are in the line of truth, there must apparently be some means by which interstellar space is kept free from minute beclouding matter. It is a fair inference that such outermost zones as this, attending all the duller and denser stars, is one of these indicated agencies. In this class of stars the spheres of attraction envelop the spheres of repellency and forestall the escape of the beclouding material, while they gather in part of what comes from the brighter class of stars. This carries the presumption that the brightest stars are losing such part of their minute matter as is pushed over into the spheres of gravitative control of the adjacent dull stars by the superior repellent forces of the bright stars. They thereby contribute to the masses of the duller stars—and this is at least a step toward celestial equilibrium.

It may be added here that all the radial pressure of light and its allies, in so far as it becomes actually effective by pushing matter outward, contributes to the potential energy of position of the matter so affected. This is another form of conservation. Paradoxically it comes about through radiant forces, usually reckoned as sources of energy loss. Perhaps all the energies of radiation, and all radial forces of any kind, are sooner or later absorbed before the borders of the universe are reached.

CONTRASTED VIEWS OF THE PLANETARY SYSTEM

It appears from the foregoing considerations that our study of the genesis of our planet and its kin is likely to turn out to be more a matter of motion and of energy than of substance and of space. The substance and the spacing are, however, much the more impressive. We commonly think of the solar family as consisting of eight globes of different sizes revolving at different distances from the sun. What this means in terms of energy is not so obvious to us. Yet it is clear that the energy required to move the substance of these bodies from the sun out to the positions they occupy is a vital matter in their formation. It will help to guard us against overlooking or misconstruing this vital factor of energy if, at the outset, we form distinct impressions of each point of view and then compare the spacing of the planets with the energy required to give them this spacing. This will be the clearer if we use merely a common unit for the planets and avoid the complication of their varying masses.

The factor that makes the deploying of the planets considered simply in terms of space, so liable to misconception, is the outward variation in the intensity of the sun's gravitation, a variation inversely proportional to the square of the distance. This rapid decline in the sun's gravitative field of force is well enough known and is a feature we have already emphasized in other relations, but it is invisible and intangible.

When this intangible potential energy of position is

brought into consideration, the differences between the potential energy of position of the planets and the spacial position of the planets appear in striking contrast.

It is one of the most familiar facts of the planetary system that the spaces between the planets increase outwardly at a high rate. An attempt has been made to find a law underlying this distribution (Bode's law). The

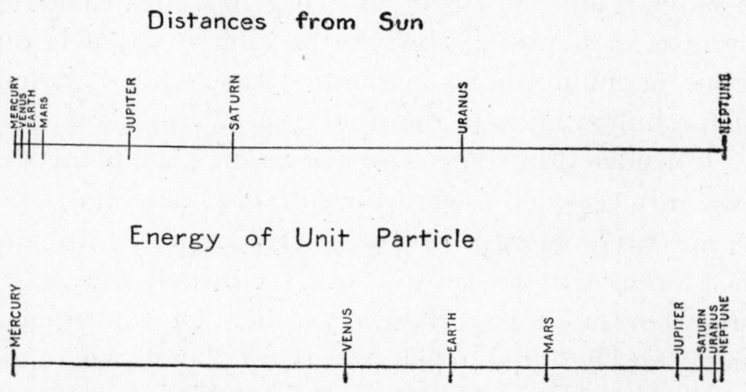

FIG. 3.—Diagram showing the proportional distances of the planets from the sun (distribution in space) and the energy required to move a unit mass from the sun to the respective positions of the planet (distribution of potential energy).

outer spaces are so great, relative to the inner ones, that it is difficult to represent them on a true scale by a diagram suited to any ordinary page.

But when the potential energies of these positions are considered (that is, the energies required to move unit masses from the sun to these positions), the difficulty of diagraming is almost precisely reversed. This is shown in Figure 3, prepared by the kindness of Dr. Walter Bartky of the Astronomical Department of the University of Chicago. The great dynamic distance of

Mercury from the sun is, of necessity, omitted, and only the deployment of the planetary zone is represented. If the deployment between Mercury and the sun were included, the planets would be crowded into indistinctness. It will be noted in particular that the dynamic separation of the planets *declines outwardly* as markedly as their distribution in space increases. It required much more energy to move a unit mass from Mercury to Venus than from Uranus to Neptune, though the simple space is only about 31 million miles in the first case while it is more than a billion miles in the second case.

Considered in respect to space alone, the planets are relatively crowded toward the sun; considered in respect to potential energy, or the energy required to place them, they are as conspicuously crowded toward the outer border of the planetary zone. Of course, more energy was required to place the outer planets where they are than the inner ones; but considered in respect to the *relative* energies, the increment rapidly declines outwardly.

It is a rather interesting, and perhaps a suggestive fact, that our planet lies near the dynamic center of the planetary belt, a little on the cool side of the center.

CONSTRUCTIVE DIFFERENCES BETWEEN CONCURRENT AND NON-CONCURRENT MOTIONS

Control is the first step toward construction. It is also an essential condition for the maintenance of any moving system after it is once formed. The occasion for control springs chiefly from motion. The chief difficulties of control spring from high relative velocities and from adverse directions of motion. Opposite and transverse motions are obstacles to control; concurrent motions yield more readily to control. The very open state of the cosmic structure gives great opportunity for motion and much room in which control may be effected without collision. Mastery by means of swings into closed orbits has put a large part of the energy of the cosmos under control in the form of revolution. This revolutional control is the chief feature of cosmic government and of cosmic construction. Concurrency of motion is the main road to revolutional control and to construction.

CLOSENESS OF APPROACH

As already noted in this chapter, the attractive and the repellent forces alike proceed from centers which are mere points relative to interstellar space. This gives vast opportunity for the motion of these centers. These centers are surrounded by fields of force, but these decline rapidly from their centers outward in all directions to points where they become submerged by the counterextensions of like forces from other centers. Enveloping fields of force move with the centers of mass and encounter one another long before the concentrated masses do, and very often when the central masses do not.

DYNAMIC ENCOUNTERS

Such encounters are dynamic. They must apparently take place many billions of times oftener than material encounters between the stars. They differ very radically from the collisions of rigid bodies. The dynamic encounters are graduated from zero to their maximum, according to the law of the inverse square of the distance. The dynamic encounters of the outermost borders of the domains of attraction of the stars must probably be very numerous in the stellar world, but encounters of the mere borders must be ineffectual. Only rarely is there a close enough approach to make these encounters effective in the genesis of planets; but when such close approaches do take place, their results are as important as their occurrence is rare.

The recognition of dynamic encounter of a high order by close approach was the first step toward that form of interpretation of the genesis of our planetary family which is set forth in the constructive chapters of this book.

Next after dynamic, non-bodily encounters, concurrency of motion, as distinguished from transverse and opposing motion, is found to be a leading constructive factor. Dynamic encounter and concurrent motions lead naturally to revolutional motions which are prime factors in the planetary system. Concurrent revolutions give rise to harmonious careers, and therein lies the stability of the planetary system. At the same time it constitutes an effective mechanism for storing energy and conserving it. It has been recently revealed that the mutual revolutions of the minutest bodies known are the embodiment of the most intense energies known. From the revolutions of the greatest bodies to the revolutions of the least bodies, constructive work takes the form of concurrent revolution within enveloping fields of force.

REFERENCES

1. T. C. Chamberlin, "On the Possible Function of Disruptive Approach in the Formation of Meteorites, Comets and Nebulae," *Astrophysical Journal*, XIV (1901), 17–20; also, *Journal of Geology*, IV (1901), 369–93.

2. T. C. Chamberlin, *Carnegie Institution of Washington, Year Book No. 3* (1904), pp. 208–53; *ibid., No. 26* (1926–27), pp. 338–45.

CHAPTER V

TESTS OF GASEOUS THEORIES BY THE LAWS OF GASES

In fairness to Laplace and his followers, let us recall again that under the constitution of gases as understood previous to the middle of last century, there was no inconsistency in supposing that a rapidly rotating spheroid of gas might, in the course of its cooling and shrinking, leave behind a succession of rings of gas. At the same time, no deferential regard for a great name justifies us in failing to follow the determinations of later research to their utmost applications. The introduction and establishment of the kinetic theory of gases destroyed the very foundation on which the concept of gaseous rings (of a planet-forming order) was founded.

By the terms of its laws, the kinetic theory requires that the molecules of a rotating body of gas should fly off individually as fast as they acquire sufficient velocity by rebounds from individual collisions. This had been urged before these studies were undertaken; and, so far as this point is concerned, they have done little more than enlarge upon the contention.

However, previous to the present century, the kinetic theory of gases was not regarded as fully established, so that this argument was subject to all the doubts that still hung about the theory from which the argument was drawn.

THE FORESTALLING EFFECT OF THE INDIVIDUAL ESCAPE OF MOLECULES

The successions of collisions and rebounds among the molecules of gases bring about cumulative effects. A certain percentage of molecules gain velocities high enough to escape from the body controlling them if they find a free path in the direction of rebound. When the velocity required to escape is much greater than the rotational velocity, the number of such escapes is relatively small; but if the rate of rotation becomes almost sufficient of itself to set off molecules, only a slight enhancement of velocity by molecular interaction is required to actually send them off. This of itself would forestall separation as a ring or in any other aggregated form. The usual argument rests here.

But another factor comes into function just before the critical instant for mass separation is reached and *prevents the rotation from rising to the velocity necessary for massive separation.* This effect springs from the well-known law that action and reaction are equal and in opposite directions. Whenever a molecule on the equatorial rim of a rotating spheroid escapes by rebound because of its exceptionally high velocity, it carries off an exceptional amount of momentum, while its partner in collision reacts in the opposite direction. The mean effect of such reactions is to *check the rate of rotation.* And since high-speed molecules are continually going off, the rotation never quite reaches the rate required to shed a ring or any other mass of gas as a mass.

THE DISPERSION OF PLANETARY RINGS INEVITABLE, EVEN IF FORMED

Not only would the molecular activity of a hot, rotating gaseous spheroid, like that postulated by the Laplacian hypothesis, have forestalled the formation of gaseous rings, but this same activity would have dispersed the rings, even if they could have been formed. This may be shown by technical and mathematical methods, but the general reader feels less able to pass upon these than on arguments drawn from natural evidences.

It is obvious that molecules of gases hot enough to keep ordinary rock-substances in a volatile state would be very active and that their collisions and rebounds would be very frequent and intense. If, therefore, we argue from cold bodies, we will leave a large "margin of safety" to cover any little qualifications that our argument may be thought to need. The satellites that in cold states cannot now hold atmospheres, cannot rationally be supposed to have held atmospheres when in a hot state, and certainly not when in a smaller growing state. If once hot enough to be wholly gaseous, such bodies as the relatively small satellites and planetoids probably could not control even the vapors of their stony material. If, therefore, any of these bodies in its present cold state does not hold an atmosphere, it is quite safe to assume that it did not do so if it was ever hot enough to be a gas.

As the sun and stars are constantly throwing out molecules, and as comets give us frequent demonstrations that the sun drives molecules out of them and across planetary space, it is also safe to infer that any planet, planetoid, or satellite that can hold an atmosphere would long since have gathered one. There was once a theory that atmospheres might be lost by being absorbed into the planets or satellites which they enveloped; but the evidences that will come out later indicate that atmospheres are being supplied from within, as also from without, when the planets can hold them. We may therefore make use of the atmosphereless bodies of the planetary system as natural credentials of the ability or lack of ability of bodies in the inner zone of the sun's domain to hold atmospheres.

THE MOON USED AS A TEST-CRITERION

Let us first make use of the moon as a test-criterion. Let us suppose the earth to be divided into moons distributed along the earth's orbit like a ring of beads. Such a ring of beads would be distinctly more capable of holding gases than a uniform cylindrical ring, for there is no form in which a given amount of matter is so capable of controlling enveloping gases as in the spherical form. A cylindrical ring about a massive body, such as the sun, is peculiarly ill fitted to control gases. In using a ring of cold beads, we are giving the supposed hot gaseous ring two distinct advantages—the advantage of temperature and of concentration.

Let us give the ring theory still another advantage by assuming that the number of moons is 82, although the earth-matter would fall a little short of that. The moons would then be 7,000,000 miles (11,200,000 kilometers) apart. But to hold an envelope of ordinary cold atmospheric gases, they should *overlap*.

If the supposed earth-forming ring were no larger than the orbit of Venus, the centers of the moons would still be more than 5,000,000 miles apart and the competitive attraction of the sun would be greater and more overlap would be required. If the ring were of the size of the orbit of Mars, the centers of the moons would be more than 10,000,000 miles apart, but the competitive attraction of the sun would be less, and less overlap would be required; but no single moon even at that distance would hold an atmosphere of ordinary gases. Mercury tells its own tale directly, for, although its whole mass is well concentrated, it does not hold an appreciable atmosphere.

But how about the great planets? Jupiter is much the largest and most massive of all the planets, is situated in the midst of the planetary series, and appears now to have the greatest envelope of gases. In these respects it is well suited to give us a supreme test. Theoretical considerations seem to imply that, even at the distance of Jupiter's orbit, the moon would not hold an atmosphere. Jupiter would make 25,778 moons; and, if distributed equally along its orbit, their centers would be more than 11,700 miles apart.

We may find an alternative test by taking the mean mass of the four Galilean satellites of Jupiter whose eclipses were watched long and carefully to determine the velocity of light and which therefore may be presumed to be unobscured by appreciable atmospheres. The mass of Jupiter would make about 24,000 of such representative satellites, and if these were distributed along Jupiter's orbit their centers would be 12,600 miles apart. The result is of the same order as before. From this mode of testing the postulated gaseous rings they do not seem even closely to approach competency to hold themselves together.

The test takes its most decisive form when applied to the smaller satellites and the planetoids, of which there are a thousand or more. None of these now have atmospheres, though their substances are concentrated into the most favorable form for atmospheric control and they are quite cold. They offer no reasons for supposing that they ever held atmospheres.

Tested in these and other ways, all gaseous lines of planetary evolution seem to prove altogether incompetent. The actual mode of building the planets must have been one by which the high velocities of molecular collision and rebound were avoided.

Destructive tests of this kind carry a positive intimation in addition to their negative determinations. They imply not only that the true line of search avoids antagonistic motions but that it lies in modes of motion that are *concurrent*.

This type of motion is thus brought definitely into working recognition as standing over against antagonistic, transverse and heterogeneous motions.

REFERENCES

1. T. C. Chamberlin, "The Tidal and Other Problems—The Bearing of Molecular Activity on the Spontaneous Fission of Gaseous Spheroids," *Carnegie Institution of Washington, Publication 107* (1909), pp. 163–67.

2. T. C. Chamberlin, *The Origin of the Earth*, chap. ii.

CHAPTER VI

TESTS OF CENTRIFUGAL THEORIES BY SPEEDS OF ROTATION

It is only little by little that man has come to realize that nature makes records of almost all that it does, and that these records are often better historical evidence than the records of man himself, for they are free from his bias. He naturally sees things from the human point of view. There was a time when man refused to recognize the validity of any historical records that antedated his own. He thought it sufficient to say that no man then lived to witness events and they could not be humanly known. He held all claims to know earlier events as purely speculative. In the less familiar realms of nature this attitude is as yet only partially abated. New views that traverse old concepts are still quite freely consigned to the limbo of "the purely speculative." But those who really think are coming to realize that the automatic vestiges of creation are the best of all evidences of the earliest events, if only they are truly read. In the intelligent world, the time has passed when the testimony of the relics of life are seriously questioned. Physical records now commonly command like confidences. The footprints of processes are accepted as good credentials quite on a par with the footprints of living creatures. Stratified beds, ripple marks, glacial grooves, the folded strata of mountains, and the stumps of volcanoes are held to tell past history as truly as fossils and footprints. But equal confidence is not yet reposed in the less tangible dynamic relics—inherited motions, for example.

It is now being revealed, as never before, that the dynamic world is the really great world; the material world is receding. Naturally enough it is coming to be seen that there are dynamic vestiges as well as material vestiges. There are rotations that tell a tale as well as the body that rotates. The revolutions of a planet may tell us more than the planet itself. Not only are there kinetic energies and momenta, but there are the much more intangible and subtle potential energies of position. All forms of these activities, as they now exist, are as truly vestiges of past events as are the material relics we read with so much greater confidence. These dynamic fossils seem less tangible and convincing. They are, indeed, less easily read. Certainly they are less obtrusive, and when set forth, are less impressive even when they are quite as conclusive, and even more fundamental. We are very slow to realize that by far the greatest energies of the cosmos are very unobtrusive. The greatest works of nature are silent and unseen. The great actors of nature do not strut on the stage.

From the nature of the case these studies have been forced more toward the dynamical than toward the material. In testing the doctrine of centrifugal separation of the planetary bodies as rings or otherwise, there was no better criterion than the dynamic vestige offered by the sun's rotation.

THE ROTATION OF THE SUN AS A DYNAMIC RELIC

When, as brought out in the last chapter, the test of the gaseous hypotheses by the dynamics of gases seemed to cut their working basis from under them, it seemed wise to try to find some other line of test not immediately dependent on the theory of gases, or on the velocities of molecular escape, or on spheres of control. Attention happened first to fall upon the slow rotation of the sun. This rotation is an inheritance from the rotation the sun had when the planets were formed, and is as truly a vestige of creation as the Silurian formations, the Cambrian trilobites, or the Paleozoic Alps. Attention was later directed to the obliquity of the sun's axis, another dynamic vestige of like fundamental nature.

It is one of the basal postulates of the Laplacian hypothesis—and, substantially, of all other hypotheses that belong to the same genus—that the nebula which evolved into the solar family had a certain rotation when it was in its most expanded condition, and that, as it cooled and shrank, its rate of rotation increased in accordance with mechanical law to preserve the value of its rotatory momentum, technically its moment of momentum. The constancy of the moment of momentum in such a rotatory system is one of the best-established principles of mechanics. It is inevitably involved in all centrifugal theories of celestial genesis, and must indeed enter radically and consistently into any cosmogonic theory, whatever its nature, if such theory is to have any claim to serious consideration. As such indispensable principle, it is susceptible of being made a criterion of

..ighest value in testing the validity of cosmogonic tenets. It is peculiarly applicable to the tenets of hypotheses confessedly founded on it. In the application of this principle, it was held under the Laplacian hypothesis —by implication, if not by open declaration—that when the parent nebula by cooling had shrunk to a diameter of about five and one-half billion miles—the velocity at its equator being then 3.4 miles per second—a ring was separated by centrifugal action which afterward gathered into the planet Neptune. When, three stages later, the nebula had shrunk to a diameter somewhat less than a billion miles—the velocity then acquired being about 8 miles per second at the equator—a more massive ring was supposed to have been separated, which later formed the great planet Jupiter When, again omitting two stages, the nebula had shrunk to a diameter about equal to that of the orbit of the earth—its equatorial velocity having risen to 18.5 miles per second—another ring was separated which formed the earth. When the nebula had shrunk to a size comparable to the orbit of Mercury, its equatorial speed had arisen to about 29 miles per second. As shrinkage continued after the separation of Mercury, the principle requires that proportionate increases of rotatory velocity should have ensued. Further separations of equatorial matter and further formation of planets might, in complete consistency with the hypothesis, be presumed to have taken place and, indeed, were presumed to have taken place by the astronomers of the last century. They made diligent search for inner planets at times of solar eclipse when the glare of the sun, that might ordinarily obscure small planets in its vicinity, was cut off. An eminent astronomer even announced the discovery of such a planet and named it Vulcan, but the observation proved illusory. Now, if Vulcan had proved to be a reality, and if the radius of its orbit had been a million miles, its velocity in its orbit, if circular, should have been about 170 miles per second, and the equatorial velocity of rotation of the parent nebula at the time of the planet's supposed separation should have been the same. The further contraction of the nebula to the present radius of the sun should have given it an equatorial velocity of 270 miles (435 kilometers) per second. *But the actual velocity of the sun's equator is only about 1½ miles (2 kilometers) per second.* In other words, the actual velocity is only about one-half of 1 per cent of the theoretical requirement. Here then is an enormous discrepancy. The discrepancy is the more notable in that it arises from the very principle on which the hypothesis is founded. Interpreted as a dynamic relic of the sun's past history and as an index of its genesis, this inconsistently slow rotation seems to imply that the sun is not the residual product of any such a system of progressive separations as the Laplacian and similar centrifugal hypotheses postulate. It is not easy to see how this conclusion can be escaped, unless it can be shown that some competent agency acting as a break, came into action after the separation of Mercury and was efficient enough to reduce the rotation of the sun to a two-hundredth part of the velocity toward which it had been trending up to this stage in accordance with one of the best-established laws of mechanics. There is an inherent difficulty in seeing just how any such agency, or the source of any such agency, could have existed in the system and have remained in abeyance during the whole active period of planetary evolution so as to permit rotation to increase systematically until all the planets were cast off, and then, but then only, have come into action of an opposite order and of so high efficiency that further contraction should not only have failed to sustain the previous habit of steadily increasing rotation, but should have reversed the effect with so much potency as to bring the rotation down to a very small fraction of what had already been attained.

However, a possible agency working somewhat in this strange way must be considered. So long as the planetary matter remained in the form of rings, its attraction had no deterrent action on the sun's rotation; but as soon as the rings were gathered into concentrated masses, as the hypothesis assumes they did, each of these masses tended to develop tides in the sun, and these tides acted as brakes on its rotation. Now, in the first place, it must be noted that as soon as any planetary mass began to act in this way, it tended to stop the planet-forming process. Too much efficiency of this kind on the part of the outer planets would have forestalled the formation of the inner planets. Now the time at which such masses could be most effective was in their earliest stages, for then the solar body was largest and its proximate side was nearest to them while its distal side was farthest from them. Furthermore, the tides of these first-formed masses were then least neutralized by the tides of the later-formed masses. The planets are distributed about the sun by their different rates of revolution and are rarely, if ever, all on a single side of the sun, or on the opposite sides, so as to conjoin their tidal effects. Their distribution is constantly changing, so that any distribution that tends to tidal efficiency is merely temporary. As a result, their several tides neutralize one another in large degree and the residual effect is small. The subject of tidal influence in the evolution of our planetary system has been elaborately investigated by Sir George Darwin, and as his working hypotheses were such as to give to tidal effects their maximum probable values, his results are assumed to be conclusive. He found that the utmost assignable effects of all the planetary tides upon the rotation of the sun, and upon the reciprocal retreat of the planets, is so trivial as to be quite negligible. Even if the age of the system be greatly extended beyond current estimates, the evolutionary value of the planetary tides does not rise to appreciable moment.

As the sun is constantly radiating away enormous quantities of heat, it is improbable that the retarding action of the planetary tides has been at any time equal to the accelerating effect of the sun's contraction, even if the solar contraction is much slower than was formerly supposed, owing to sources of heat then undiscovered. It is, however, impracticable to determine this positively in the present state of knowledge relative to the sun's sources of heat.

If there were any doubt as to the incompetency of the planetary tides to account for the great discrepancy between the actual rotation of the sun and the theoretical rotation it should have under the Laplacian hypothesis, this doubt should prompt us to a search for other grounds on which to test the hypothesis by the application of fundamental principles, for discrepancies are almost sure to insinuate themselves under the mantle of any hypothesis that does not tally with the historic reality. While no doubt is here entertained as to the incompetency of tidal action to explain the great discrepancy disclosed by the rotation of the sun, an independent line of inquiry, undertaken to cover, so far as possible, any weaknesses that might be supposed to lurk in this argument and in the preceding atmospheric test, will be the subject of the next chapter.

It was only after such a supplementary inquiry had been made that the implications of the second of the sun's significant vestiges, the inclination of its axis to the planes of the planets, arrested serious attention, and so, if strict historic sequence were followed, this feature should be discussed later; but while we are considering the dynamic vestiges of the sun, it is convenient to refer briefly to the inclination of its axis. It must be quite obvious to everyone familiar with ordinary mechanics that, if the sun, by reason of its rotation, "threw off" parts of itself by centrifugal action, they should have taken paths lying in the plane of its equator; much more is this evident if the center of the nebula simply shrank away from the outer rim, the true picture. This holds whether these parts were left behind as rings or as individual particles, or in any other natural manner.

But as a matter of fact the plane of the earth's orbit is inclined $7^\circ\ 10'.5$ to the plane of the sun's equator. The orbits of all other planets are also inclined to the plane of the sun's equator, some more, some less than this; some of the planetoids very much more than this. If, however, these varying inclinations were such as completely to offset one another so that the mean plane coincided with the sun's equator, the conditions of the theory might still be regarded as fulfilled; but the "invariable plane" of the planetary system which summarizes the total inclination values of all the planetary orbits is also inclined to the sun's equator about 5°. While this is not a very large angle, the inertia represented by the motion of the planets is so enormous that even this small deviation represents a rather grave discrepancy between theory and fact, though it does not rise to the serious nature of the preceding discrepancy. It will be necessary to recur to this feature when later we turn from destructive criticism to the much more difficult task of constructing a hypothesis to meet, if possible, this and the many other significant features of the actual system.

REFERENCES

1. Sir George Darwin, "On the Tidal Friction of a Planet Surrounded by Several Satellites and on the Evolution of the Solar System," *Philosophical Transactions of the Royal Society of London*, Part II (1881), pp. 491–535.

2. T. C. Chamberlin, F. R. Moulton, C. S. Slichter, W. D. MacMillan, Arthur C. Lunn, Julius Stieglitz, "The Tidal and Other Problems," *Carnegie Institution of Washington, Publication 107* (1909).

3. T. C. Chamberlin, *The Origin of the Earth* (1916), chap. ii.

CHAPTER VII

THE LAPLACIAN HYPOTHESIS TESTED BY THE LAWS OF MECHANICS

When, as recited in a previous chapter, the nebular hypothesis, as well as all other gaseous theories, betrayed serious weaknesses under the application of the kinetic theory of gases and under the principles of celestial control, and when, as recited in the last chapter, the centrifugal factor of these hypotheses seemed to disclose even more declared incompetencies under the test of rotation, there arose a strenuous urge to test the Laplacian hypothesis by still other and, if possible, more decisive criteria. It could not be lightly assumed that a hypothesis which had been so widely accepted for a century was fatally weak in its own fundamentals. It was more natural to assume that the inquirer had himself fallen into error or misconception. However, the call to proceed till the error or the misconception, wherever it lay, should be disclosed was none the less imperative. The call was perhaps all the more urgent because the weaknesses of this, the leading gaseous hypothesis, seemed to involve all other gaseous hypotheses as well as all quasi-gaseous hypotheses and perhaps all centrifugal hypotheses. Indeed, it seemed to raise doubt as to the possibility of even framing any centrifugal hypothesis that could fit the facts of our planetary system. This does not, of course, imply that some other planetary system might not arise from centrifugal separation, but merely that *our* planetary system, being what it is, did not arise in that way.

Dr. Moulton had, as previously stated, furnished me with tables and formulas of parabolic velocities for the earth, under different conditions of volume and rotation, as an aid in the gaseous inquiry; and I had sought his good opinion relative to the significance of the sun's slow rotation. He was now good enough to join seriously in the inquiry and to take the leadership in testing the tenets of the Laplacian hypothesis by means of the laws of dynamics, a line of investigation in which the skill of a master in celestial mechanics carried a value of the highest order. The new tests were singularly fertile in disclosing discrepancies.

SPECIFIC DEFECTS OF THE LAPLACIAN HYPOTHESIS

1. For a first trial, the nebula postulated by the Laplacian hypothesis as the parent of the solar system was restored by Dr. Moulton as faithfully as possible by a theoretical conversion of the entire mass of the present system into gas and by assigning to it such a deployment as would be required by the accepted laws of gaseous distribution. In doing this he endeavored to give the hypothesis the benefit of every doubt and to allow a liberal margin of safety in every case of quantitative uncertainty. To this restored nebula he assigned the full value of all the momentum the system now possesses. Comparison was then made between this representative nebula and the actual solar system in regard to the respective values of their momenta. These values are funda-

mental in nature and should tally closely with one another if the Laplacian hypothesis were true.

The first stage selected for comparison was naturally that at which the restored nebula had, by hypothesis, shrunk to the size of the orbit of Neptune and was ready to cast off a ring to form that planet. The value of the momentum in the nebula and the value of the momentum that would be necessary to bring about the separation of the postulated ring by centrifugal action were each computed and were found to be widely discrepant, the momentum of the nebula having less than a two-hundredth of the value required for separation. A similar trial was made at the stage when the matter for Jupiter should have parted from the nebula, and it was found that the nebula then had less than a hundred and fortieth of the momentum required to separate a ring. At the stage assigned for the setting off of the earth-moon ring, the nebula had about an eighteen-hundredth of the momentum necessary. At the Mercury stage, it had about an eleven-hundredth. It will be seen that these are discrepancies of a very high order and are quite comparable in this respect to the discrepancy disclosed by the sun's slow rotation.

While these inquiries of Dr. Moulton were entirely independent of previous investigations in like lines, as was natural from the special way in which he was led to make them, it was found later that Babinet had detected discrepancies of the same type many years previously. Though his conclusions had been reached in a somewhat analogous way, the methods pursued were not identical. It does not appear from what can now be learned that Babinet pushed his inquiry so far as to become convinced that the discrepancies were fatal to the Laplacian hypothesis. On the contrary, he seems to have regarded the incongruities merely as difficulties which must be met in some way by the hypothesis which he appears to have continued to accept.

2. In the tests of Dr. Moulton, each stage in the evolution of the nebula was considered by itself, such masses as had been separated previously to form planets outside the one under consideration being subtracted from the nebula, following in this, as in other respects, precisely the terms of the Laplacian hypothesis. Each case was thus, in some sense, an independent one. To apply the test in a somewhat different way, it was assumed that the whole mass of the system remained in the nebula until the rate of its rotation became sufficient to force the separation of the rim as a ring in accordance with the assumptions of the hypothesis. It was found that the centrifugal component would not rise to equality with the centripetal force of gravity until after the nebula had shrunk within the orbit of the innermost planet.

As all these tests were based on well-established dynamical laws, the conclusions could not fairly be regarded as much less than rigorous, except perhaps in so far as they were dependent on the accuracy of the restoration of the nebula, which was guided by the accepted law of distribution of gases. This law, while probably rigorous under ideal conditions, shows some tendency to break down in cases where the state of the gas is near the border line that marks the transition from the gaseous state to some other state; but in all known cases, the departures from the strict terms of the law were found to be such as to bear *against* the hypothesis, so that here, as in other cases, the assumption of the complete integrity of the law gave the hypothesis the benefit of the doubt. The critical reader will readily see that the true law of distribution might vary widely from the accepted law without removing in any large measure the great discrepancies disclosed.

3. Although there was thus no tangible ground for apprehending that any falling away from the law of distribution of gases could essentially weaken the rigor of the conclusions reached by Moulton's dynamical inspection, it seemed none the less desirable to find a test whose working factors were not derived from the law of distribution of gases, and thus cover by such alternative inquiry any doubt that might seem to arise from this source. I endeavored to find such a test in a comparison of masses and momenta as they now exist. The method proceeded on the assumption that the masses and the momenta alike remained essentially constant throughout the evolution, an assumption inherent in the principles of the Laplacian hypothesis. Exchange of momentum between the members of the system is not, however, excluded, and there will be something to say of the possible extent of this after the mode of trial and its results have been outlined. The method may be concretely illustrated in the case of the great planet Jupiter, which fairly represents the general tenor of the results in other cases. Jupiter, including his satellites, now carries a little less than one-thousandth (1/1,024) of the mass of the solar system exclusive of the planets outside Jupiter which do not enter into this comparison. The mass of the nebula just

before the Jovian ring was separated from it, was, according to the Laplacian hypothesis, identical with the combined masses of Jupiter and the bodies within its orbit. For the purposes of the inspection the momentum values now carried by the Jovian family and the bodies within were taken from the computations of Sir George Darwin, and thus the results were made to rest on authoritative data wholly independent of the computations of my colleague. Now the reader will find little difficulty in forming a mental picture that roughly represents the proportions of momentum and of mass in the different parts of a symmetrical rotating body such as the nebula must have been; at least he can picture disproportions in the different parts so great that they would not be developed in a natural evolution, and so he may limit to his own satisfaction the *range* within which the true case must lie, without assuming to know precisely what the exact fact is. If skilled in mechanics, he may use a series of hypotheses that fix more definitely the range within which the true case must fall. The nebula at the initial stage of partition must have formed an oblate spheroid rotating at such a rate that the outer one-thousandth part was just ready to separate to form Jupiter and his moons. The next thousandth part lay just inside that and was rotating at a proportional rate, which was somewhat slower; the next thousandth lay next within and was still slower, and so on down to the last thousandth which had almost no rotatory momentum at all. The value of the momentum in each case is measured by the product of the mass, the speed, and the length of the arm on which each part was rotating, and the comparison is to be between the outer thousandth and the *sum* of all the remaining nine hundred and ninety-nine thousandths. If the reader has fixed upon the highest proportion of the total momentum that could possibly, in his judgment, be carried by the outer one-thousandth part of the nebula, he will be prepared to appreciate how far the hypothesis is credible when, by recourse to the data of Sir George Darwin, it is found that Jupiter and his moons now carry 96 per cent of the whole momentum, leaving to the remaining nine hundred and ninety-nine parts only 4 per cent. In some respects this remarkable disproportion is quite as convincing evidence that Jupiter was not separated by simple centrifugal action as the more rigorous determination by the previous method which showed that the existing momentum is one hundred and forty times more than the same matter would have carried in the restored nebula.

When this alternative method was applied to other planets, similar disproportions between masses and momenta were disclosed; in some cases even a greater relative disproportion was revealed than in the case of Jupiter.

4. Inspections of the foregoing kinds that direct specific attention to the conditions under which separation should take place force the conviction that a certain regularity and symmetry in respect to the masses of the successive rings must have resulted from the centrifugal process, if it obtained. But very striking irregularities in the masses of the planets are observed. If the mass of the earth be taken as unity, the order of the planetary masses from the outermost to the innermost is 17; 14.6;

94.8; 317.7; 0.1073; 1; 0.82; 0.0476. This irregularity has of course long been known and the incongruity recognized but not thought fatal.

5. Rings shed from the rim of a rotating spheroid should have been strictly circular when they were first formed, and no wide departures from circularity should probably have followed in the course of subsequent evolution. The orbits of most of the planets approach fairly closely to circularity and no severe indictment of centrifugal hypotheses can be based on the ellipticities observed, though some of them are rather notable. The orbits of the planetoids, however, are often much more eccentric, and their planes diverge more notably from the invariable plane of the system. The attraction of their powerful neighbor Jupiter is sometimes held responsible for this. There is, however, a singular fact about the orbits of the planetoids that is not met by this plausible hypothesis. Bodies shed from a nebula by centrifugal action should have orbits strictly concentric with one another; no orbit should loop through any other. The orbits of the planetoids, however, are so singularly interlooped that, if they were solid rods, the lifting of one would lift the whole group.

6. If we turn to the supposed evolution of the satellites from the planets by centrifugal action, some features as strikingly incongruous as any of the preceding are encountered. Under the centrifugal theory, all the satellite rings should have rotated precisely as their parent nebulae did, and when the rings were condensed into satellites these should have revolved in the same direction as their primaries. Each inner ring should have rotated

in less time than the rings outside it, while the central body should have rotated in a shorter period than any ring. The principle is the same as that already considered in relation to the rotation of the sun. But Phobos, the inner satellite of Mars, revolves around that planet more than three times while the planet rotates once. This is a very singular, telltale vestige of Mars's early history. While this anomaly has been known ever since Hall discovered the satellites in 1868, and has been recognized as puzzling, its force was largely avoided or palliated by the hypothesis that the rotation of Mars was indeed high at the outset but has been so reduced in the course of time by the tidal action of its moons that the present strange state of affairs was reached. Nolan, however, insisted that this explanation was inadequate. Moulton added piquancy to the anomaly by pointing out that the little bodies which make up the inner border of Saturn's innermost ring revolve in a period only about half that of Saturn's rotation. Moulton further pointed out that, even if a tidal scheme could be made to fit the case of Mars, it would not, at the same time, fit the case of Saturn, unless it were assumed that Saturn is something like three thousand times as old as Mars.

7. Though it is not in proper historical order here, this is a convenient place to remark that three even more telltale cases of strange behavior on the part of satellites have been discovered since we were led by the foregoing and other considerations to abandon the centrifugal theory of satellite origin and to adopt a new one. Among the new satellites that have been discovered by photography, it appears that Saturn has one and Jupiter has

two that revolve in a *retrograde* direction *contrary to the rest.* Nothing would seem more obvious than that a planetary spheroid, rotating so fast as to shed a series of rings by centrifugal action to form satellites, should impart to them all its own direction of motion. Such a result is so obvious that it was formerly taught that a single exception would be absolutely fatal to the Laplacian theory; the writer was so instructed in his college days. It now appears that, while the majority of the satellites revolve in the same direction as their primaries, a minority take the opposite course, and that these contrary habits are found in the same family of moons in two cases.

8. Among the older objections to the ring theory was the inference that a gaseous spheroid would not cast off a definite ring, even if its rotation were so increased that separation in some form was inevitable. It was felt that the molecules would go off separately, or at the most in small groups, and that such small separations would follow at short intervals, so that the whole would form a disk rather than a series of distinct rings. The molecules of gases are held together by gravity in spite of a tendency to fly apart by reason of rebounds from collisions with other molecules, and hence so soon as gravity at the outermost rim of the rotating nebula was neutralized by the increasing centrifugal force, the molecules should have gone off individually into orbits. There was no agency to hold them back until the other molecules requisite to make up a ring great enough to form a planet should also have reached the state requiring separation. A ring of sufficient magnitude to form the greater planets should have had some millions of miles of depth

and the differences in the ratio of rotation to gravity in its outer and in its inner edges respectively should have been rather large. This objection is so obvious that some surprise may naturally be entertained that the formation of rings was ever made a part of the hypothesis. There seem to have been two reasons, doubtless seemingly cogent at the time, for the introduction of the ring feature.

One of these was a supposed logical necessity to meet the facts of planetary rotation. All the revolutions of the secondary bodies of the solar system were in the same direction as their primaries, that is *forward*, so far as known when the Laplacian hypothesis was framed. It was reasoned that if a ring rotated *as a unit*, the outer part of which moves faster than the inner, the rotation of the globe into which the ring gathered would also be forward; but if, on the other hand, the ring were made up of small bodies revolving independently, the inner bodies in this case moving faster than the outer, as they must, the rotation of the resulting globe would be in the opposite or *retrograde* direction. This cogent logic seemed to warn everyone away from any theory that started with particles pursuing independent revolutions. To all such hypotheses it seems to have served as a lion in the way, effectually warning off cosmogonic pilgrims. The warning seems to have been religiously heeded throughout the last century. The question will arise later whether it was anything more than the skin of a lion, but let that pass here.

The other reason was naturalistic. The rings of Saturn were very naturally thought to be vestiges of the evolutionary process, and, correctly interpreted, they were certainly entitled to be so regarded. There can be little doubt that they were really the foster-parents of the ring theory. In Laplace's time, it was not unnatural to suppose that they were gaseous. It required the acumen of later mathematics and the analyzing power of the spectroscope to prove that the rings are in reality composed of little bodies revolving independently, satellitesimals, if you please, the very class of bodies that were supposed to give rise to *retrograde* rotations. For a hypothesis built up so naturally in response to the apparent teachings of such lovely celestial objects as the Saturnian rings to find at length that it was the victim of misplaced confidence was indeed a cruel fate.

9. But our study of the case did not leave the issue simply with the conviction that the rim of the nebula would separate continuously into a disk; it went farther and raised two much more radical questions, the first, whether the passing off of the molecules individually would not *forestall* the state at which the centripetal force of gravity would be overtaken by the centrifugal force of rotation; the second, whether the molecular orbits would really be circular, as assumed, or whether on the contrary, they would not be so far elliptical as to vitiate the reasoning by which the rings were regarded as logically necessary.

In the second chapter, the ways in which the common collisional atmosphere passes into an ultra-atmosphere of vaulting molecules, and the ways in which a part of these vaulting molecules pass into an ultra-atmosphere of molecules in orbital flights, were set forth. Now it is clear that centrifugal action aids the passage of the collisional molecules into vaulting molecules and also aids the passage of some of these vaulting molecules into orbital molecules. Every increase of rotation, by increasing the centrifugal tendency, increases the transfer of molecules from the collisional to the vaulting, and from the vaulting to the orbital, states. This transfer is at the expense of the momentum of the rotating body, for the orbital molecules require a higher mean value of momentum than the mean value of the momentum of the molecules of the collisional atmosphere. If the process is closely followed, it will be seen that as the centrifugal tendency increases almost to equality with the opposing centripetal force of gravity, the number of molecules that are driven by collisions into vaulting leaps and orbits is increased. The momentum requisite for the orbital movements is taken from the molecules from which the last leaps were taken. The loss of these molecules is equalized later with the rest of the nebula. The inference from this is that increase of rotation, in such a body, necessarily finds issue in increasing the number of molecules that pass into orbits, and that the nebula, because of its constant loss of momentum, would never reach the state at which molecules will be separated *simply* by centrifugal action; they would rather be separated by *molecular activity* superposed on the high rate of rotation attained. If this seems a too subtle distinction, it is to be observed that the molecules which go off through molecular activity pursue orbits that have a great variety of eccentricities so that their subsequent aggregation into planets and satellites is conditioned by these eccentric orbits and is not amenable to the logical deduction relative to rotation cited above as playing so important a part in cosmogonic thinking for the past century. Reference must be made to a later discussion on rotation for the full meaning of the distinction between aggregation from circular concentric orbits and aggregation from heterogeneous elliptical orbits respectively.

10. Moulton has shown that, even if a ring were formed, the breaking of this ring at some weak point and the collection of the whole into a globe, as postulated in the Laplacian hypothesis, if it does not traverse the laws of celestial mechanics, is at least attended with grave difficulties. Even if a large nucleus were formed at some point on the ring to serve as a collecting center, it probably could not gather to itself bodies in independent circular orbits from an angular distance of more than 60° without the co-operation of some other agency. The considerations in this case are too technical to be introduced here. So also are some other criteria developed by Dr. Moulton in the course of his inquiry.

If then the probabilities are strongly against the formation of a coherent ring by centrifugal action, and if such a ring, granted that it be formed, could not hold the lighter molecules at the postulated temperatures in such a case as that of the earth, and if, in addition, the mechanical difficulties of segregation into a single spheroid were highly adverse, if not insurmountable, even under the most favorable circumstances, this line of genesis offers little in its favor to offset the grave incongruities and discrepancies disclosed in the mechanics of the system.

It would, however, no doubt leave an unfair impression of the hypothesis of Laplace, and of its unsurpassed simplicity and beauty, and of the great service it has rendered the progress of thought, if there were no recognition of the fact that there is a long list of general harmonies between the salient features of the solar system and the broader terms of the hypothesis. On such general harmonies the hypothesis was founded, and from these it gathered to itself a wide adherence. All this was meritorious in its day. It was only by the progress of discovery —to which, indeed, it had itself made noble contributions—and by advance in analytical inquiry, that these broader harmonies were found to be merely general, while specific incongruities of a grave nature were disclosed. In some notable measure, though not wholly, these incongruities were veiled at the time the hypothesis was given to the world by the great French astronomer and mathematician.

Before passing to the next phase of our inquiry, a word is to be said relative to some of the cosmogonies that preceded the admirably specific theory of Laplace. Only general reference has been made to these thus far, for they really took almost no part in the inquiry. There were specific reasons for this. For the greater part, they had not been worked out into specific details that could be applied closely to the peculiar dynamic features of the earth and its planetary kin, and, for this reason, they were not fitted to play any serious part in an inquiry that tried to proceed naturalistically on the specific testimony of the dynamic vestiges borne by the planets. It was of some interest, to be sure, that these general cosmogonic theories were more or less susceptible of being made the point of departure for some new view of the genesis of the earth that was specific, if one felt that the facts of the dynamic record made such an effort promising. But the views actually offered for consideration were, in general, too vague to take their places beside the clear and sharp tenets of the Laplacian hypothesis. As earlier intimated, the Laplacian hypothesis stands alone among the older views in its laudable definiteness.

THE LESS SPECIFIC HYPOTHESES

To a notable extent, though not universally, the other older cosmogonic theories centered on the profound problem of original creation, or, at least, on the primitive state of celestial matter. Following back along the line of terrestrial evidence, as our inquiry did, and clinging as closely as possible to the evidence of the earth's automatic record, it would have been an unwarranted leap into the depths of speculative assumption to have presumed that, when we had reached the stage of planetary genesis, we had also reached the beginning of things. Nothing whatever had been found in the record to imply that the birth of the earth was a feature of the absolute beginning of the universe. As intimated already, once and again, there seemed no ground to assume that the origin of the earth stood as the only type of origin of secondaries in the great universe, or that it was a part of primitive creation, however naturally it may have been assumed by the ancients to be a creative *ultima Thule*. There had not even appeared in the record any clear evidence that there was a primitive creation *ex nihilo*, as distinguished from an indefinite backward extension of cycles of celestial evolution. The trend of our inquiry—a trend that will appear even more distinctly in its later stages—lay rather in the latter direction. The inquiry had been leading—and it continued to lead—step by step to the impression that the creation of our planetary system was but an incident in the history of our sun, while even the genesis of the sun might not improbably be but an incident in the history of our stellar galaxy, and the genesis of that perhaps only an episode in the evolution of the real universe that undoubtedly lies chiefly beyond our ken. It appeared, therefore, that, while our inquiry might lead on ultimately to some consideration of the evolution of our stellar galaxy, and to the modes of genesis of the stars and their attendants—which, springing from surpassingly rich resources of energy and activity, might follow many different lines—only a small part of this broad complex problem lay within the specific field of our inquiry. This fraction, however small relative to the whole, was none the less all too great for our investigative resources.

To a large extent, as intimated, the older cosmogonic views centered upon the speculative concept of primeval chaos, or a modified view of it, and made this chaos the initial stage of stellar history. Under this assumption there usually lay the postulate of absolute creation, but this was not always the case. Creation *ex nihilo* was accompanied, or followed, putatively, by endowments of energy, activity, and the various properties of matter; and these led on to a series of events which brought the sun and the planets into being. The whole solar system was thus made the direct offspring of a primitive series of events. The sun and the planets were assigned a common birth. The details and special stages were more or less successive, indeed; but the whole was one great unitary evolution. This general postulate of a common, and essentially contemporaneous, evolution of sun, stars, planets, and satellites was a feature common to most of the older cosmogonic theories. In this they were at one with the Laplacian hypothesis. A departure from this prevailing conception appeared, however, in the latter part of the eighteenth century, in the collisional hypothesis of Buffon. To this we shall refer later.

Where primeval chaos, or any form of a universal diffuse condition was taken as the original state, some form of segmentation must necessarily have followed as a means by which appropriate volumes of the diffuse matter came to be separated from the rest in a form suited to gather later into the several stellar systems—the solar system being the case of particular interest to us. The mechanics assigned for such a segregation were very obscure, or altogether neglected. Even the segregation itself was passed over lightly. If original uniformity was assumed, as obscurely implied in most cases, as definitely stated in some, the assigned agencies that actuated such sub-segregation rested on doubtful bases. If in any case departure from original uniformity was implied, no specific asymmetry suited to produce just the right kind of segregation seems to have been postulated in any instance. Such dynamic insight was perhaps more than could be expected from the attainments of the earlier ages in mega-mechanics.

Passing this by, the dynamics of the later processes by which the subdivisions of the universal chaos gathered into stars and planets were often scarcely less obscure. When definite, they were usually untenable.

Aside from the great historical interest that attaches to these earlier attempts at the solution of the great problem of the genesis of the heavens and the earth, and apart from the genuine admiration they awaken for the ingenuity and breadth of view some of them display, notwithstanding their shortcomings, only one among them has claimed the serious attention of modern scholars, the Kantian hypothesis, and that not very widely. If our inquiry had been a study in general cosmogony, instead of a search for the genesis of our planet, the Kantian view might perhaps have had certain claims to take precedence over even the Laplacian hypothesis, for the latter purposely stopped short of a comprehensive philosophical view of celestial evolution; it neglected to assign an origin, or to delineate the early history, of the nebula with which it dealt; it started with an assumption; it simply postulated a nebula of given mass and physical state; it did not, even by speculative hypothesis, connect this nebula with its own origin or antecedent history, much less with an absolute beginning, or even with a general parental state, as did the Kantian hypothesis.

Unfortunately the Kantian hypothesis was made to rest on the untenable view that the rotatory momentum of the system would arise inevitably from the centripetal action induced by gravity and the reaction of atomic repellency. Other mechanical infelicities crept in also. These inhibited any modern building on the Kantian basis, unless its dynamic foundations were replaced by sound tenets; and tenable substitutes did not offer themselves that were not, in essence, abandonments of the Kantian concept. It has been seen that the rotatory momentum of the planetary system is not only a very radical, but a very discriminative, element in the dynamic constitution of the solar system. It has already appeared—and the observation will gain in force as study proceeds—that the dynamic endowments of the sun, on the one side, and of the planets, on the other, are in such striking contrast that they seem to imply that these two sections of the solar system had different histories, or, at least, that some differentiating agency entered into their histories in such a way as to give them contrasted and incongruous endowments of momentum. The critical considerations that grew out of a study of these differential endowments, far from leading back toward a simple evolution from a common apportionment of primitive chaos, seemed to point quite specifically in the opposite direction. The observed apportionments of mass and momentum in the solar system were found to depart widely from the apportionments naturally assignable to a systematic mode of evolution from a single common mass segregated from the primitive chaotic universe. The Kantian hypothesis seemed, therefore, so completely excluded, not only by the fallacious mechanical concept on which it was based but also by its evolutionary unfitness to meet the requirements of the case, that it held out no inducement to serious consideration. Even if its mechanistic infelicities could be replaced by sound mechanics, it was obvious that it would encounter at once the more serious of the difficulties that were found to bar out the Laplacian hypothesis. Whatever place, therefore, the Kantian views may be entitled to hold in general cosmogony, they did not seem, while our inquiry was in its early stages—still less do they now seem—to have any serious claims to consideration as an account of the way the earth and its fellow-planets came to be what they are.

REFERENCES

1. F. R. Moulton, "An Attempt to Test the Nebular Hypothesis by an Appeal to the Laws of Dynamics," *Astrophysical Journal*, XI (1900), 103–30.

2. M. Babinet, *Comptes rendus*, LII (1861), 481.

3. T. C. Chamberlin, "An Attempt to Test the Nebular Hypothesis by the Relations of Masses and Momenta," *Journal of Geology*, VIII (1900), 58–73.

4. Nolan, *Nature*, XXXIV, 287.

5. T. C. Chamberlin, "On the Bearing of Molecular Activity on the Spontaneous Fission of Gaseous Spheroids," *Carnegie Institution of Washington, Publication 107* (1909), pp. 161–67.

PART II

THE GENESIS OF THE PLANETARY FAMILY

It is pleasant now to turn from the unwelcome task of destructive criticism, however unavoidable, to the story of constructive effort. *To build up* now becomes an obligation upon us, in as much as we have heretofore torn down. If the gaseous and centrifugal theories do not fit the requirements of the case, what interpretation satisfies them better?

We may at least at once adopt a new method. We may make the vestiges of the genetic events serve as our guide. All the peculiarities of the planetary system that have seemed to point away from the inherited hypotheses should also serve as system-pointers to the true interpretation. In the course of our destructive criticism, certain features of the planetary system have seemed to stand forth as peculiar and, hence, as significant. They may be really distinctive and may thus serve as intimations of the interpretation we seek. Our first step in constructive effort is then to list these features and to derive as much guidance from them as we may.

CHAPTER VIII

DESTRUCTIVE CRITICISM TURNED TO CONSTRUCTIVE SERVICE

Among the features of the planetary family that have been made the basis of adverse arguments against the inherited theories of planetary origin, and which may now be cited as criteria to be met and as guides to tenable interpretation, are the following:

1. The total mass of the planets is less than one-seventh of 1 per cent of the mass of the sun. This implies relatively mild action on the part of the formative agency.

2. The family embraces four large outer planets of low density (probably largely gaseous)—Jupiter, Saturn, Uranus, and Neptune.

3. It embraces also four small inner solid planets with limited atmospheres or none at all—Mercury, Venus, Earth, and Mars.

4. There are, in addition, perhaps a thousand planetoids none of which hold observable atmospheres.

5. There are twenty-six satellites distributed between six of the planets in numbers ranging from one to nine. They seem to be solid and naked, or nearly naked, bodies.

6. All these bodies revolve in the same direction about the sun, though a few of the satellites have retrograde motions relative to their primaries.

7. These bodies not only revolve thus concurrently but keep within a closely appressed disk.

8. This arrangement in a disk fits, in a general way, the centrifugal theories, and no doubt suggested them and greatly helped to give them currency; but in precise detail it so far fails to fit them as to be their most decisive weakness.

9. The orbits of the planets are subcircular but yet in some cases notably eccentric. The eccentricities of the planets vary from 0.00687 (Venus) to 0.2056 (Mercury); those of the planetoids vary from 0.00 to 0.65.

10. The orbital planes of most of the planets lie within 2° of the invariable plane of the planetary system, but Mercury is inclined as much as 7°. The inclinations of the planes of the planetoids range up to 38°. But none of these are large compared with the inclinations of the orbits of comets, meteorites, and chondrulites which may be said to range through the whole 360° and to revolve either backward or forward.

11. The equator of the sun is inclined to the planes of all the planets and to the invariable plane of the planets which represents the whole family in a dynamical sense.

12. Though the sun carries $\frac{744}{745}$ of the total mass of the whole system, it carries less than 2 per cent of the revolutionary moment of momentum. This is perhaps the most significant of all these finger posts.

CHAPTER IX

FUTILE EFFORTS TO AMEND THE GASEOUS AND CENTRIFUGAL THEORIES

When some fundamental faith on which one has long rested gives way beneath him and he finds himself plunged in a sea of doubt, it is in the natural order of things that he should flounder awhile in the endeavor to find a new bottom or a new float. His stress is all the more keen if he also awakens to a realization that unconsciously he has built freely upon his faith and that many a pet edifice must sink to wreckage if the foundation is really gone. No one quite realizes how much of accepted doctrines, of current interpretations, and of working assumptions has been built subconsciously upon the nebular hypothesis and upon the derivative doctrine of a gaseo-molten earth. No small part of the traditional tenets of geology are imperiled when the gaseo-molten state of the primitive earth is really brought into question.

While there was only partial appreciation of this at the time, it was felt to a disturbing degree. At first, however, one could find some comfort in the feeling that there were many alternatives upon which it was easy to fall back if the old view proved untenable. If the earth did not arise from a gaseous nebula, belief could shift to an origin from a meteoritic swarm that masqueraded as a nebula, or to an aggregation of meteorites gathering in from the four quarters of the heavens. Perhaps stars have collided and re-formed into a new system, or nebulae have encountered one another and started a special evolution, or some other of the possible permutations and combinations of celestial agencies may have functioned in a genetic way. With such a plethora of alternatives it was easy to persuade one's self that our geologic tenets might be transferred to some new cosmogonic base and still be entertained, if the old foundation could carry them no longer.

And yet the question continued to rise insistently: How many of these alternative concepts had really escaped the stress which dynamical laws put on the most symmetrical and complete of all the inherited hypotheses, not to say the hypothesis most honored by an eminent parentage and a noble clientèle? Were the vague alternatives any better grounded than the definite and beautiful hypothesis of Laplace? Obviously, there was no logical resting-place for one's confidence short of some definite foundation that would stand the searching tests of dynamics, or at least seem to do so.

It is idle to say that we can proceed without basal concepts. If they are not consciously adopted, *they unconsciously insinuate themselves* and thus take on their most deceitful forms. The unctuous feeling that one is dealing "only in solid facts" is often merely a cloak for subconscious speculations that swarm in the turbid substratum of thought. It is easy to be content with current opinion and take no heed of the assumptions on which it floats. It is easy to feel quite sure of the obtrusive and be quite unconscious of the speculations and even superstitions which may be its only buoy. The nearest approach to security that can be attained lies in tracing all tenets back as far as possible, with critical examinations of their grounds, yielding assent to them only in proportion as they link themselves with the best-established principle that condition natural phenomena.

INQUIRY ALONG OTHER GASEOUS LINES

In the attempt to find a tenable view of the origin of our planetary system—an attempt which naturally followed loss of faith in the Laplacian and related hypotheses—no success was had along gaseous lines. The tests based on the kinetic theory of gases and on the laws of dynamics seemed to cut a deadly swath through all assignable outgrowths of gaseous states *so far as these had to do with our own planetary system.* I beg that this distinction between *our* planetary system and other *possible* planetary systems be kept in mind. There is no question that a certain group of the nebulae are gaseous, and there is ground to believe that such nebulae develop secondary systems along consistent lines; but the evidence brought out by the previous inquiry seemed to leave no ground to believe that *our* planetary system arose in this way. All efforts in gaseous lines appeared not only to be futile but there seemed to be no encouragement for further efforts with any allied medium over which laws of the collision-rebound type presided.

INQUIRY ALONG METEORITIC LINES

To this last category belong all meteoritic hypotheses of the quasi-gaseous type, that is, all meteoritic hypotheses in which the deployment of the meteoric swarm is supposed to be maintained by collisions and rebounds of the constituent meteorites. Sir George Darwin had attempted to show that if meteorites were assembled so as to collide and rebound in a miscellaneous way, as do the molecules of gases, and if, in such collisions, essentially perfect elasticity was brought into play by the generation of gas at the points of impact and the instant expansion of this gas, the whole assemblage would follow the laws of a gaseous body. He held that the meteorites, at least up to sizes comparable to the cannon balls of former days, may be treated as gigantic molecules. The uncertain point in this deduction lies in the doubt whether meteorites in collision would, as a matter of fact, develop the elastic recoil essential to the validity of the conclusion. If not, the collapse of the assemblage would apparently be more rapid than that of a true gaseous body and the evolution of heat would be faster; the liability to pass into a true gaseous condition would thus be imminent.

But, whichever alternative obtained, the behavior of a quasi-gaseous swarm of meteorites would follow the same general course as the evolution of a gaseous nebula. In neither of these meteoritic alternatives should the swarm normally have a larger ratio of angular momentum to mass than does a gas—nor should the momentum be better distributed. Now Moulton's trenchant studies have shown that a gas, normally distributed according to the law of gases, does not carry enough moment of momentum, or the right distribution of moment of momentum, to develop into such a planetary system as ours. At first sight, the quasi-gaseous form of meteoritic hypothesis has its attractive features, but on closer scrutiny it appears that it is not more promising than the true gaseous hypothesis—if, indeed, it is not in some respects less promising—even if we ignore all grounds of doubt as to the reality of such a nebular constitution.

There were, however, other meteoritic hypotheses. The most strictly meteoritic of them all is that old view which took its cue from the observed habit of the "shooting stars" that nightly streak our present skies. From these the reasoning ran backward as follows: The earth now gathers in meteorites daily by millions; there must be just so many millions less in open space today than there were yesterday; there must have been millions more at each earlier interval than in each later one; more were picked up daily in early times than now; in the very early days, the accretion was very rapid and the growth fast. This seems logical thus far; but the hypothesis halts or grows vague just when it should press on sharply to the initial stage on which everything hangs. Up to its halt the working basis is the *pre-existence* of the earth and its service as a collecting center. The hypothesis spends its force upon an unquestioned source of growth, but it fails to point out *the origin of the mechanism* of which this growth is an incident. When scrutinized relative to the essential initial condition, it seems specially incompetent, for meteorites are seen to be plunging through space with various velocities, in various directions and in a very sporadic way. The velocities of the meteorites are so various and so high as to imply a dispersive rather than a segregative tendency. They offer no suggestion as to how a planetary nucleus could spring from them. Their momentum is so vastly superior to their gravitative power that the conditions they offer appear to be distinctly hostile to segregation, except as they are caught by some masterful body.

Even if this fundamental difficulty could be avoided, it does not appear that there is any systematic preponderance of infall from any one direction. But a marked preponderance is prerequisite to the disklike arrangement of the planetary revolutions, one of the most pronounced characteristics of the system.

At best, then, this line of search merely leads back to the vital questions: What gave origin to the planetary *centers of collection?* What made the planets revolve nearly in the same plane? Efforts along the meteoritic line as just sketched—the only observed line—seem therefore futile, if the search is for the *origin* of the planetary system. This meteoritic hypothesis merely lays emphasis on a mode of growth—undue emphasis, it would appear, on what is probably a merely incidental rather than an essential mode of growth. Meteoritic growth at present is so extremely small as to be practically negligible, as shown by Woodward and others. There is little or no specific support for any presumption that such meteoritic growth ever rose in geologic time to appreciable quantitative value. The discussion in Part III will throw much additional light on this and all other phases of the meteoric concept.

INQUIRY ALONG COLLISIONAL LINES

More than a century ago the naturalist Buffon advanced the theory that our planetary system arose from the collision of a great comet with the sun. While later knowledge of comets has rendered this view quite untenable, Buffon gave definite initiation to the collisional genus of cosmogonic hypotheses. Collisional views of genesis of various, less obviously untenable types have been entertained since. Without doubt the possibilities of collision are entitled to a place among cosmogonic studies, for encounters undoubtedly occur and almost inevitably they must be followed by some form of reorganization or recollection of the scattered matter, though this does not necessarily, nor perhaps generally, imply a reunion into a single body or group of bodies. The question in hand, however, is the simpler one: Did any form of collision initiate the conditions out of which our planetary system arose? Here, as before, the decisive criteria are to be sought in such vestiges as are borne by our planetary family.

The conditions to be met are definitely fixed; the collision must yield a central mass of the magnitude of our sun; this must be surrounded by eight rather large masses and a multitude of small masses, all in subcircular revolutions. These planetary masses must together equal about $\frac{1}{745}$ of the solar mass. This small factor must carry 98 per cent of the moment of momentum of the whole system.

Now center-to-center collisions, or anything approaching such collisions, seem to be excluded by these conditions, for if the impinging body were small, it would be simply swallowed up in the great solar mass; if it were sufficient in mass or in velocity completely to traverse the solar body, the result probably would partake of the nature of a vortex of the smoke-ring type. The ring nebulae may possibly fulfil the requirements of such a case, though other possible interpretations of these singular objects may be entertained. Extreme dissociation no doubt would follow such a piercing stroke, since the velocity of collision would be high if the mass of an average star were involved.

It is difficult to imagine a case of head-on collision that could leave its wreckage in a state suitable for gathering into a system like our own, for radial dispersion is the normal result of a head-on collision. The only case of promise is a glancing collision; that at first seemed to be quite hopeful and was industriously tried.

In cases of glancing collision certain conditioning features are inevitable and need to be taken seriously into account. The course of the impinging body at the time of impact is a sharp curve, not a straight line as sometimes pictured. This curvature is further conditioned by a severe tidal strain due to the differential attractions of the two bodies when very close together. This alone involves danger of disruption. If the impinging body is affected by elastic compression, expansion enters also into the combination of conditions. Only in an exceptional case, if at all, is it safe to assume that an impinging body at the instant it nears collision with a massive body of the order of the sun would maintain its integrity under the disrupting influences. If it is gaseous, it must yield freely to the dispersive tendencies.

The velocities at which collisions would normally take place are forbiddingly high, and excessive dispersion becomes almost inevitable. The case in hand requires at least a mass as great as the sun plus the mass of the planets. A planetary body merely falling under gravity from some point outside the sun's normal sphere of control would have a velocity at the instant of collision of the order of 385 miles per second. It is possible to escape some of this troublesome velocity by assuming that the solar body was in an expanded condition. A glancing impact would then take place at a greater distance from the center of gravity, and the velocity would be correspondingly lower. It is scarcely permissible, however, to assume that the expansion reached the orbit of the innermost planet about to be formed, for that would prevent the deployment of that planet. And so the velocity of collision could not well be reduced below 50 miles per second by postulating expansion. Even this would incur incidental difficulties, for the outer border of so expanded a sun would be very attenuated and formed chiefly of the lightest gases, which would not be the right kind of material for forming the earth.

It is difficult to picture the effects of collisions at velocities ranging from 50 to 385 miles per second. Extreme dispersion would be inevitable and would perhaps involve atomic dissociation. The lines of dispersion should radiate from the point of impact. One can scarcely imagine the formation of aggregates to serve as centers for the collection of planets in such dispersed matter. As only a portion of one or both bodies is supposed to be in direct collision, the rest might limit the dispersion in its direction and give the dispersed matter a semiradial form such as seen in several cases in the heavens, of which the two great nebulae of Orion are the most notable examples.

These may possibly have been co-partners in a mutual collision.

Before serious inspection, the case of a small meteoroidal nebula driving nearly tangentially into the very attenuated border of a larger solar nebula seemed to me to present a hopeful basis for a planetary hypothesis, and considerable constructive effort was spent in the endeavor to find consistent working conditions that might eventuate in our planetary system; but in addition to the infelicities of dispersion arising from high velocities of collision, other formidable obstacles arose.

It is a law of celestial mechanics that bodies thrown into orbital paths by encounters must, in completing their courses, return to the point of collision, which, in this case would be the edge of the sun, or of the body that was to form the sun. Of course, bodies might be driven off so violently as to fly beyond the sphere of control of the solar mass and be irrecoverable, and this would be a rather imminent contingency; but all such dispersed matter as remained under the solar control—and this, of course, included, all that could enter into the formation of planets—was compelled to come back to the point of collision and be subject to renewed collision, and so on indefinitely. Some partial escape from these fatal conditions might arise in the case of such molecules or other highly elastic bodies as experienced secondary collisions in the course of their flights and, by reaction from these, established new orbits, with a necessity of returning to the point of this collision where the chance of a new encounter might be lessened. There might also be some escape when the attraction of the impinging body, after collision, drew the flying matter into new orbits, if the impinging body remained in a sufficiently aggregated state to exert any appreciable centralized attraction. The effectiveness of either or of both of these diversions working together is very doubtful. In any case the new orbits would be likely to remain very eccentric and to have their perihelion points near the sun.

There are ways in which eccentric orbits may be reduced to subcircularity; but the extreme eccentricity of the orbits that would arise from collision, and the difficulty of finding any applicable and adequate agency for the reduction of these orbits to the requisite subcircular form, seemed to be so insuperable that constructive effort in this line was abandoned.

This disappointing outcome, however, had a suggestive value. The results pointed to the general direction in which a successful hypothesis might lie. They suggested that spiral nebulae were promising forms for study. Celestial collisions were indeed one of the sources to which the origin of spiral nebulae was then referred. While such a genesis of spiral nebulae could not be regarded as supported by the considerations just reviewed, *some related source* might perhaps be found to fit both the origin of the spirals and the genesis of our planetary system. The supreme weakness of referring spiral nebulae to eccentric collisions lies in the fact that such an origin implies *a single spiral arm* or a set of arms, springing from the side of the nucleus at which the collision took place; whereas spiral nebulae habitually show two arms or sets of arms arising from diametrically opposite sides of the central mass. Some other origin of spiral nebulae, and of our planetary system alike, seemed to be indicated by the study of collisional effects.

But there seemed to be "a lion in the way" here. Each knot, and each other scattered part of a spiral nebula, must obviously move in an independent path and be supported by its own moving force. All such bodies, it was said, should give rise to retrograde rotations, whereas most of the planets have forward rotations. If this "lion in the way" was a real lion, it was idle to waste time on spiral nebulae, unless it could be shown that the lion was chained to some special condition which rendered him harmless.

REFERENCES

1. Sir George Darwin, "On the Mechanical Conditions of a Swarm of Meteorites, and on Theories of Cosmogony," *Philosophical Transactions of the Royal Society of London* (1888), pp. 1–29; *Nature*, XXXI (1884–85), 25.

2. T. C. Chamberlin, *Carnegie Institution of Washington, Year Book No. 2* (1903), pp. 261–70; *ibid., Year Book No. 3* (1904), pp. 195–208.

3. T. C. Chamberlin, *The Origin of the Earth* (1916), chap. iv.

CHAPTER X

FROM STERILE FIELDS TO A BARRED PROVINCE

Thus far our inquiry had related to cosmogonic states held by one inquirer or another to be possible, if not probable, sources of origin for our planetary system. On scrutiny, they had proved to be sterile ground, unprofitable for further cultivation. The list includes (1) the gaseous state; (2) quasi-gaseous assemblages of meteorites; (3) the actual meteoritic state; and (4) body collisions, whether central, eccentric, or merely glancing. It was not denied that these states might give origin to some other kind of planetary system than ours, but they seemed to lack elements necessary to such a planetary growth as that of the earth and its kin.

In fairness to the hypothesis that had received the widest acceptance (the Laplacian), it is to be noted that some of its untenability arose from the kinetic theory of gases, which was only advanced some decades after the hypothesis had been put forth and generally accepted. It seemed reasonable enough to postulate rings of gas until the kinetic concept showed that it was otherwise. Saturn had a beautiful set of rings which were then supposed to be gaseous. These lay between the planet and a fine family of satellites. This no doubt suggested that these rings were the embryonic states of moons-to-be. What seemed so true of satellites springing from a planet might reasonably be assumed to be true of planets springing from a sun. There seems no doubt that both Kant and Laplace took their cues from the rings of Saturn. The combined Kantian-Laplacian hypothesis was widely accepted and taught in the schools long before Keeler and others proved that Saturn's rings are formed of small solid discrete particles in individual orbits. But what has the difference between a gaseous and an orbital state to do with the generation of planets?

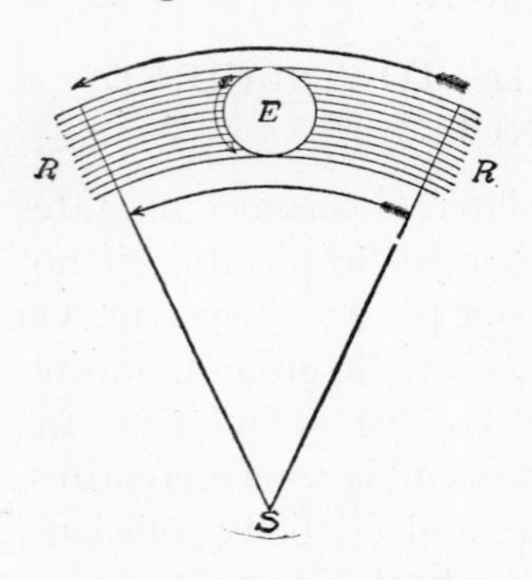

FIG. 4.—Diagram illustrating forward rotation arising from a gaseous ring. *RR* represents a ring of gas revolving as a unit. If it contracts normally into a spheroid, *E*, centrally located, the resulting rotation will be forward, as represented by the arrow, because the outer part is moving faster than the inner part.

THE RESPECTIVE BEARINGS OF GASEOUS AND ORBITAL STATES ON PLANETARY GENESIS

Not only in respect to the genesis of planets, but in the on-goings of celestial affairs generally, there is a radical difference between the gaseous state and the orbital state. The reader is urged to grasp and hold firmly in mind this critical difference. The orbital state embodies much the greater angular momentum, is much more varied in its combinations and in its action, and much more distinctive and individual in its results. It was too close a following of the gaseous analogy that, as we are about to show, barred out an adequate study of the most promising of all cosmogonic fields for half a century. The reasoning was sound enough as far as it went, but it did not take account of the varied resources of the orbital state. The inadequate reasoning ran in this wise:

In the revolution of a ring, the outer part moves faster than the inner part; and hence if any symmetrical section of it gathers normally into a sphere, the outer part inevitably swings around the inner part and gives it a rotation *forward*, that is, in the direction of its previous revolution. In reality this was already taking place, for in every revolution of a solid ring, its outer part swings around its inner part once per revolution. The condensation of the section only concentrates and intensifies what is happening already (Fig. 4).

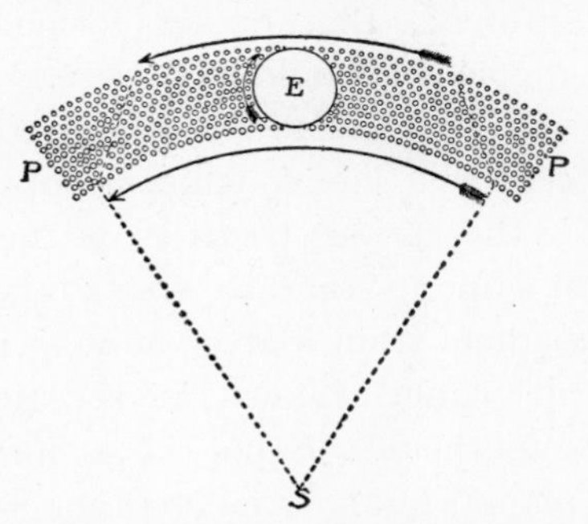

FIG. 5.—Diagram illustrating retrograde rotation arising from the concentration of discrete particles in revolution. *PP* represents free particles such as planetesimals revolving concentrically about the sun, *S*. It has been held that if these collect normally into a spheroid, *E*, the resulting rotation will be retrograde, as represented, because the inner bodies move faster than the outer ones.

On the other hand, if a ring is formed of discrete particles, each revolving independently in its own orbit about the center of the ring, the inner particles are necessarily moving faster than the outer ones to give the higher centrifugal force needed to match the higher centripetal force arising from their greater nearness to the center of gravity. And so it was reasoned cogently that if any symmetrical section of such a ring were collected into a sphere, its rotation would be *retrograde* (Fig. 5).

The reasoning was sound, and on this basis the broad inference that planets formed from discrete particles in revolution would have retrograde rotations was accepted with practical unanimity up to the close of the nineteenth century. The conclusion appeared as standard doctrine in the various treatises on the subject. On this account, it came to stand as a bar to the origin of forward-rotating planets from matter moving in independent orbits, and all planets known at the time Laplace advanced his hypothesis rotated in a forward direction. Only the planets Uranus and Neptune, later discovered, have retrograde rotations.

When these planets were discovered and found to have retrograde rotations, it was easy to assume that they were formed from discrete bodies and still hold that all the other planets had been formed from gaseous rings. This left the earth still under ban. Much ingenuity was shown in trying to avoid the application of the ban. It was urged that if the section of the ring that formed the planet did not concentrate symmetrically, but gathered about some eccentric point, the result might be forward rather than retrograde rotation. But as all concentrations were referred to gravity and as the action took place freely in open space, it was not obvious why the concentration should not be normal. Attempts to lift the bar along this line were unsatisfactory, though they were given a place in the literature of the subject.

Even when it was found, by Keeler and others, that

the constituents of the rings of Saturn are discrete particles moving in independent orbits about Saturn, the theoretical bar did not seem to be wholly broken down, for it had also been made almost certain by Roche and Maxwell that the matter of the rings was forced to take the form of discrete particles by the strong differential attraction of Saturn. The Saturnian case was therefore an exceptional one. It left the general problem of planetary genesis much as it had been.

And so, while the rigor with which an origin of the earth from discrete orbital particles had been barred out was somewhat relaxed, it still stood in the way of free postulation in orbital lines. It seemed to make the orbital field a forbidding, if not wholly forbidden, domain.

Cogent as the reasoning seemed, there was yet enough ground to doubt its complete applicability to warrant further scrutiny of the grounds of the prohibition. Did the reasoning, however good in the cases in mind, hold in all the cases in the cosmic field? It was soon seen that the reasoning had been based on *circular* rings and naturally enough carried over to *circular* orbits. All the planetary orbits are, however, eccentric. What kind of encounters might arise between belts of discrete particles moving in elliptical orbits?

CHAPTER XI

FROM THE BARRED PROVINCE TO A FIELD OF PROMISE

When once attention was turned to the matter, it was readily seen that the planetary problem relates mainly to elliptical motions rather than to circular motions. The fascinating display of discrete particles in the beautiful rings of Saturn were, after all, less representative than prepossessing. None of the planets has a strictly circular orbit though most of them are subcircular but some are rather eccentric. It also came to mind that circular orbits are unstable, in the sense that any disturbance makes them elliptical; while elliptical orbits are stable, in the sense that when disturbed they merely take on new elliptical orbits with new eccentricities. It thus appeared that the properties of elliptical motions not only constituted the actual problem, but that they were superior in resources of adaptability and stability. It was then clear that to attack the real problem of planetary rotation and its bearings on planetary genesis it was necessary to consider what kind of rotation would arise *when discrete bodies in elliptical orbits came together to form a single planetary body.*

Further study showed that the conditions of the case might vary considerably within the known range of planetary phenomena, and that, like most natural evolutions, the actual case was rather complex. We must therefore go somewhat into detail.

The four planets known to have forward rotations, Earth, Mars, Jupiter, and Saturn, form the middle section of the planetary family. If the discrete particles that formed them had orbits much more elliptical than their present orbits, as was probable, some of the orbits would be likely to overlap or interpenetrate one another more or less, and such overlaps would be shifted by precession. Encounters should take place where the orbits overlap; indeed, they should be more common there than elsewhere. How these encounters would take place and how such encounters would affect rotation must now be considered.

As a first step, let Figure 6 represent three planetary orbits of this class. These are a little more elliptical than the actual orbits, but they are about as near the true order of ellipticity as is suitable for illustration.

Bodies moving in orbits like these cannot come together at all unless the outermost (aphelion) swing of the inner body coincides with the innermost (perihelion) swing of the outer body. Of course, orbits might be chosen in which the aphelion and perihelion portions would overlap so that crossings would occur, but in all such cases there could only be crossings where *a more or less aphelion portion of an inner orbit overlapped a more or less perihelion portion of an outer orbit.* The general order of effect would be that illustrated by the simple case chosen for illustration. Now, on referring to the diagram the reader can see for himself, without any formal celestial mechanics, that at any point where a body in an outer

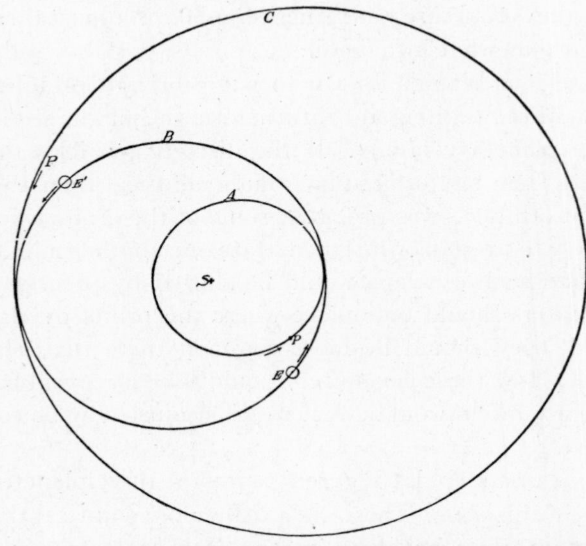

FIG. 6.—Diagram illustrating the conditions under which collisions may take place in elliptical orbits of the planetary type. *S* represents the solar mass at the center of the system; *E* a planetary nucleus; *B* its orbit; *p* a particle in the orbit *A*, smaller than *B;* and *P* a particle in orbit *C*, larger than *B*. The case has been so chosen as to represent at once the smallest and the largest orbits of typical eccentricity that can come into contact with the orbit of the planetary nucleus. The minimum extreme is found when the aphelion point of the small ellipse *A* coincides with the perihelion point of the orbit of the planetary nucleus *B*. In no other position can the orbit *A* touch the orbit *B*. The maximum extreme is found where the aphelion point of *B* coincides with the perihelion point of *C*. In no other position can these orbits touch. Between these limiting phases represented by the orbits *A* and *C*, there are an indefinite number of possible orbits that might cut the orbit *B;* but in all cases, except where the orbits were like *B*, conjunction could arise only when *a more or less* aphelion portion of an inner orbit touched or crossed a more or less perihelion portion of an outer orbit. If the orbits were equal, the velocities at the crossings would be equal and the rotating effects would be *nil*, or neutralized; and if they were nearly equal, the difference would be slight, so that the effective cases are those of the extreme classes represented.

orbit comes into collision with a body in an inner orbit, the former is moving faster than the latter, for if no collision took place, the body in the outer orbit would swing *away* from the center, S, the controlling body, and describe a large loop, whereas the inner body would *drop back* toward the center and describe a smaller loop.

By inspection of this and similar kinds, supported by mathematical investigations by Moulton, the conclusion was reached that *at the points where collision is possible, bodies in the larger orbits move faster than bodies in the smaller orbits*, a conclusion precisely opposite to that reached in the case of concentric circular orbits. There is no difference in the *principles* of the elliptical and of the circular orbits; the apparent difference lies wholly in the application of these principles. In so far as elliptical orbits exceeded circular orbits in the planet-forming field, these deductions have superior value as guides in inquiries of this kind.

THE BALANCING OF OPPOSITE EFFECTS OF INFALLING BODIES

Whether a particle falling on a globular planet tends to give it rotation forward or backward depends on the side of the axis of rotation on which it happens to fall. It may tend to give forward, or it may tend to give backward, rotation; it may tend to give rotation from right to left or left to right; or there may be an exact balance of effect and no rotation at all. This in a sense is promising, for it seems possible to find a fit for any actual case, if appropriate infalls can only be postulated. But of course only the infalls that actually took place had anything to do with the actual result. Our solution must be an actual, naturalistic one, not a merely possible one.

The mode of action in typical cases in the middle of the planetary system is illustrated in Figure 7. A sphere, *E*, is here introduced to represent a growing planet revolving in a median orbit like that of the earth about a controlling body, *S*, together with two belts of particles each moving in independent orbits about *S*, one set in larger orbits than that of the planet, and the other set in smaller orbits, the general arrangement being the same as in Figure 6 previously discussed. It will be seen that in one case (right-hand) the particles overtake the planet, and in the other case (left-hand) the planet overtakes the particles. Belts of particles have been chosen wide enough to show that part of them will strike the planet on the side rotating *from* the particles and will thus add to the rotation (if the rotation is not equal to or faster than the orbital motion of the particles, which would only rarely be the case), while part of them will strike on the side rotating *toward* them and the collision will tend to reduce the planetary rotation. Similar diversity of action will take place in the encounters represented at the right. This offsetting action is in itself not favorable to much rotation; it is definitely unfavorable to a very high rate of rotation.

To fully realize the precise issue, it is necessary to go even closer home to the details of the case. With this in view, the figure has been shaded so as to show the areas within which the belts of particles can overtake or be overtaken by the planet, respectively. It will be noted that in such cases as are represented by the figure, the areas that represent strokes favorable to forward rotation

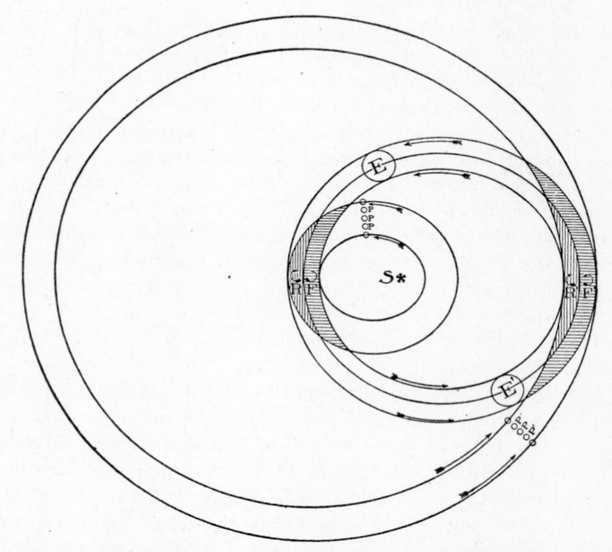

FIG. 7.—In this diagram, S represents the sun; E, a representative planet of the middle of the system, moving toward the perihelion of its orbit and about to encounter small discrete bodies (ppp) in the aphelion portion of their elliptical orbits, which are smaller than the orbit of E and are hence moving slower than E. E is to be imagined to be spherical, and its track to be cylindrical. E' represents another position of the same planet moving toward the aphelion point of its orbit and about to be overtaken by small discrete bodies ($p'p'p'$) in the perihelion parts of their elliptical orbits, which are larger than that of E', and are hence moving faster than E'. For simplicity, only belts of the breadth of E and E' are represented. To make a complete inspection, it is only necessary to draw similar belts between the two chosen until the whole orbit of E, E' is covered. On the left-hand side of the figure, the shaded area represents the only portions of the paths of E and of the little bodies (ppp) that belong to a common belt and are in the aphelial portion of their orbits, where alone collisions with E can take place. Since E is here moving faster than ppp, it is obvious that encounters on its inner half favor forward rotation while encounters on its outer half favor retrograde rotation. R represents retrograde effect, and F, forward effect.

Inspection shows that the inner section of E within which collisions favoring forward rotation can take place is notably greater than the outer section, within which collisions favoring retrograde rotation can take place; and hence, if there is an equable distribution of the small bodies, E is likely to acquire a forward rotation.

On the right-hand side, the small discrete bodies, $p'p'p'$, move faster than E' and, in overtaking E' on its outer side, tend to give it forward rotation; while if they strike on the inside, they tend to impart retrograde rotation. The preponderance of space here favors forward rotation as before. Inspection shows that the same would be true of the additional belts required to cover the whole path of E, E', but the difference of effect would be less in these interior belts. The belts chosen are those in which the difference of effect would be greatest.

These conclusions are drawn on the assumption that E had no rotation at the start.

If E already had forward rotation, inspection of the figure shows that the rotation would tend to increase the force of the impacts favoring retrograde rotation and to diminish those favoring forward rotation and hence would be, to this extent, unfavorable to increase of forward rotation, as explained in the main text. If E already had a retrograde rotation, inspection shows that the force of the impacts favoring forward rotation would be increased and that of those favoring retrograde rotation reduced. The accessions would then tend to arrest the retrograde rotation and ultimately to reverse it.

are larger than the areas within which strokes favorable to retrograde rotation can occur. If, therefore, these areas truly represent the number and value of the strokes, forward rotation would be favored; and this seems really to represent the general probabilities of the case. If, however, the distribution of the particles in orbits were other than symmetrical and correspondent to the areas of striking possibilities, a retrograde rotation or none at all might be favored.

It should be noticed that the case represented is one in which the growing planet has an elliptical orbit as well as the particles, and that it is assumed to be in the midst of a great assemblage of particles in elliptical orbits. These are the conditions almost certain to have arisen from the nebularization of the middle planetary zone later to be described.

On the outer border of the nebularized disk the orbits of the particles will be more nearly concentric and, if a collecting planetary nucleus has a nearly circular orbit, retrograde rotation would be likely to arise, as in the second case set forth in the previous chapter.

It appears, then, that forward rotations would be likely to arise in the midst of a discoidal assemblage of discrete particles in elliptical orbits, as in the observed cases of Earth, Mars, Jupiter, and Saturn, but that retrograde rotations would be likely to arise at the same time in the outer reaches of the system. It is important to observe further that the rotations that would arise are due merely to the *balance* between the opposite effects of infall on the two sides of the growing planet. There is no one-sided action; and as the difference of effects on the two sides could not well be great, a high rate of rotation is not only not favored but is definitely counter-indicated.

A TENDENCY TOWARD EQUILIBRIUM

If a really high rate of rotation were attained at any stage, further growth would be likely to subdue it. Looking at Figure 7, it will be seen that if the planet, *E*, is rotating rapidly, the collisional velocity on the side moving in the same direction as the particles will only be accelerated by the *difference* between the velocity of the particles and the rotational velocity of this part of the planet, while on the opposite side the velocity of the collisions will be the *sum* of the velocities of the particles and of the rotational motion of that part of the planet. If the infall of particles is equal on the two sides, the effect would tend to subdue the rotation. The mechanism is such as to forestall cumulative effects and to restrain progressive acceleration; it favors oscillation about an equilibrium rate, or, at most, merely moderate divergence from it.

THE SMALL PROPORTION OF THE ORBITAL MOMENTUM CONVERTED INTO ROTATIONAL MOMENTUM

How small a dynamic factor rotation really is appears from a comparison of the rotational momentum with the total momentum of revolution of the planets. For example, according to Moulton, the angular momentum embodied in the revolution of the earth is 3,700,000 times the angular momentum embodied in the earth's rotation. If the planets were formed from particles in revolution about the sun, only a multi-millionth part of their revolutionary momentum would need to be converted into rotational momentum to give the existing rotations.

REFERENCES

1. The initial statement of the essence of this doctrine of rotation was published as a footnote to an article entitled "A Group of Hypotheses Bearing on Climatic Changes," read before the British Association for the Advancement of Science, Toronto, Canada, August, 1897, and published in the *Journal of Geology*, V (October–November, 1897), 669.

2. Chamberlin and Salisbury, *Geology*, II (1905), 72–77.

3. T. C. Chamberlin, *The Origin of the Earth* (1916), pp. 93–100.

CHAPTER XII

THE POSTULATED DYNAMIC ENCOUNTER—THE CLOSE APPROACH OF A PASSING STAR

The bars to a possible orbital genesis being thus let down, the inquiry turned into the neglected field and took a path of its own. The choice of this path was determined chiefly by certain dynamic peculiarities of the planetary system that had been disclosed in the course of the previous destructive criticisms. There had seemed to be two sets of genetic factors, and these appeared to imply a twofold parentage. The concentration of mass in the central body contrasted strangely with the small masses of the planetary bodies, individually and collectively. The mean mass of the individual planets, planetoids, and satellites was found to be less than one-millionth of the mass of the sun; their combined mass to be only one-seventh of 1 per cent of that of the sun. A similar strong contrast had been noted in the distribution of the masses. The well-centralized sun stood over against planetary bodies scattered out over a disk five billion miles in diameter, the outermost seventy-five times as far from the sun as the innermost. A still more significant contrast had been found in angular momentum. The central mass had been found to have only about one-fiftieth of the whole, and the planetary bodies the remaining forty-nine fiftieths. When this dynamic contrast was set over against the contrast in mass, the real issue began to emerge. Very high mass and low angular momentum were arrayed on one side; very low mass and high momentum were arrayed on the other side.

And yet the bodies on both sides, so far as knowledge went, had essentially the same chemical composition—sun, planets, planetoids, satellites, and all. There appeared no ground to question the close kinship of the material of all parts of the solar system. This kinship had indeed been generally recognized and had been made a factor in nearly all genetic theories.

But in the face of this nearly identical composition, the dynamic endowments of the planetary factor had been found to be a high multiple of that of the solar factor. The contrast seemed to imply that the sun had furnished the substance and some incidental part of the momentum, and that there had been another parent from which the planetary offspring had inherited their special dynamic endowments. To detect this other parent was clearly the crux of the problem. It was clearly implied that this endowment was chiefly or wholly dynamic.

COLLISION EXCLUDED

Physical collision between the two parental bodies was counter-indicated, for in such a case both the central body and the scattered bodies should have participated proportionately in the distribution of the material and of the dynamic qualities. Besides, the considerations urged in chapter ix made it clear that the planetary system did not arise from any form of bodily collision. The results of collisional action of the celestial sort were *qualitatively* unfit. As already indicated, to fit the case under study, the second parental agency must have acted chiefly, if not wholly, without material contact. It must apparently have been a force acting from a body at a distance.

THE OCCURRENCE AND THE COMPETENCY OF PURELY DYNAMIC ACTION

It had long been known that celestial bodies acted dynamically upon one another at great distances, as when the sun and the moon produce tides upon the earth. It was easy to see that the distance of the sun was of the right order, and there was no question about its reality. But at first thought, action of the tidal type seemed inadequate. More careful study, however, brought out the fact that in the natural approaches of heavenly bodies to one another there were many possible combinations of mass, distance, and modes of motion, and that some of these might even be too vigorous to fit the case of planetary formation.

POSSIBLE OVERCOMPETENCY OF PURELY DYNAMIC ACTION

Many years ago, Roche, by mathematical investigation of an idealized case, showed that if a satellite were made to approach its primary on an inrunning spiral, it would not hold together until it came into contact with the primary, but that at a distance of 2.44 times the radius of the primary it would be pulled apart by the strong differential attractions of the two bodies, *provided* both primary and satellite were of the same homogeneous constitution, cohesion and other modifying conditions being neglected. While this, strictly interpreted, was a purely imaginary case, simplified to make mathematical handling possible, it gave some insight into the real effectiveness of certain possible approaches of celestial bodies. It made it clear that approaches of great bodies like stars might not only be competent to separate from the smaller body such small masses as were required to form planets but might be destructive to the smaller body. It was obvious that such destruction would be specially imminent if the smaller body were gaseous and already predisposed to eruption, as in the case of the sun.

Roche's mathematical conclusions were supported by the fact that the rings of Saturn lie within the Roche limit of Saturn, while Saturn's innermost satellite lies just outside it. These seemed to show that there is a real Roche limit nearly coincident with the computed one. It is this *real* limit that is used in naturalistic discussions, not the idealized mathematical one. If Jupiter were to pass between the rings of Saturn and its innermost satellite, apparently the whole Saturnian system would be wrecked, for the Roche limit of Jupiter is much larger than that of Saturn. So, likewise, if a star twice the mass of the sun were to pass it at less than the Roche limit of the star, the sun would be dispersed and the star would be likely to carry off most of the wreckage.

Dynamic encounter appeared, then, not only competent to draw out planetary matter from the sun under assignable conditions, but competent to go far beyond that and give rise to destructive as well as constructive effects.

A SOMEWHAT DISTANT APPROACH INDICATED

The problem of the derivation of the material of our planetary system from the sun's substance appeared thus to be one in which extremes were to be avoided. Restraint, equipoise, and careful consideration of agents and conditions, seemed to be required. If the passing star were more massive than the sun, it must not be supposed to approach so near the sun as to cause wreckage or even overprojection. If the passing star were smaller than the sun, it must come close enough to cause the eruption and adequate propulsion of at least one-seventh of 1 per cent of the sun's mass. And there must be room for the deployment of the planetary bodies without their falling permanently into the sphere of control of the passing star and being carried away by it.

THE MODE OF TIDAL ACTION BY A PASSING STAR

If a star and the sun approached one another with sufficient nearness to interact mildly in a tidal way, the first effects would be tidal cones drawn out on the side of the sun toward the star and on the side from the star; and there would be a *compressional belt* between these, due to a transverse component of the tidal pull. The proportions and directions of the tidal forces are shown in Figure 8, which is the standard diagram used by tidal experts. The arrows represent the stresses on the surface. According to Sir George Darwin, the stresses increase toward the center in the ratio of 1:3 on an equatorial radius, and 1:8 on a polar radius, from which we infer that the stresses produced by a passing star would favor deep eruptions. The mean specific gravity of the sun is only

1.4, on the water standard, the temperature of its radiation surface is 6000° C., and hence it is generally assumed that the sun is largely gaseous. If so, its body may be pre-

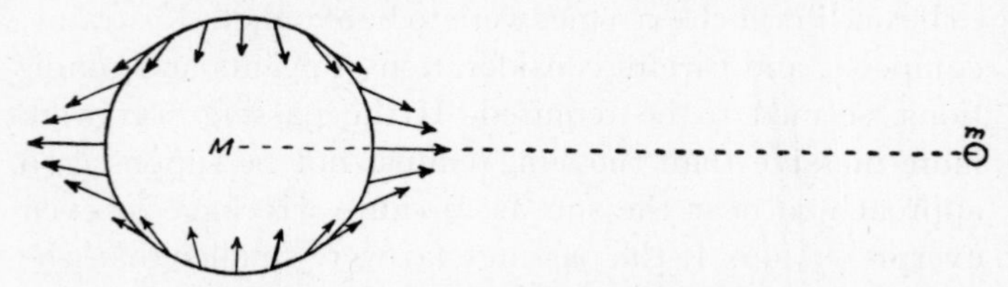

FIG. 8.—Diagram of tidal forces, showing lifting forces in due proportions and directions to and from the moon and the girdle of compressive forces at right angles to these. Note that the direct compression is half that of direct lifting. Prepared by F. R. Moulton.

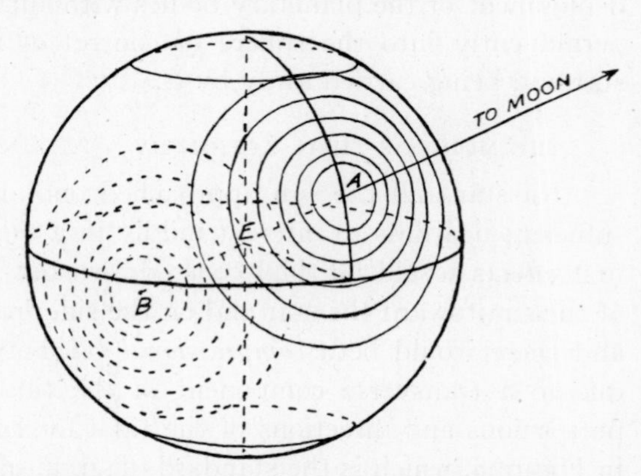

FIG. 9.—Diagram showing the tidal cones, *A* and *B*, pointing to and from the moon. Prepared by F. R. Moulton.

sumed to have yielded readily to the pressure under the compressional band and to the pulls toward the two cones (Fig. 9) and thus to have favored large concentrated eruptions. This combination was well fitted to restrain eruptions in the compressional belt and promote eruptions at the points of the cones.

THE ERUPTIVE AND PROPULSATORY POWER OF THE SUN

The turmoil and eruptivity of the sun are so well known that we need only cite a few of the later developments and take note of the general trend of opinion, as research progresses, relative to its projective and propulsatory competency.

When our view of the expulsion of planetary substance from the sun was first entertained—near the opening of the century—there was some question as to the competency of the sun to project portions of its substance so far out as the planets. As a mere matter of *eruptive* projection, such doubts might still obtain; but the additional propulsatory powers of the sun now recognized—whether in the form of radiation-pressure, electric and magnetic charges, electronic and protonic propulsion, or other agencies, or combinations of these—so greatly increase knowledge of the sun's total projective potency that its competency can scarcely be questioned at the present time. The trend of opinion has been reversed. It is now urged by some investigators that the sun is throwing itself away. Views of this type are being pressed so zealously that one feels almost instinctively an impulse to step on the brakes to save our faith in our luminary.

The agencies engaged in pushing solar matter away from the sun are held to be almost in equilibrium with the sun's gravitative power, so that only a relatively small additional propulsive force gives it competency to

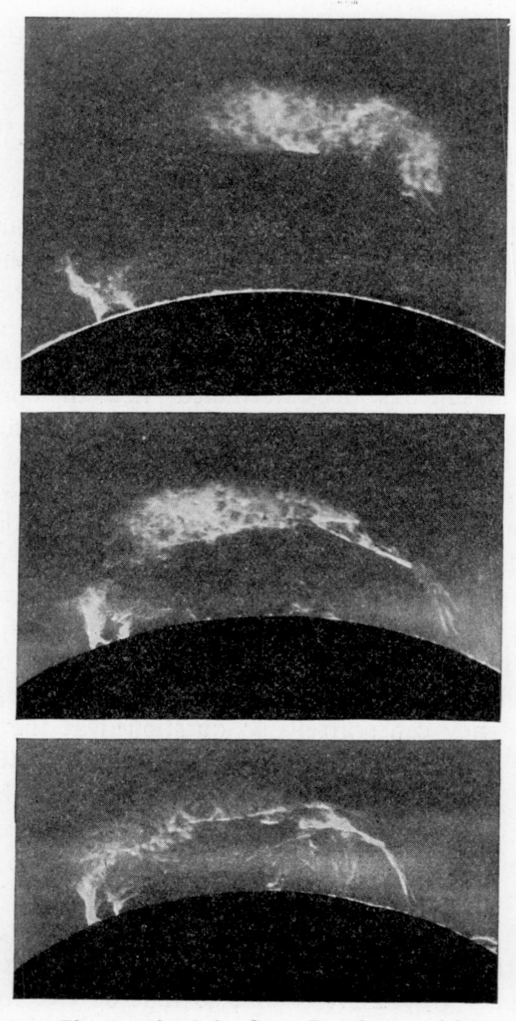

FIG. 10.—Photograph of the Great Prominence of May 29, 1919, showing propulsion after eruption.

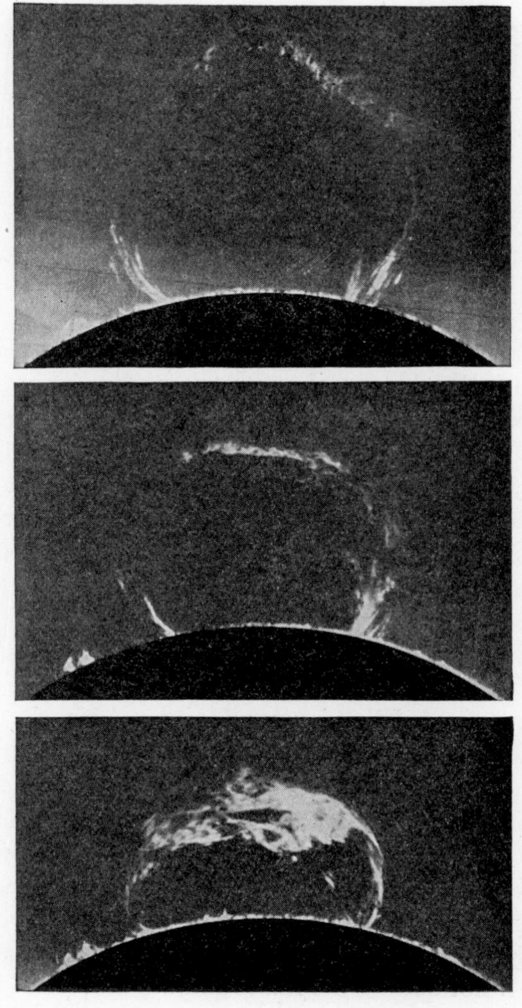

FIG. 11.—Photograph of the Great Prominence of July 15, 1919, showing propulsion after eruption.

send solar substance, or selected portions of it, to the limit of the sun's control.

It is now apparent that eruptive and propulsatory forces combine in action, and that the propulsatory forces sometimes exceed the eruptive. This is strikingly illustrated by the discovery of Pettit at the Yerkes Observatory that solar matter, *after* eruption, is sometimes pushed away from the sun in a succession of impulses that give it *increasing velocity* as it rises, in spite of the sun's attraction. Three stages of ascent are shown in Figures 10 and 11. It is to be noted that the light by which the photographs were taken came from calcium, a common and fairly heavy constituent of terrestrial rocks. The first projection was observed on May 29, 1919, and the second on July 15, of the same year. The first disappeared in the course of its ascent (probably by cooling or dispersion) at 760,000 kilometers above the sun's surface; the second at 720,000 kilometers; that is, both of them had risen more than the radius of the sun before they vanished from sight. More than three-fourths of the theoretical attraction at the surface of the sun had been overcome. What is even more surprising, the centers of the arches were then going upward faster than when they left the sun's surface. The first was ascending at 60 kilometers per second, the other at 163.9 kilometers per second when last observed. This is an extraordinary revelation. It leaves little room to question that substances as heavy as the constituents of common rock are sometimes even now driven far out into interplanetary space, if not quite to its limits and beyond. So far as we know, Pettit, pending further data, has not as yet offered

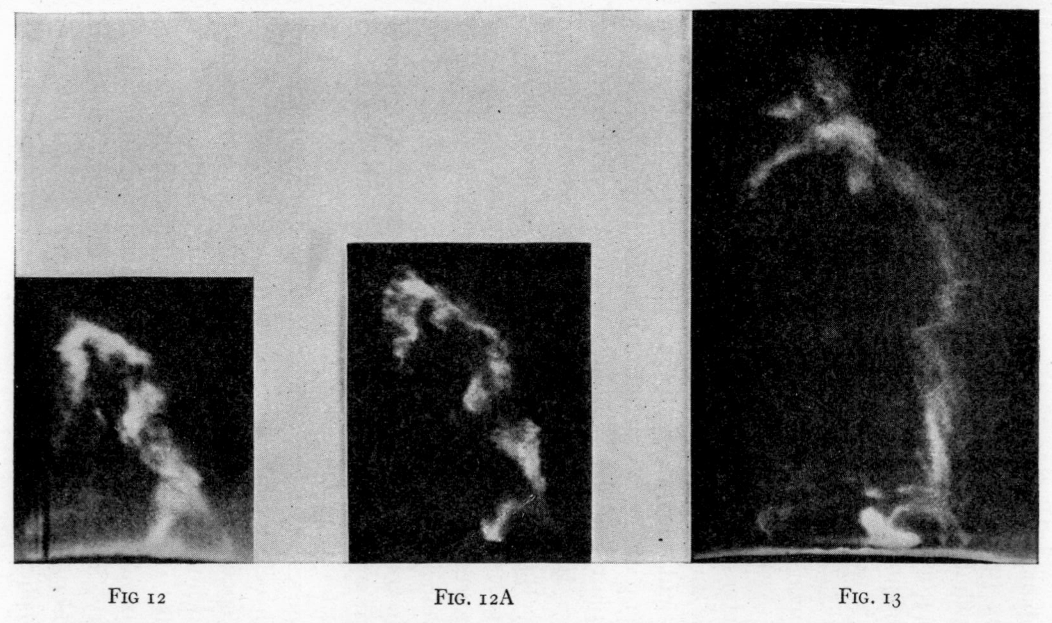

FIG 12 FIG. 12A FIG. 13

Three stages of an eruptive solar prominence taken with the spectroheliograph by Ellerman at Kenwood Observatory on March 25, 1895. Prominence at 10h, 40m (Fig. 12), 162,000 miles high; at 10h, 58m (Fig. 13), 281,000 miles high. Mean rate of ascent, 6,600 miles per minute. (Per kindness of Ellerman and Frost.)

any opinion respecting the source or nature of the actuating forces in this case. Much as we would like to know what it is, only the fact of such propulsion is material to our present study.

The amount of matter actually driven forth in these cases is not known. Some intimation of the masses involved in the Pettit illustrations may be gathered from the dimensions of the arches. That of May 29 was transverse to the sun's equator and had a chord of 584,000 kilometers; that of July 15 also straddled the equator, but in an oblique attitude, and yet its foreshortened chord had a length of 363,000 kilometers. Figure 43, in chapter xxix, shows an active prominence, 140,000 miles high, photographed at Mount Wilson Observatory, July 9, 1917. In this illustration the earth is shown as a white disk in the lower right-hand corner. The projections in these cases were certainly not trivial affairs.

Figures 12 and 13 show a more vertical eruption at high velocity, in which connection with the sun's surface is still retained. It is to be noted that the high speed of 119,000 miles in 18 minutes takes place above 162,000 miles from the sun's surface.

Figures 14 and 15 show a detached projectile moving at high velocity far above the surface of the sun.

Respecting the vortical nature of the sun's turbulence, Hale, who has so long and successfully studied the sun, regards "a sun spot as a solar storm, resembling a terrestrial tornado, in which the hot vapors, whirling at high velocity, are cooled by expansion, thus accounting for the observed changes of the spectrum lines and the presence of chemical compounds." He has recently announced

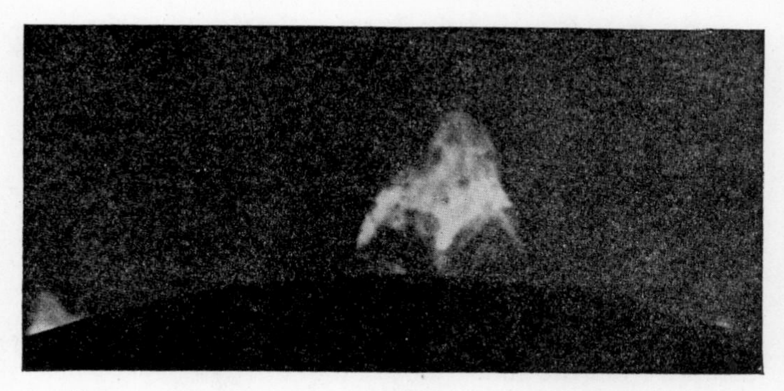

FIG. 14.—Eruptive prominence of the sun photographed at Yerkes Observatory March 25, 1910, at 4h, 14.7m.

FIG. 15.—Same prominence as above, photographed March 25, 1910, at 4h, 57.9m, or 43.2m later.

that his newly invented spectro-helioscope reveals many tornado-like projections at various points on the face of the sun.

In the light of these and other revelations that have been disclosed in recent years, there seems no longer any good ground to question that solar substance to the relatively small amount of the planets may have been propelled to planetary distances under the stimulus and aid of a star of ordinary size passing at a considerable distance from the sun.

REFERENCES

1. Edward Roche, *Mémoire de l'Académie Montpellier*, Vol. I.

2. T. C. Chamberlin, "On a Possible Function of Disruptive Approach in the Formation of Meteorites, Comets, and Nebulae," *Astrophysical Journal*, XIV (1901), 17–20; also, *Journal of Geology*, IV (1901), 369–93.

3. T. C. Chamberlin, *Carnegie Institution of Washington, Year Book No. 3* (1904), pp. 208–53.

4. T. C. Chamberlin (with R. D. Salisbury), *Geology*, II (1905), 60–80.

5. F. R. Moulton, "On the Evolution of the Solar System," *Astrophysical Journal*, XXII (1905), 165–81.

6. F. R. Moulton, *Introduction to Astronomy* (1906), pp. 463–87.

7. G. E. Hale, *Ten Years' Work of a Mountain Observatory*, p. 37.

8. Edison Pettit, "The Great Eruptive Prominences of May 29 and July 15 (1919)," *Astrophysical Journal*, L (1919), 206–19.

9. G. E. Hale, "Nature of the Hydrogen Vortices Surrounding Sun Spots," *Publications of the Astronomical Society of the Pacific*, XXXVII (1925), 244–75.

10. G. E. Hale, "Visual Observations of the Sun's Atmosphere," *Proceedings of the National Academy of Sciences*, XII (1926), 286–95.

11. V. Bjerknes, "Solar Hydrodynamics," *Astrophysical Journal*, LXIV (1926), 1–29.

CHAPTER XIII

TWIRLING MISSILES

The whole surface of the sun shows signs of vigorous turmoil, but the larger and more systematic cyclonic motions are mainly restricted to belts lying on both sides of the solar equator between about 5° and 30° solar latitude. It is in these belts that the sun-spots, faculae, and flocculi

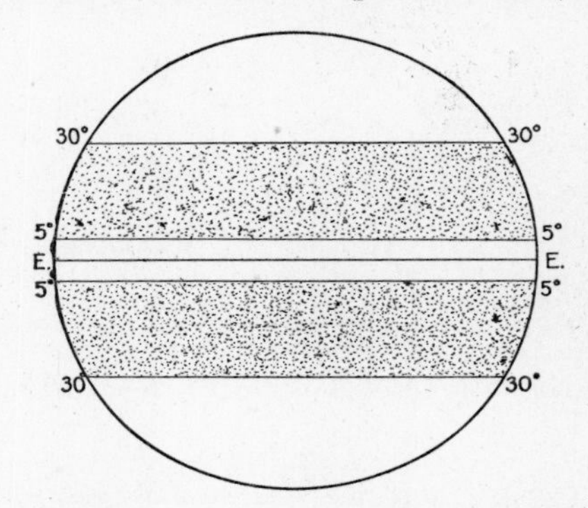

FIG. 16.—Diagram showing the chief eruptive belts of the sun

—all of which appear to be affected by whirling motions—most abound, though they are not wholly confined to these latitudes. These belts bear the most demonstrative features of the sun's circulation and are given the leading place in our special interpretations. We are not directly concerned with the sun-spots, though they are the most conspicuous features, for downward cyclonic motions appear to dominate them and these cannot be the immediate source of the planetary projections; but ascending whirls are closely associated with them, and these are objects of prime interest. Often the solar cyclones present the singular phenomenon of pairs, as shown in Figure 17. Our study is not concerned with this feature except in so far as it illustrates the tendency of moving fluids in

FIG. 17.—A bi-polar sun-spot group photographed at Mount Wilson Observatory on August 10, 1924, by the Hα hydrogen line.

such a seething rotating body to whirl more or less in cyclonic fashion.

Solar substances that stand out from the sun's surface as though projected are commonly called, conservatively, merely "solar prominences." These are the subject of most special interest to us. Some of them are "quiescent," in which the elevations remain but little changed for considerable periods and the motions seem relatively slow. They appear to represent an approach to a balance between forces pushing from the sun outward and the

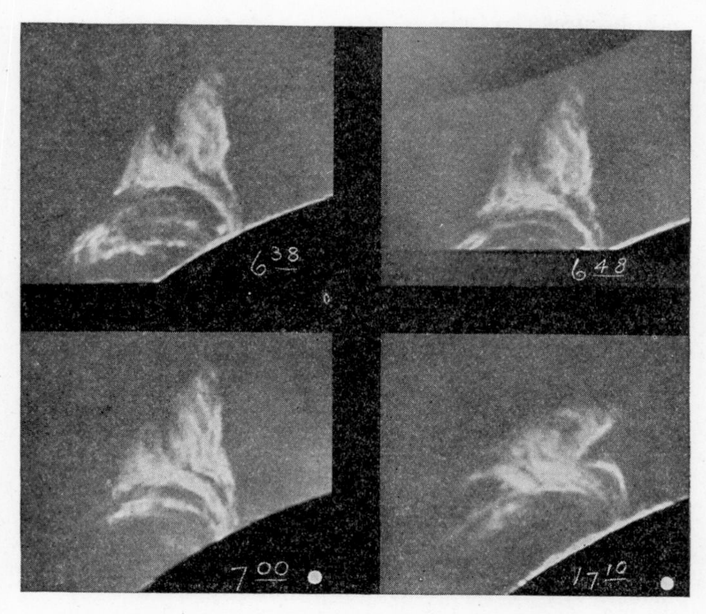

FIG. 18.—Four successive views of a "quiescent" prominence 110,000 miles high, photographed with the H*α* Hydrogen line at Mount Wilson Observatory, June 10, 1917. The small, white circle shows the relative size of the earth. The reader may judge for himself the amount of twist involved in even this "quiescent" prominence.

attraction of the sun pulling backward. Figure 18 shows four views of one of these "quiescent" prominences photographed at intervals of 10, 12, 10 minutes, respectively. This shows that while the elevation and general form was not radically changed, there was much change of detail; and among these details are evidences of twisting motions, which is the matter of special interest here. If there is swift outward propulsion, it stretches and obscures the twist.

ROTATIONS INHERITED BY THE PLANETARY BOLTS

It is a well-established law of mechanics that a rotating fluid body, in ascending or in descending, must take on cyclonic motion. This law is all too well illustrated in the violent tornadic twists of the earth's atmosphere. In these extreme cases, portions of large, relatively slow cyclonic movements are concentrated into close spiral whirls of great intensity. This usually takes place when general pressure over a large area is forced to find relief through a small exit. The development of the intense motion of the tornado from relative slow motions is often strangely sudden.

Since all the turbulence of the sun is probably cyclonic in some degree even when it does not manifest itself as such, it seems safe to assume that all massive propulsions of solar substance inherit some form of twisting motion as they leave it.

In the special eruptions assigned to the stimulus of the passing star, the inward pressure over the whole middle belt of the sun co-operated with the tidal pull which was greatest at the points of the cones. This was a combination of the same order as that which gives rise to tornadoes. The inward pressure, however, was general, the points of exit were large, and the tidal pull graded away in all directions to a vanishing feebleness, so that intense, sharply-defined tornadic bolts can scarcely be said to be specifically indicated. But ejections distinctly larger and more definite than ordinary solar eruptions seem to be fairly implied.

All these considerations support the important conclusion that all masses of sun-substance shot forth under the stimulus of the passing star *rotated about axes in the line of their projections much as do the missiles of a rifled cannon.* Such rotation gives a definite concept of the bolts, as well as mechanical guidance in tracing out the later history of these twirling masses. The most piquant feature of the case, however, is the startling fact that this *gives to the planetary bolts rotations such as none of the planets now have.* The deduction of such a rotation seems to be a logical necessity. Stated in another form, all the planetary bolts rotated about axes lying in the planes of their revolution. Most of the axes of rotation of the planets now stand at high angles to the planes of their revolutions. Jupiter, the greatest of all the planets, has an axis about as far as possible removed from its primitive axis as thus deduced. We seem to be headed for the brambles at the very start, but is not the deduction a necessary one? Must we not face its consequences, wherever it seems to lead?

AN EVORTICAL FACTOR ALSO

Precisely as there seems to be no escape from the inference that each planetary bolt would rotate about an axis in the line of its projection, there seems no escape from the conclusion that there was a fore-to-aft rolling of the exterior of the bolts due to drag at the contact between the bolt-material and the surrounding mass of the sun. Such an effect is very familiar and, like the

Fig. 20.—8:14 A.M

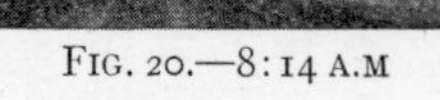
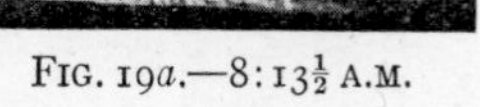
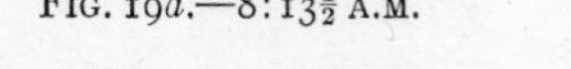

Fig. 19.—8:12 A.M.

Fig. 19*a*.—8:13½ A.M.

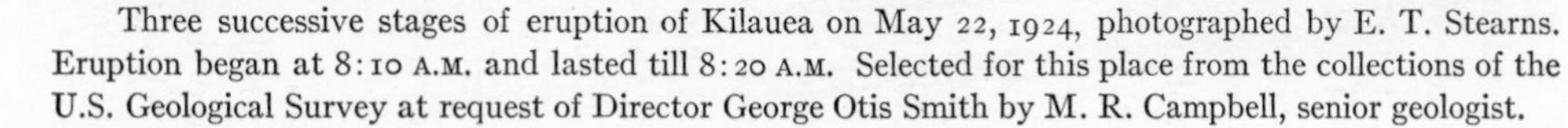

Three successive stages of eruption of Kilauea on May 22, 1924, photographed by E. T. Stearns. Eruption began at 8:10 A.M. and lasted till 8:20 A.M. Selected for this place from the collections of the U.S. Geological Survey at request of Director George Otis Smith by M. R. Campbell, senior geologist.

preceding, is quite inevitable. It is seen in a mild form in the "boiling clouds" that are so common on a hot moist day. It is very impressively shown in volcanic eruptions. The outrolling-inrolling convolutions in this latter case have given the highly descriptive but uncouth designation, "cauliflower-like." The outrolling-inrolling feature is strikingly displayed in the typical eruption shown in Figures 19, 19*a*, and 20. Figure 30, chapter xxi, shows the effects of two closely succeeding eruptions in which the outrolling-inrolling motion is very declared. Practically all volcanic eruptions show convolutions of this kind. Their motions belong to the vortex type; but as they present themselves in natural phenomena, the type motion is so far modified and made so intricate that it would be misleading to call these convolutions vortex motions. We shall try to avoid this by merely calling them evortical, for our interest is chiefly in the outrolling-inrolling feature. The evortical motion probably could not have penetrated as deeply into the planetary bolts, relatively, as in volcano eruptions, for volcanic gases are forced to escape through a rigid, or at least a viscous orifice, and the rolling motion is thrown wholly on the escaping gas. The outroll in "boiling clouds" is more comparable, for the rising currents in the clouds are of the same nature as the air through which they rise and the rolling motion is divided between the two, though we *see* only the outrolls of the cloud-fog. For the purpose of our study it is sufficient to know that this evortical motion was inevitable, and important more because of its nature than its massiveness.

The rotatory and the evortical motions of the planetary bolts must have combined into spiraloidal motions, but the effects of each type of motion would persist in the composite form into which they merged and be susceptible of analysis. That is all that it is strictly necessary for us to know, however much more about the merged product we would like to know.

REFERENCES

1. T. C. Chamberlin, "The Growth of the Earth," *Carnegie Institution of Washington, Year Book No. 25* (1925–26), p. 376.

2. T. C. Chamberlin, "The Growth of the Earth," *Scientia*, XLII (1927), 6.

CHAPTER XIV

THE SPIRALIZATION OF THE SOLAR PROJECTILES

To fashion a full picture of the projectiles from the sun it is necessary to combine the rotatory twist of the main projection with the evortical drag-effect. To these two dominant inheritances there are to be added such trailings and scatterings as would attend events of this kind. The main planetary bolts naturally took the lead as bunched heads, while the rolling drag was a lag factor. Some of the dragged parts doubtless kept close with the main bolt, merely rolling into its rear; other parts probably were detached and fell behind to various distances. Of this detached portion, a part should have kept near enough to the head bunch to enter with it later into planetary and satellite formation, while yet other portions fell back to greater distances. All together, these may be pictured as a head bunch and a trail, attended by more or less scattered material.

A close succession of such heads and trails would overlap and be merged by irregularities, and thus take on the semblance of a knotted arm, though the alignment and the continuity would not be likely to be good.

With the warning that all the spiral nebulae here introduced as illustrations are of a much larger—and in some respects a different—order from the spiralization of the planetary bolts of the sun under study, the reader is invited to inspect the spirals illustrated in Figures 21,

22, and 23, and to gather a general impression of spiralization as it appears on an immense scale in the distant heavens. The spiralization of the little bolts shot out

FIG. 21.—An unusually symmetrical spiral nebula, M 74 Piscium, showing a typical nucleus and well-defined knots along its two arms. Not so symmetrical in the outer as in the inner parts. Photographed at the Lick Observatory.

from our sun to make our planets was relatively a very small affair, but it was *our* affair. We will later have a little to say about the big spirals, but only by way of analogy.

THE TIDAL FACTOR

In our little planetary problem, the tidal pull of the passing star should have given rise to cones on either

FIG. 22.—The whirlpool nebula M 51 in the constellation Canum Venaticorum. The inner part is quite symmetrically spiral; the outer part, much more elongated. Yerkes Observatory.

side of the sun and a squeezed belt between. The stress conditions should, therefore, have favored two bunch-and-trail arms issuing from opposite points of the sun's

FIG. 23.—A spiral nebula with a much larger ratio of nucleus to arms which are formed of large knots closely assembled about the nucleus. M 94 (N.G.C. 4736). Mount Wilson Observatory.

body and curving concentrically in the direction of the mutual swing of sun and star. The arm extending toward the star should have been the stronger and should have reached out the farther. The spirality of the arms was simply the mechanical effect of the mutual attraction of the sun and star swinging about their common center of gravity. If the sun and star had been stationary relative to one another, the bolts and trains issuing from the cones would simply have gone out so far as their projectile forces would have carried them and then have returned to the sun; *unless* the bolts were projected far enough to enter the sphere of control of the star, in which case they would have been drawn on toward the star and have been lost to the solar system. It is obvious that the star might be so massive and have come so close that it would have stripped the sun of its projectile matter or even have wrecked it.

But neither the sun nor the star was stationary or could be stationary under the conditions that prevail in the heavens. During their approach to one another they were swinging about their mutual center of gravity and were increasing their speeds at every instant.

If it is found difficult to understand how a tide can be raised on the opposite side of the tide-distorted body, it is only necessary to picture that body as being swung around the mutual center between itself and the tide-raising body as shown in Figures 24 and 25. The part of the distorted body nearest the tide-raising body is obviously drawn more effectively, and takes a sharper curve, than the center of the distorted body, and that in turn takes a sharper curve than the distant part of this body and *so pulls away from it.* This has the same distortional effect as though that part were pulled away from the center of the body just as is the side nearest the distorting body. The reader who is versed in the dynamics of the case will see readily enough that if the near part, the center, and the far part of the distorted body were *three bodies* merely held together by mutual gravity, such tidal separation would take place *even more readily*. This is a rather vital matter in the interpretation of the great

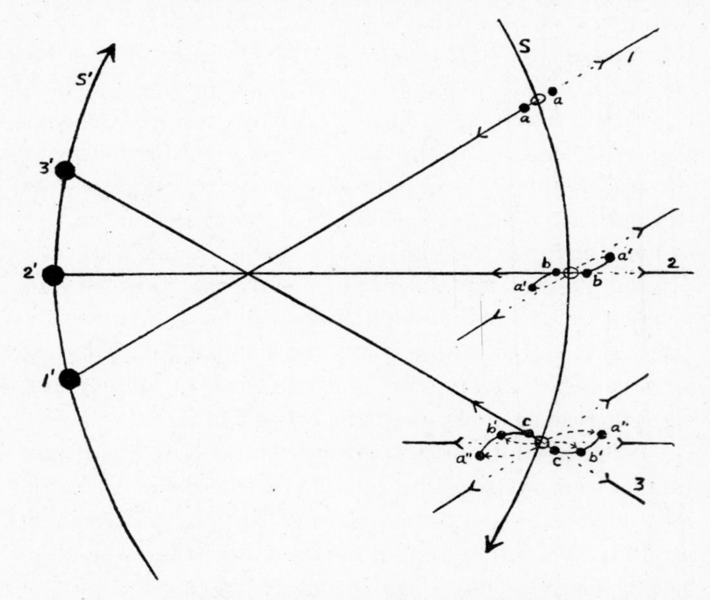

FIG. 24.—Diagram showing one of the assigned modes of developing a spiral nebula from an eruptive body.

nebulae which are the only observed ones available for illustration, though they do not exactly fit our case. We shall come back to this point later. Just now let us follow the general courses of the solar projectiles, whether planetary bolts or subwhirls or scattered matter or otherwise.

THE POSSIBLE COURSES THAT MIGHT BE TAKEN

The planetary bolts projected directly toward the star suffered some little lag; but as the star was moving forward, it pulled them forward also in the direction of its own motion. The amount of this forward pull de-

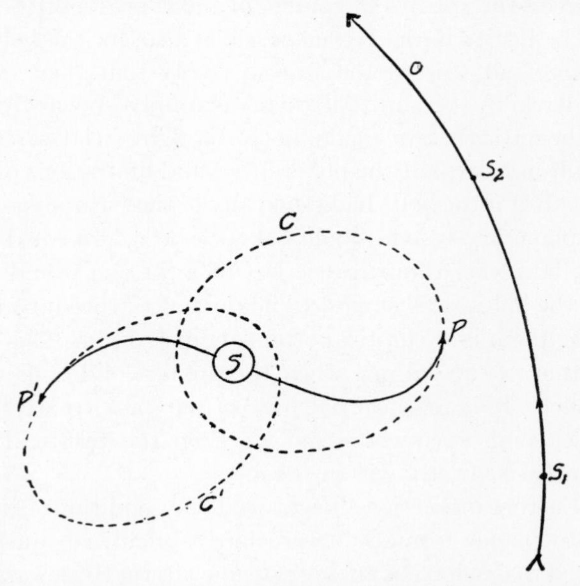

FIG. 25.—Diagram showing another of the assigned modes of developing a spiral nebula. (Moulton.)

pended on the relative mass of the star, on the nearness of its approach to the sun, on their relative velocities, on the eruptive and propulsive power of the sun, and on the direction and distance of the bolts as the movement proceeded. It was possible for the bolts to be drawn entirely away from the sun and to take no part in planet formation. This would be the case if the bolts were driven effectively into the sphere of control of the star. It was possible also for the bolts to be shot out so that the attractions of the star and the sun balanced one another, in which case the projectiles would go off in a tangent between the spheres of control of the star and of the sun and be lost to both. It was possible, also, for the bolts to be shot out toward the star so feebly that they would fall back to the sun. All this was amply shown by the mathematical tests made in forty-eight trial cases by Moulton to exploit the possibilities and limitations of the case. But if the bolts had taken any of these three courses, our planetary system would not have been formed. There was, however, a fourth case in which the sun would control the bolts at all stages, while the pull of the star would swing them into elliptical orbits about the sun. This case became the actual one when the proper conditions were fulfilled. It is an essential part of our task to see what those conditions were, and to keep the terms of our hypothesis strictly within them.

Further inspection showed that the conditions favorable to planet formation were fairly broad, so much so indeed that selection among possible alternatives was also a part of our task. The possible orbits ranged from those that were perfectly circular to those that were long, narrow ellipses. All the present planetary orbits are elliptical, but some of them approach circularity rather closely, and none of them are very highly elliptical. In the later revisions of our working hypothesis we have tried to choose relations that would give the bolts open subcircular courses from the start. The evolution of such a system would probably tend toward circularity, but its effectiveness is uncertain and we have tried to avoid dependence on it. In other words, we have regarded the subcircular ellipticity of the orbits of the planets as a hereditary trait that should be satisfied directly by the postulates of our hypothesis.

DETAILS OF THE SPIRALIZATION

If a series of projected bolts were shot forth from the sun in succession toward the star while all were being pulled forward by the star *but in different degrees*, the train they formed would obviously be curved in a spiroidal manner. Similar conjoint actions on the trailing parts and the scattered matter would bring them into some measure of accord with the leading parts. Differential effects of the same sort on the opposite side of the sun would give spirality to the arm on that side, with curvature in a like direction. Thus the whole would take on the form of a two-arm spiral (Fig. 24). As the sun was relatively large and was only slightly reduced by the drawing out of less than 1 per cent of its mass, we should, perhaps, regard the result as a nebulous star rather than as a nebula.

At best, the spiral could only have been temporary. The sun's relatively great mass and the relative nearness of the inner bolts would force these to revolve much faster than the outer bolts, and so the spiral would have wrapped up rapidly into a disk so closely coiled that its spirality would be undetectable. An observer on a neighboring star, with the best of telescopes, would probably never have made it out.

AN INCIDENT RATHER THAN AN ESSENTIAL

The spiral form is thus more a matter of interest than of importance in the formation of our planetary system. The evolution of our planets depended solely on the mechanics of the case, and the temporary form assumed was a mere incident. When the planetesimal hypothesis was first offered, it was announced—and the announcement emphasized by italics—that the hypothesis did not stand or fall on the theory that spiral nebulae are formed by dynamic encounter during the close approach of celestial bodies. This view was then, and is still, held by us, but not as an essential part of our hypothesis of planetary genesis. The spiroidal deployments in the heavens seemed then, and seem still, to be examples of dynamic encounter, and hence to lend strength to the special view of planetary origin here set forth. The encounters that gave form to the great spiral nebulae outside our stellar galaxy must have attained a vastly higher order of magnitude than anything that could arise in the relatively crowded spaces within our galaxy. Spiral nebulae of such small sizes and such short lives as could be formed within the spheres of control of the individual stars of our galaxy would be quite unlikely to be distinguishable from nebulous stars, unless observed in the very process of nebularization. Such an event as the birth of our planetary system would not even rise to the dignity of a nova, for there was no general catastrophic action. In the production of our planetary system the sun merely emitted a succession of minute fractions of itself; their present average size, even as adult assemblages, is now less than a millionth part of the mass of the sun. The overgrown body of the largest is now less than a thousandth of the sun's mass. We can scarcely emphasize too strongly the meager proportions of the planetary genesis. The birth of our little planet was a very quiet affair. It made no great stir in the universe. It is not at all likely that even the star neighbors felt any "thrill" by reason of the event.

NON-ERUPTIVE SPIRALIZATION

It does not belong strictly to our story to take note of types of spiralization other than that of our planetary system, but to forestall confusion of ideas, we may perhaps turn aside long enough to recognize that the *eruption of a sun or any other gaseous body is not essential to spiralization;* indeed, as already pointed out incidentally in connection with tidal distortion, a group of bodies already separated may respond to the spiralizing whirl of two centers of gravity even more freely than an eruptive body from which the spiralized matter must be shot forth. The shooting forth only brings about the conditions of spiralization; the spiralization itself is due to the dynamic encounter.

Recent studies have shown that some of the spiral nebulae that have been under observation since the days of Herschel are much larger affairs than formerly supposed. It has been claimed quite recently on cogent grounds that the outer part of some of them is made up of stars. This, of course, does not prove that when they came into existence they were not in a more primitive state. But the state of the material when spiralized is less a matter of interest than the source and mode of spiralization. The crux of the whole matter is *the spirality of the spirals.*

The bigness of the spiral may not make a radical difference in the mode of its origin. We have already noted that if the central mass and the two cones of a tidally distorted body were separated into three bodies—in lieu of three parts of a single body—the tidal distortion would be all the more effective. If a cluster of stars passes within

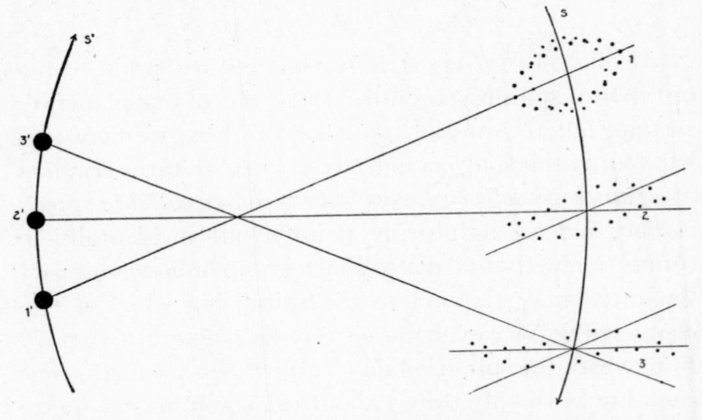

FIG. 26.—The spiralization of a star-cluster. Diagram of progressive distortion of an ideal circle of stars (dots back of first stage of distortion, upper right hand) in swinging about the center of gravity between it and a more massive cluster of stars or other great mass (black circle).

the strong differential attraction of the gravitative center of another group of stars, spiralizing distortion may be postulated as freely as if one or both were gaseous and eruptive. Figure 26 is drawn with a view to making this tangible in a simple case. The figure was fashioned on the pattern of Figure 24, which was made to fit the case of planetary eruption, and may be compared with it.

Organized star-clusters have centers or centroids of

mutual gravity, and these may undergo encounters of the same fashion as other centers of gravity and be attended with like gyrations. The stars of our galaxy and of most known star-clusters are so far apart that two such assemblages may pass through one another with very few, if any, star collisions. Such passages may be eccentric in any degree, and the combinations of their inertias and gravities should produce spiroidal effects of great variety and effectiveness. The symmetry of globular clusters seems to fit them singularly well for symmetrical spiralization, while such great heterogeneous assemblages as the Magellanic clouds stand in contrast as fit subjects for irregular redistribution. The galaxies of the higher order of magnitude should be able to effect spiralization in smaller clusters penetrating them without very marked reciprocal effects. As already stated, it is no part of our task to explain the great extra-galactic nebulae. It is only appropriate here to forestall the impression that either solar concentrations or eruptive states are more than incidental conditions in spiralization.

REFERENCES

1. T. C. Chamberlin, "Planetesimal Hypothesis," *Carnegie Institution of Washington, Year Book No. 3* (1906), pp. 203–53.

2. Chamberlin and Salisbury, *Geology* (1905), II, 36–81.

3. F. R. Moulton, *An Introduction to Astronomy* (1916), pp. 421–36.

4. T. C. Chamberlin, *The Origin of the Earth* (1916), pp. 101–29.

5. T. C. Chamberlin, "Synopsis," *Carnegie Institution of Washington, Year Book No. 26* (1926–27), p. 339.

CHAPTER XV

POSITIVE ASSETS AND RESIDUAL WORKING HYPOTHESES

The rarity of effective disruptive approaches of one star to another is by no means evidence that such approaches do not take place. If the motions of the stars of our galaxy are in any notable way discordant, as they are known to be, effective approaches are inevitable in time, however far apart these may be, while ineffective approaches are probably frequent. The certainty that such approaches do take place rests upon the same process of reasoning that proves the rarity of effective approaches. The hypothesis that our planetary system arose from such an event carries two valuable assets.

Our planetary family had an aristocratic birth. It was no everyday affair, even if it did not make much stir in the universe.

The rarity of disruptive approaches makes our future the more secure. In times past, mankind has suffered much from fear that "the end of the world" was close at hand. If close approaches of stars are as rare as they are computed to be, another approach is not due under the law of chance for a long time to come. Let us be at peace on this point.

If we care to inspect our special situation, it will appear that no star is near enough to the earth to endanger our planetary system for tens of thousands of years, even if one were coming this way, and none of the near stars seems to be doing this. The splendid orderliness of our planetary system shows clearly that no star has been within disturbing distance since the system was formed.

In addition to the atmosphere of complacency which these considerations throw over our view of our planetary ancestry, it is pleasant to note that its quiet biparental birth was unattended by disaster to any other known organization. It is also pleasant to contemplate that, so far as time and living conditions are concerned, our race is quite sure to have an opportunity to work out whatever good there may be in it.

THINGS YET TO BE DONE

Coming down from these congenial considerations to our own day's work, not yet done, we may plead that there are to be other days in which to do it; and then, too, there are generations yet to come. All phases of the planetary problems cannot be solved at once. Like the system itself, we on our part must be content with close approaches—if, indeed, they are close. The nativity of our planet and its kin has many aspects. The tokens of heredity in the heavens hint that there were many possible phases of spiralization, even though all rest back upon dynamic encounter. Certainly there could have been many varieties of approach, for there were all sizes of stars; there were many degrees of approach; there were possible differences of form, of orbit, and of velocity, and there were other possible variations of relationship.

THE LINE OF EFFORT AND THE STAGE OF PROGRESS

As a first step toward the details of the dynamic encounter, Moulton exploited the field by working out mathematically forty-eight special cases intended to stake off the ground that might perhaps prove productive and might distinguish it from the ground that was quite certainly unsuited, if not inimical. These preliminary tests narrowed the field very greatly, but it still remained large; it still offered many possible combinations. This preliminary inquiry made it evident that to work out the precise combination of mass, distance, orbit, speed, and other qualities of the co-operating bodies would necessarily involve a large amount of time and labor. In attempting this, either the naturalistic or the mathematical phase might precede or both might run concurrently. Both would ultimately be necessary, for the realistic idiosyncracies and the dynamic actuation must be qualitatively and quantitatively matched. If the more abstract inquiry preceded, it would be quite sure to develop many solutions of seeming applicability in addition to the true one, so that discrimination between the true one and the rest would remain to be decided by the naturalistic evidences. Such is the extraordinary power of mathematics, when untrammeled by naturalistic bondages, that it can furnish not merely one solution but many possible solutions, as urged by Poincaré, whose penetration and frankness led him to say that for any given set of data relative to a problem competent to give any solution at all, *an indefinite number* of mathematical solutions can be found, all correct and precise from the point of view of mathematics alone. Realistic features must be brought in to detect and exclude such assumptions as are untenable from the realistic point of view. On the other hand, it is unnecessary to urge that naturalistic interpretations may seem to fit the facts of the case and yet be mathematically untenable. When naturalistic concepts are reached, they need to be tested by the touchstone of mathematics. In the case in hand, it was foreshadowed that many possible combinations of the variables of the case would give planets of some kind and that the peculiarities of the actual system alone could determine the true from the merely plausible. Parallel work in the two essential lines was preferred, and followed through the early critical stages, but circumstances of the nature of a higher call to service, rather than preference, decided the mode of procedure in the later stages.

The more deliberate scrutiny of the planetary system which has been made in recent years has revealed combinations and relationships not suspected in the earlier studies, though they lie quite within the bounds at first marked out. The diligent use of the method of multiple working hypotheses in its application to the theories to which these gave rise has excluded most of them, but several remain plausible. These seem to point the way toward the ultimate solution, but they have not passed (1927) beyond the state of alternative working hypotheses. It does not seem important to force them to premature decisions, since most of the practical issues that depend upon them seem certain to hold true whichever of the alternative views may ultimately be approved. In the next chapter we will outline one of the most promising of these alternative sub-hypotheses, as an indication of their general nature.

CHAPTER XVI

HYPOTHETICAL CO-OPERATION OF SUN AND STAR

The following sub-hypothesis of the joint action of the passing star and the sun in propelling from the latter the planetary bolts which were later to grow into the planetary system, is offered merely as the most promising of the group of such hypotheses still entertained as possibly tenable. It is held with confidence that some combination of this order gave rise to the planets. This particular one serves to show how many peculiar requirements are to be satisfied.

The passing star is assumed to have belonged to one of the more numerous classes and to have been somewhat less in mass than the sun. This is assumed partly because it is statistically probable but chiefly because it seems best to fit the requirements of the case. A star distinctly more massive than the sun, if brought near it, would not only endanger too serious a disruption to suit the smallness of the mass of the planets (one-seventh of one per cent) but would be likely to strip the sun of such projectiles as were drawn forth from it. To accord with the observed natural division of the planets into two groups, an outer one of four large low-density planets and an inner one of four small high-density planets, it is assumed that the large outer planets arose from projectiles shot *toward* the star and that the small inner planets arose from projectiles shot in the opposite direction from the opposite side of the sun. This accords well also with the break between these groups. These two groups of four bolts each are supposed to represent the systematic response of the sun to the differential attraction of the star as it passed obliquely over the two specially eruptive belts of the sun on either side of its equator. It is assumed that there were two

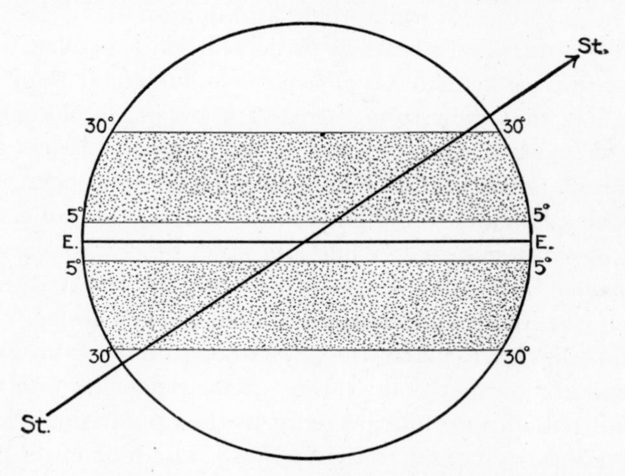

FIG. 27.—Diagram showing the assumed path of the passing star relative to the eruptive belts of the sun.

shots toward and two shots from the star in crossing each belt, making, in all, four great missiles sent far out past the star in its rear and four smaller missiles shot shorter distances from the opposite belts on the far side of the sun (Fig. 27). We thus postulate only four main double shots.

The planetoids are supposed to have arisen from small irregular projections stimulated on the far side of the sun by the passing star before it reached the specially eruptive equatorial belts. The solar tracts outside the main eruptive belts are very turbulent but in an irregular, much-divided way. They are known to be affected by gyratory swirls of smaller and more intricate nature than the solar cyclones of the subequatorial belts. Counterpart eruptions of this irregular type on the side toward the star may possibly be represented by undiscovered bodies beyond Neptune, of which there are some signs.

The planetary bolts as projected and propelled from the sun are held to have been far less unequal than the planets that grew from them. The import of the whole study points to much growth of the great planets and scantier growth of the smaller planets. In general, the outer planetary bolts were favored in the collection of gaseous material, while the inner ones were largely stripped of their gaseous constituents. Jupiter and, next to it, Saturn were specially favored by their positions, while Mars and particularly the planetoids suffered from great Jupiter's competition. (Many little particulars of this kind bobbing up unexpectedly in the application of the hypothesis give much satisfaction.) The four outer projectiles shot toward the star may be likened to the great shells of heavy ordnance; the four inner ones shot away from the opposite side of the sun, to solid shot from smaller ordnance; and the planetoids, to bird-shot from a shotgun.

THE ORIGIN OF DIFFERENCES BETWEEN THE OUTER AND INNER GROUPS OF PLANETS

The separation of the planets into two such natural and diverse groups suggests that the line of passage of the disturbing body lay inside the great group and that the larger order of planetary bolts shot toward the star were given sufficient momentum by the joint push of the sun and pull of the star to shoot past the latter, necessarily some distance in its rear, since the star was speeding on while the bolts were coming from the sun. The star pulled these bolts outwardly and forward until they passed it, and then forward and backward till it passed to an ineffectual distance. The forward pull was very effective while the bolts were passing in its rear, and this tended to give circularity to the revolutions of the bolts. If this forward pull had been too effective, the bolts would have been carried off by the star. To fit the case this forward pull must have been less than the sun's pull toward itself, but it might have approached the solar pull to any degree, and so the resulting orbits may have approached circularity to any degree. In this lies the basis for the subcircularity of the large outer planets. As there is supposed to have been much interchange of planetesimals in the later evolution, the subcircularity of the orbits of the great planetary bolts would doubtless have been sufficient to have given the orbits of the little planets subcircularity also; but the reciprocal swing of the sun is believed to have given them subcircularity from the outset. The general nature of these developments is shown in Figure 28. It is, of course, quite impossible even to approximate the true proportions of the planetary system in a diagram of this sort, but it may be helpful in realizing the radical differences in the conditions of formation of the outer and of the inner groups. Figure 28*a*, whose import is the same as that of Figure 3, is introduced here to call again to mind that exaggerations in space are offset in some degree by exaggerations in potential energy in the opposite direction.

While the precise location of the paths of the star and the sun and their relative masses are not fixed by such naturalistic considerations, they seem to be hemmed within rather narrow limits by them.

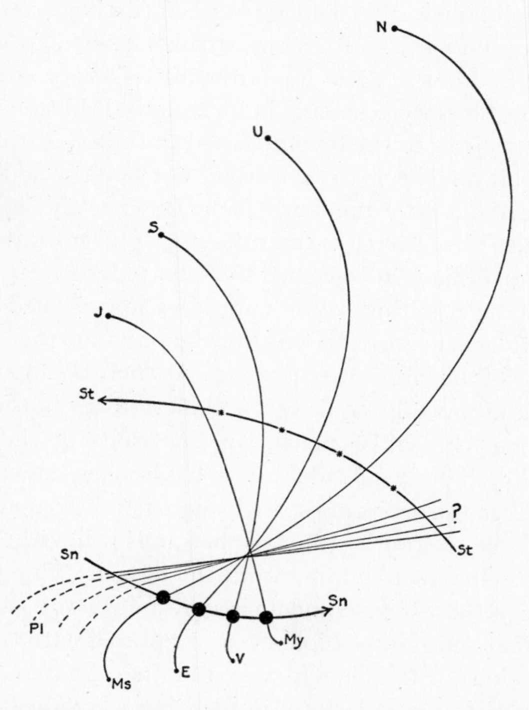

FIG. 28.—Hypothesis of formation of planets by joint action of the sun and the star. *Sn*, path of sun; *St*, path of star; *My*, Mercury; *V*, Venus; *E*, Earth; *Ms*, Mars; *Pl*, planetoids; *J*, Jupiter; *S*, Saturn; *U*, Uranus; *N*, Neptune. Four stages of double eruption of the sun give rise to planet pairs, Mars-Neptune, Earth-Uranus, Venus-Saturn, and Mercury-Jupiter. Planetoids assigned to eruptions previous to ejection of Mars-Neptune pair.

If the star had been as eruptive and propulsive as the sun, it would probably have suffered loss of substance and the sun would have gained substance from it. This may have been the fact, but we find little or no signs of it. This

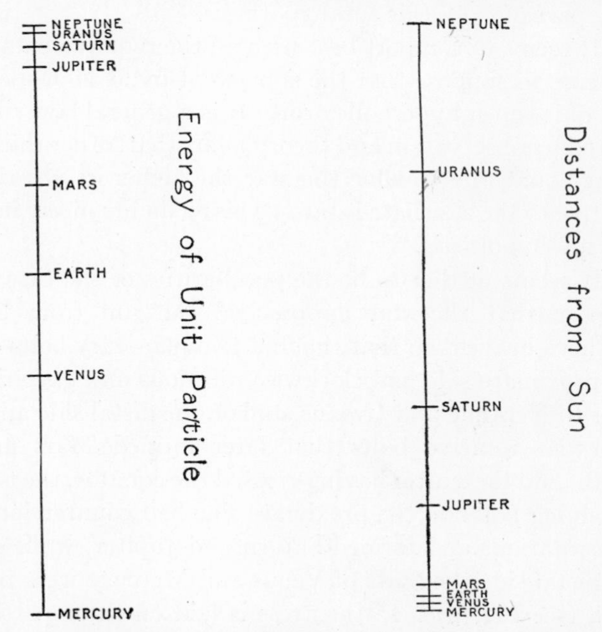

FIG. 28*a*.—Diagram showing the relative distances of the planets from the sun compared with the relative energies required to move unit particles from the sun to their respective distances.

absence of evidence in turn suggests—as does, also, the smaller mass postulated—that the passing star may have been a far-cooled dull, or "dark" or "dead" star. And perhaps we should interpret a dark star not so much as a cooled sun as the residue of stellar wastage, and therefore small as well as dark. This, at least, is in line with the current disposition to view stars as continually dispersing themselves by radiant and other forms of projectivity.

While all this fits in rather happily, it is not a necessary part of even this sub-hypothesis.

It seems to comport best with all the requirements of the case to suppose that the star swept by at high speed in a quite open hyperbolic orbit. It is a general law, supported by observation and theory alike, that, other things being equal, the smaller the star the higher its velocity relative to the associated stars. This again fits nicely into our sub-hypothesis.

It seems further to fit the peculiarities of the case to suppose that the star approached the sun from the southern heavens so that the first two planetary bolts on the proximate side had clockwise rotations and gave rise later to Neptune and Uranus, and on the distal side anti-clockwise rotative bolts that later formed Mars and Earth; and that, after having crossed the equator, the two remaining bolts on the proximate side had counterclockwise rotations and formed Saturn and Jupiter, while on the distal side the bolts of Venus and Mercury were put forth (see Fig. 27). Little stress is laid on these particular phases of the sub-hypothesis. We are merely trying to follow it to great lengths to bring out the details that must be met by a satisfactory sub-hypothesis. These intricate matters are beyond the province of a little book, except as they illustrate the intimate nature of the case. This particular sub-hypothesis seems, however, to gain strength by every test of its competency to meet all these peculiarities.

CHAPTER XVII

THE PROCESS OF NEBULARIZATION

The propulsion of solar bolts into planetary space and the drawing of these into orbits by the joint action of the sun and the passing star (the spiralization) was only the beginning of the process of giving organization to the cloud or nebulous envelope about the sun (nebularization) which led on to the formation of the planets. The spiralization was a deploying process rather than an organizing cloud-making process. The distinction between a spiral and a cloud or nebula is worth emphasis because there may be spiralization that is not nebularization. In the present case the spiral was ephemeral and unimportant as such; the nebularization furnished the immediate basis for the later processes. A clear concept of the nebularizing process and its results is essential to a close tracing of subsequent events.

ASSORTMENT AND EVOLUTION INTO PLANETESIMALS AND RESIDUAL SWARMS

The projection of the planetary bolts was followed by a stage of assortment which led on to orbital organizations of the material. This in turn controlled the processes of re-collection. The re-collecting processes in their turn constituted the actual formative process of the planets.

Foremost in the process of nebularization was the escape of a part of the bolt material from bolt control and its dispersal into great orbits about the sun. The combined forces acting on this widely dispersed matter were such as to permit only very slow regathering into planets. The process amounted to the dynamic storage of food for the future planets in a form that could only be drawn upon little by little during a long period.

At the same time, the assorting process led to the assemblage of a select residue consisting of heavy accretions which, for a time, served as the special infantile food of the young planets-to-be.

This assorting and reorganizing process began as soon as the planetary bolts emerged from the sun, and continued until it was essentially complete and the re-collecting process took its place. For simplicity, we will follow the evolution of the earth-bolt chiefly and only refer incidentally to the building of the other planets.

THE FORMATION OF PLANETESIMALS

As the earth-bolt emerged from the sun into open space, it was subjected to a formidable combination of dispersing influences. These included (1) expansion because of escape from the pressure suffered by the gases while in the sun, (2) enhanced molecular velocities arising from successions of collisions and rebounds, (3) divergence of projection, (4) the centrifugal component of the rotational motion of the bolt, and (5) the centrifugal component of the evortical motions of the bolt. This is, indeed, a formidable array. One could easily jump to the conclusion that the bolt would be entirely dissipated, but there is another side to the picture, presently to be drawn. Just here let us reserve a place for whatever residue may be found able to withstand this formidable combination, and merely follow the effects of the latter.

It appears clear at once that, in a mass no greater than the earth-bolt, the lighter constituents would escape from the control of the gravity of the bolt. The sphere of the bolt's control was zero as it left the sun. At that stage the bolt matter was kept together chiefly by the inertia of its own projection. As the bolt receded from the competitive attraction of the sun, its sphere of control grew. In this growth lay one of the compensations that saved a remnant of the bolt from dispersion. It is a good example of the unseen agencies that so often play a subtle part in nature's methods.

The alternative between control by the sun and control by the bolt was merely one of *first* obedience as against *secondary* obedience, for the sphere of control of the sun always enveloped the sphere of control of the bolt, so that whatever escaped from first obedience to the control of the bolt immediately entered the enveloping sphere of control of the sun and yielded direct obedience to it (see chap. iv). The escaping particle merely cut loose from its bondage to the bolt and took up an orbit of its own about the sun. The constituents that remained under the control of the bolt continued to revolve about the sun as a matter of secondary obedience, while they yielded first obedience to the bolt.

All constituents of the bolt that escaped from its control and took individual paths about the sun behaved as little planets and have hence been named planetesimals. We shall see later that it is quite inadmissible to confound these with meteorites. The one indispensable criterion of a planetesimal is that *it behaves like a planet.* It follows a subcircular orbit as the planets do and in the same concurrent way. The dynamical part of a planetesimal's definition is much more important than the physical part. Its physico-chemical makeup does not form a criterion. A planetesimal may be an atom, a molecule, or any one of several different sorts of accretions. It will be easy to see why most of the planetesimals that formed the earth were minute accretions of stony and metallic material. Let us turn at once to the way these accretions were formed.

COOLING AND AGGREGATION INEVITABLE CONSEQUENCES OF DISPERSION

Recalling the nature of the dispersive agencies previously listed, it becomes clear that their expansive effects must have led to rapid cooling, not merely on the exterior but throughout the bolt material. The simple radial expansion of a solar mass of the magnitude of the earth in passing from the sun to the distance of our planet would increase its volume more than 8,000,000 times. This of itself should remove all doubt that the ordinary stony and metallic substances would quickly lose the vaporous temperatures they had in the sun and pass down through the various temperatures of their liquid states into those of their solid states. Such a passage would give conditions ideally suited to the formation of small accretions, for the constituents were in collisional relations to one another for a time. The accretions thus formed constituted the critical feature of nebularization, for it was these accretions, not the invisible gases, that formed the cloud or nebulous envelope about the sun. The formation of these accretions is so important that it requires further statement.

FREE ACCRETION IN OPEN SPACE

The inevitable cooling of the solar gases from rapid expansion must have led to those special phases of accretion that are peculiar to the conditions of free space. These were singularly well fitted to give rise to minute accretions ranging up to certain sizes, beyond which the conditions became unfavorable. While in the sun, all the constituents that were to form the earth may be assumed to have been in a vaporous or gaseous state and to have been intimately mixed with one another. As the mass was shot into almost vacuous space and rapidly expanded, it cooled *throughout* so that the constituents in passing down through their temperatures of liquidity into those of solidity were at the same time colliding with one another and offering opportunities for aggregation. At first, these collisions numbered billions of times per second, later the frequency declined, but yet high frequency continued until the progressive dispersion separated the constituents so far as to forestall further intimate collisions of this kind. This type of accretion was thus limited. Less frequent and less systematic collisions continued so long as the constituents were assembled as a cloud, but even this was limited.

Not only does such accretion and such limitation of accretion seem inevitable, but the testimony of chondrules seems clearly to indicate that it is and long has been a common cosmic process. Chondrules make up much the larger part of the stony meteorites. They are small accretions ranging from minute grains up to the size of walnuts, the mean size being about that of millet seed. There will be much occasion to consider these chondrulitic accretions later (chap. xxix), for they seem to be the units that make up comet heads as well as meteorites, and to be the source of "shooting-stars." They are so commonly broken as to leave little room for doubting that they were formed as free-moving bodies subject to frequent collision. They seem to tell us by example what sort of little bodies would be formed by planetary material cooling from an original gaseous state as it was being dispersed into open space. And yet a few further particulars are needed to bring out the peculiarities of the case.

THE SPECIFIC NATURE OF THE PLANETESIMALS

As previously stated, all the constituents of the original earth-bolt that acquired too high velocities to be controlled by their own mutual gravity escaped into the sphere of control of the sun and pursued orbits of their own about it. They had previously been revolving about it as constituents of the bolt, but after escape they took independent orbits. They then became, in effect, little planets, that is, planetesimals. It will scarcely be doubted from the previous considerations that the larger part of the earth-bolt escaped from its control and became planetesimals. These were to be the main source of feeding of the planets. The slow feeding in of the planetesimals was one of the key features of the whole process of planetary formation. Some small part of the planetesimals undoubtedly acquired such high velocities that they escaped from the control of the sun, but these may be neglected.

The passing star not only called forth the planetary bolts and gave them orbits but it kept modifying these orbits as time went on. It also kept modifying the orbits of the planetesimals as soon as these were formed, and these modifications were not quite the same as those of the bolt. After the star passed on, the planetesimal orbits were further modified in much the same way as the planetary orbits now are by the attractions of all the other bodies of the solar system. It thus follows—and it is important to note this, because of its bearing on the ingathering process—that the planetesimal orbits came to vary much from one another and from the orbit of the bolt from which they were derived. This not only dispersed the nodes between the collecting body and its planetesimals but in many cases it eliminated such nodes entirely and made a very slow ingathering inevitable.

THE FORCES THAT FAVORED THE BOLT

It has been frankly conceded—or urged, as you please—that the forces which tended to disperse the earth-bolt were formidable. If the effects of these are now clearly in mind, we are prepared to consider the forces that favored the maintenance of the bolt in spite of the losses it suffered from the escape of planetesimals. The forces that favored the bolt had certain strategic qualities that forestalled its total dispersion.

The mutual attractions of all the constituents of the bolt were a constant—though not very powerful—force ever present and ever active in holding the bolt together. Since gravitation is instantaneous, it was always effective to its full value however the constituents might be moving. It persisted even in the very act of escape and limited the measure of escape. Gravitation acted on the constituents quite without regard to whether there was matter at the center of the bolt or not.

The gravity of a cluster of accretions was like the gravity of a cluster of stars. It was not the attraction of a commanding mass at the center, but was the weighted summation of the mutual attractions of the constituents for one another as they happened to be related at the instant. It was migratory as the constituents varied their mutual relations. In any case, the greatest gravity *stress* was not usually at the center. When considering the gravity hold of an open cluster on its own members, *the gravity near the outskirts of the cluster is the critical factor.* Whenever escape or non-escape is the alternative, any natural mode of distribution of the matter within the cluster is less material than the gravity *at the border.* To illustrate, the most intense gravity of the earth is now found a little below its surface; the gravity at the earth's center is zero. If the earth-substance were expanded to a sphere with a radius of 1,000,000 kilometers, the gravity at the level of the present surface would be greatly reduced, because the matter moved from within to the outside would no longer pull inward. The inward pull at the new surface, 1,000,000 kilometers from the center, would be nearly the same as before. It would be the gravity *there* that would decide whether a constituent would escape or not. Considerations of this kind are necessary to understand how a comet's head, for example, can hold together without a persistent core or central body of any moment. As will appear later (chap. xxx), we have a concrete source of appeal in the actual phenomena of comets' heads in support of the open organization of the residue of the earth-bolt to which our logic is leading us.

The law that action and reaction are equal and in opposite directions played a strategic part in holding together a residue of the earth-bolt. If a collision between two constituents of the bolt took place near its surface, and the rebound of one was outward—the main direction of escape—and led to escape, the reaction of its partner in collision was inward, and this placed the partner in a position more favorable for retention. Thus some gain stood over against the loss.

Still more strategic was the action of *the law of equipartition of energy* when rebounds arose from collisions, for this had an assorting effect; indeed, it was in some sense the key to the success of the bolt in holding a *selected part of itself* while it was losing the rest. In every collision and rebound of equally elastic constituents, the more massive and the less massive must each carry away equal parts of the energy of rebound. Hence, in a succession of collisions and rebounds the more massive bodies tend toward slower motions, while the less massive tend to accumulate faster motions. As time and repetition of collisions went on, the lighter constituents of the bolt tended more and more to escape, and the heavier more and more to be held under control.

This selective action was also favored by the nature of the accretions. On the whole, metallic aggregates were less brittle and elastic, and more prone to cohere by welding, than the stony accretions. The tendency was thus to concentrate and hold the metallic elements. They are therefore supposed to have formed the leading constituents of the residual bolt.

At first the contest between retention and escape lay mainly between free molecules and accretions. The molecules readily acquired high velocities and largely escaped. In encounters between molecules and accretions, the accretions were kicked back into the residual swarm. After the free molecules had mainly escaped, the contest lay between the lighter accretions and the heavier, and at the last it settled largely into a contest between the heavy stony accretions and the still heavier metallic aggregates, in which the latter had the advantage. Further selection came into action in the collecting process, but *complete* assortment cannot be assigned to these processes, and there is no evidence that complete assortment exists in the interior of the earth.

THE DYNAMIC STATE OF THE BOLT RESIDUE

As already indicated, a select part of the heavier accretions, largely metallic, remained as constituents of the earth-bolt even when it had reached its most depleted state. Under the conditions of the earth-bolt, complete self-dispersion is specifically counterindicated. At the same time it is essential to keep in mind that the residue, in emerging from a struggle against a prevailing and powerful tendency to escape, inherited the slow state of motion that made it successful in that struggle. Some of these residual accretions must therefore have been following paths about as near the limit of the bolt's sphere of control and power of control as was consistent with any control at all. Others were following paths deeper within the sphere of control. All had been forced to be revolutional in their earlier state, and all had played their part in the general nebularizing process. This is the key to the dynamic state of the residue. Far from any tendency to collapse, the constituents had all along been in danger of flying off. The residual accretions were swinging about their mutual center of gravity, as they had been doing through the whole history of the bolt. In this orbital motion there was a centrifugal component always pressing each constituent away from the center. This was small because only motions too slow to carry the accretions beyond their mutual control were retained; all higher motions led to planetesimal orbits. There is no reason to suppose that this state of things was in any way radically changed, much less reversed, when the residue had purged itself of its overswift members and started on a collecting career. On the contrary, the previous revolutional state was inherited, and persisted far into the later evolution.

These considerations, deduced from the earth-bolt, apply with even greater force to all the smaller bolts, those of the minor planets, planetoids, and satellites. They are probably not applicable to the four great planets whose bolts were with little doubt massive enough at all stages to hold gases and to evolve on less restrained lines.

THE RESIDUE AN ORBITAL SWARM

The group action of the accretions thus selectively retained as the residue of the earth-bolt was not unlike that of a swarm of bees circling about their queen, except that in this case there was no queen; there was merely a center of composite gravity without material embodiment. When bees are swarming out of the hive, their circlings are often quite irregular, but they are *not collisional*. Bees do not bump into one another and rebound or fall dead. Their motions are not quasi-gaseous. I once watched a swarm adjust themselves for a long flight. At first irregular, their circlings grew more and more symmetrical and concurrent; and as they moved off, they whirled about their queen in a well-ordered disk which was preserved for the half-mile through which I was able to follow them. Swarms of gnats and swirls of dust illustrate the fact that concurrency in action is a prerequisite to the permanent maintenance of a small assemblage of this type. In the residual swarm under study, the basis of control was the dynamic center; it was simply the center of mutual gravity of the swarm irrespective of the swarm's concentration.

If anyone is tempted to call this interpretation of the residue of the planetary bolts of the smaller order merely theoretical or speculative, perhaps he may find concrete instruction in comet heads which appear to exemplify just this kind of assemblage. They seem to make amends for the terror they once inspired by serving as star witnesses in this matter of critical importance. As is well known, comets have singularly low mass and open structure; stars are seen through great depths of cometic matter. That they are formed of discrete matter is implied by the absence of refraction. It seems to be demonstrated by the meteor showers into which they degenerate. In many cases there is not even much concentration toward the center of the comet's head; and never, we believe, is there any permanent solid core of even planetoidal dimensions. The nucleus, when present, does not seem to be a continuous solid, but merely the brighter portion of the open structure somewhat concentrated. Often there is no nucleus. This is not the place for an adequate discussion of this significant phenomenon (see chap. xxx), but we cannot wholly pass the testimony of these concrete illustrations of an open orbital swarm.

THE RESULTS OF THE NEBULARIZATION

When the process of nebularization had reached its climax, its main results were (1) a system of planetesimals moving in great orbits about the sun, and (2) a residual assemblage of heavy accretions organized as an orbital swarm. This swarm was to be the special foster-parent and feeder of the core of the earth in its infancy, while the planetesimals were to be the more lasting source of food for the growing planet.

REFERENCES

1. T. C. Chamberlin, "The Growth of the Earth," *Carnegie Institution of Washington, Year Book No. 23* (1924), pp. 376–87.

2. T. C. Chamberlin, "The Growth of the Earth," *Scientia*, XLII (1927), 3–16.

3. T. C. Chamberlin, "Synopsis of Planetary Evolution," *Carnegie Institution of Washington, Year Book No. 26* (1926–27), p. 339.

CHAPTER XVIII

THE PROBLEM OF THE EARTH-CORE

It is natural enough to take for granted that a core would form at the center of the residual swarm as soon as that was assembled. But if cores form spontaneously in the natural course of things, there should be plenty of samples in the great domain under the control of the sun. A diligent search outside the planetary disk fails to reveal a single core even of the smallest planetoidal size. "Shooting-stars" give daily demonstrations that there are multitudes of bodies there that might form cores if they were prone to do so or if that were the cosmic habit of their habitat. The inner planetary region is traversed also by comets whose heads seem to be made up of accretions already assembled in a loose way; but even when thus assembled, they are not known to gather into single solid cores. These comet heads stand for ages of opportunity; yet they fail to demonstrate any tendency to coalesce, even slowly, into cores—much less to gather together so vigorously as to form molten balls. All the cores of the planetoidal type known in the whole solar domain, little and least, infantile and adolescent, are found in the planetary disk. That the vast environment of the sun should be core-barren and planet-barren *except in the narrow planetary disk* is clearly an index of untoward, if not hostile, conditions of some sort pervading all the region outside this disk, and perhaps within it also when not overcome in some way.

The logic of nebularization, as we have followed it in the case of the earth-bolt, has not led us to a solid core as something that would be directly and quickly formed. On the contrary, it has led to an open swarm of revolutional accretions. This swarm was the sifted residue of the bolt material that had been undergoing strong dispersive influences, so strong that they had led to the escape of most of the planetary material. The residue embraced only those heavy accretions whose self-gravity barely held them back from escape. There was not only no compelling trend toward the center, but a trend outward that was overmatched only in selected cases by the self-gravity of the swarm. Instead of being a matter of course, and a matter of precipitate plunge to the center, the formation of a core turns out to be a matter of contingency in the case of all the small bodies of the solar system. In bodies of the smallest order—which are greatly in the majority—it turns out to be a critical problem. For the little and the least, the conditions seem to be hostile to core formation rather than friendly. It is a case of infantile hazard in the celestial world. Why should none of the hundreds of comets have succeeded in gathering its "nucleus" of a rather ambiguous sort into a solid, lasting core, and why should not this core have further grown to the size and stability of the modest planetoids and satellites? Why has no meteorite ever demonstrated an ability to grow into a rival of even the least of these midgets?

On the other hand, why should the residual swarms of even the small planetary bolts have succeeded not only in developing a core but in making some growth and attaining a place in a system that promises great perpetuity?

The solar environment may be assumed to be intrinsically as unfavorable to one as to the other. The solution lies in the bodies themselves. It seems to lie in a combination of causes already set forth in the preceding discussions. One factor is mass; another, dynamics. The planetary bolts were more massive than those from which (as we will try to show later) the comets sprang. This was one of the contributions of the passing star. Besides this, the passing star gave the planetesimal constituents *concurrent* revolutions, and concurrent revolutions are specially favorable for aggregation.

In this concurrency there was also a mutual aid liable to be overlooked. Not only were the individual bolts, projected under the stimulus of the passing star, large as a class but they gave rise to large belts of planetesimals, whose orbits overlapped, especially in the middle of the system, so that in a sense they formed *a common stock of food* on which the little swarms as well as the large could draw material for growth. This was especially true of the heart of the system, where most of the planetoids and little satellites are found.

It is easy enough to understand why the larger bolts should have formed cores under almost any conditions of the environment, for these bolts were probably massive enough to control the collisional activities of gases as well as the gently revolutional motions of the residual swarm of accretions, and so were able to concentrate directly and rapidly because the gases killed the independent revolutional motions of the constituents and gave gravity full play. But in the case of the small knots, the gases escaped in the process of nebularization. The residual swarms, thus freed, longer retained their revolutional states and resisted concentration. When we consider bodies too small to hold atmospheres, even in their adult states, the problem of the formation of cores becomes very definite. The very small residual swarms from which they grew would remain indefinitely as swarms or be dispersed, as shown in the case of comets, except for the special favoring influences just named.

CONDITIONS TRIBUTARY TO THE FORMATION OF PLANETARY CORES

The kinds of matter best fitted for being gathered into planetary cores were those that were toughest, most pliant, and most likely to weld, or coalesce in some form, when the mild encounters of the constituents of the swarm took place. Those most unfitted were the brittle and highly elastic constituents. Concretely, the metallic constituents were specially suited for core material; the tougher silicates less so; while the brittle, highly elastic silicates were relatively unsuited. The process by which residual swarms were formed tended in itself to retain the former class and eliminate the latter, so that the residual swarms were already fitted for core formation.

THE MODE OF CORE FORMATION

It is now easy to understand the mode by which residual swarms made up mostly of heavy, welding, coalescing accretions slowly gathered into solid cores. While in a general sense the members of the swarm moved in concurrent orbits, their individual paths were not strictly parallel. In the case of evortical motions there was a general type of concurrence with convergent and divergent factors. Besides this, the heterogeneities of motion of the original bolts were not wholly eliminated in the previous assorting processes. There were occasional encounters of the mild overtake or converging order. These could not be violent under the conditions that controlled swarm selection. The motions of the members of the swarms were necessarily slow. These slow encounters led to more or less adherence and coalescence. There was necessarily some loss of orbital motion. By the indefinite continuation of this slow process, concentration into a solid core took place.

THE FORMATION OF THE CORE—THE POTENTIAL ORIGIN OF THE PLANET

When a substantial core had been formed in the residual swarm of the earth-bolt and was being duly fed by the swarm and by such planetesimals as were able to hit the little target, and when both swarm-food and planetesimal-food had been fairly organized and were feeding in slowly, the genesis of our planet was *potentially* accomplished. All the rest was predetermined by the mechanism already in action. To be sure, there was yet a long period of growth ahead. In so far as we have found the process of genesis deliberate and early growth slow, by so much the story of this growth must be long—too long to be told in this little book. And so it is reserved for another volume.

But if we should drop the story just here, we would miss the meaning of some of the features we have labored to develop, especially the meaning of the earth's inheritance of rotation in the plane of its revolution, and the significance of the evortical motion. Let us, therefore, take a glance at the first stage of growth; let us see the infant planet a little way on its course.

REFERENCES

1. T. C. Chamberlin, "Formation of the Core," *Carnegie Institution of Washington, Year Book No. 25* (1925–26), p. 379.

2. T. C. Chamberlin, "The Starting of the Core in the Residual Swarm," *Scientia*, XLII (1927), 12.

3. T. C. Chamberlin, "Synopsis," *Carnegie Institution of Washington, Year Book No. 26* (1926–27), pp. 340–45.

CHAPTER XIX

THE FIRST STAGE OF THE EARTH'S GROWTH

It will be recalled that as the earth-bolt was shot from the sun it was given rotation about an axis in the line of its projection. In pushing out through the substance of the sun, another motion was added by the drag at the contact of the bolt with the adjacent matter of the sun. This drag gave rise to a fore-to-aft outrolling-inrolling motion. Rolling motions of this type are shown mildly in "boiling" clouds on a hot, moist day. In these an ascending warm central column rolls outward and is made visible by convolutions in the fog of the cloud. More violent motions of this kind are shown in volcanic eruptions, as illustrated in Figures 19 and 20, chapter xiii. The fundamental type of motion is of the vortex order; but these "cauliflower-like" convolutions are too imperfect to be called vortices, and we are merely styling them "evortical." This evortical motion is not confined to the mere contact face but extends more or less deeply into the adjacent gases on either hand. If the bulk of the gas that is pushing out is not too large nor its motion too swift, the turbulence is likely to permeate nearly the whole mass, as it obviously does in volcanic outbursts and in "boiling" clouds. In the case of the earth-bolt, the stress that forced the eruption did not have sharp borders, as in volcanic eruptions. Neither the compressional band nor the tidal cones concerned in forming the bolt were abruptly limited.

The border zone between the gas that was forced out and the gas that stayed behind was likely to have been rather vague and the limit of turbulence poorly defined. While it is well to try to weigh these details, there is no need to lay much stress on them, for the importance assigned to the evortical motion is not due so much to its mass as to the peculiar differentiating effects assigned it in this first stage of growth.

As first formed, this evortical motion was a roll from the front toward the rear. At the same time the rotation of the bolt about its axis lowered the central pressure so that as the backward rolling motion turned inward toward the axis at the rear end, it came under the influence of this lowered pressure and found in it a line of least resistance that promoted a general inrolling-outrolling movement of the bolt material. This movement is not supposed to have gone so far as to convert the bolt into anything remotely approaching a ring or a symmetrical vortex motion, but it tended in that direction. It is supposed to have merged more or less with the rotatory motion of the bolt, resulting in a composite evortical-spiroidal twist. We need not strain over the difficulty of picturing precisely the details of such a composite twist, for composite motions of this kind retain their potentialities in the combination and are amenable to the method used in the composition and resolution of forces. This makes it possible to follow the effects of the particular factor that is vital to the problem.

DIFFERENCES OF GROWTH AT THE TWO ENDS OF THE CORE

Neglecting other factors for simplicity, let us picture the accretions in evortical motion as running in convergently at one end of the axis of the core (the stoss end) and as running out divergently at the other (the lee end). The convergence at the stoss end of the axis and the divergence at the lee end are the essential features. Let us consider how this would affect the heavy, tough, welding metallic accretions on the one hand, and the less dense, more brittle, more elastic, and less coalescent stony material on the other hand. As the accretions converged toward the stoss end of the core, encounters would be more frequent than elsewhere and growth at this end relatively fast. The metallic accretions on encountering one another would coalesce and take a compromise path which would be, as a rule, toward the stoss end of the core. The lighter, more brittle and more elastic stony accretions would rebound as a rule more vigorously and perhaps be scattered by breakage. They would thus diverge more freely from the stoss end of the core and contribute less to growth there. The preponderant growth at the stoss end would thus come from the metallic constituents.

On the lee end of the core, the conditions for growth would be less favorable for both classes, but less favorable to coalescing accretions than to those whose rebounds were more miscellaneous. The united courses of the coalescing accretions would be systematically directed *from* the core.

This differential action was a very trivial matter cosmologically, but far-reaching geological consequences are assignable to it and it will be more fully treated in the book in preparation on *The Growth of the Earth*.

Considered as a part of the history of the earth's genesis, the point of special interest in this minor process

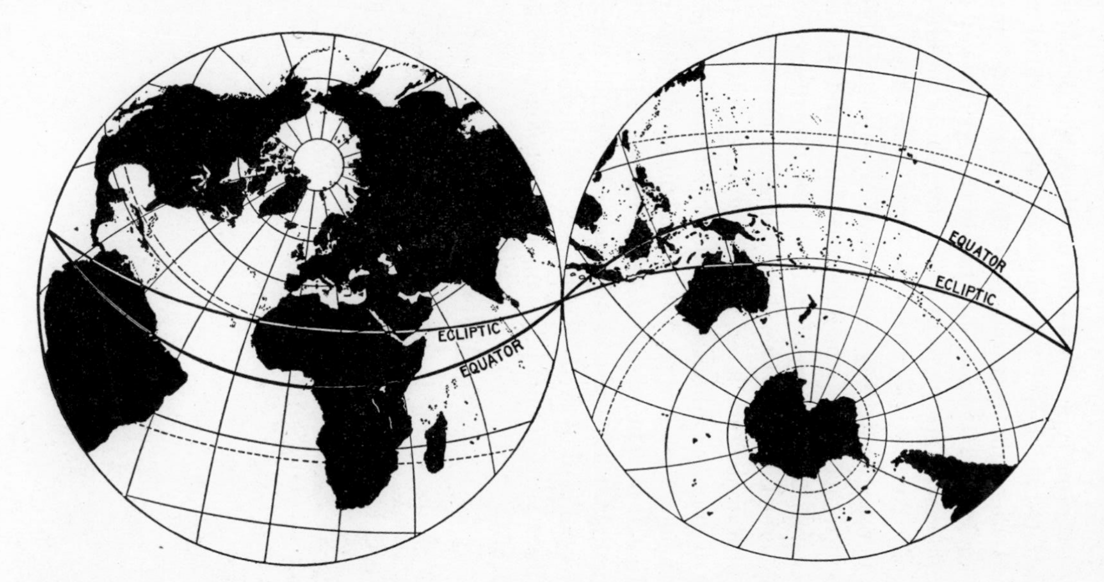

Fig. 29.—Map of the land hemisphere and the water hemisphere, drawn under the direction of Professor J. P. Goode

is that the same type of assortment which had previously concentrated the heavy material and had separated and directed the light material into the larger and more miscellaneous orbits was continued in this special way into the process of growth, and in so doing made one end of the infant core heavier than the other. The amount of this difference of density is supposed only to have been sufficient to inaugurate the difference now found between the oceanic basin hemisphere and the protrusive land hemisphere (Fig. 29). The planetesimal mode of growth came into dominance later, and there were shifts of the center of gravity and a series of deformations; but these, on the whole, worked with this original differentiation and perpetuated it. The total difference between the heavier and the lighter hemispheres now seems to be only a fraction of 1 per cent of their total masses; but the difference, small as it is, is profoundly important geologically and biologically.

REFERENCES

1. T. C. Chamberlin, "The Growth of the Earth," *Carnegie Institution of Washington, Year Book No. 25* (1925–26), pp. 375–82.

2. T. C. Chamberlin, "The Growth of the Earth," *Scientia*, XLII (1927), 3–18.

3. T. C. Chamberlin, "Synopsis," *Carnegie Institution of Washington, Year Book No. 26* (1926–27), pp. 338–41.

CHAPTER XX

THE GROWTH-CREEP OF THE AXES OF THE PLANETS

Small, slow shiftings of the axes of rotation of the planets are inevitable, and are constantly in progress; but large shiftings in any short period of time are improbable from lack of adequate available energy to cause the shift. The gyroscopic stability that arises from the rotation of the earth, for example, is a very formidable obstacle in the way of any great change in the direction of the axis in even a geologic era.

But the question here raised is new. The changes of axes recognized in the literature of the subject relate to the *adult* planet and arise from some environmental influence or some internal shift of the planet's material. The new question arises from an increase of the planet's material by growth. It is really the addition of the unassembled part of the planet—which has potential rotation—to the assembled portion which is already in rotation. It is the formation of a series of new axes to combine the rotational components of the added material with those already assembled. It is only when the growth is complete that adult rotation begins.

The well-known adult shiftings of the axes of rotation belong to two quite distinct genera. In the first, the well-established astronomical nutation, the axis, or "the pole," shifts with the planet, the two "nod" together, while the relations of pole to planet remain unchanged. In the second, geographic nutation, the axis, or its end, the pole, shifts its position in the body of the planet. This is "the wabbling of the pole."

We are not concerned with either of these here. They are short cycles, and probably much more rapid in action, limited as their movement is, than the growth-creep here under consideration. But this growth-creep was persistent in a given direction throughout the whole period of growth. It was too nearly infinitesimal, in any short period, to be called a "shift," besides being something other than a simple shift. It was a formative adaptation, a growth-creep.

THE MODE OF AXIAL CREEP

It appears from the considerations set forth in chapter xiii that the planetary bolts shot forth from the sun inherited rotations about the axes of their projections. In the course of the evolution of these twirling bolts, their swifter constituents escaped from the control of the bolts and became planetesimals. This of course included constituents that had high rotational velocities, but the constituents whose velocities were low enough to permit their retention as members of the residuary swarm, gave to the planetary core, as it formed, an inherited rotation about the axis of projection which lay in the plane of planetary revolution. This was a slow rotation by virtue of the selective process. It affected merely the residual swarm and the core formed from it.

From the considerations offered in chapter x, it appears that the balance of effect of the infall of planetesimals, in the middle of the planetary system, was to give forward rotation about an axis normal to the planetesimal disk. The axis of rotation of the ideal core at the start, and the axis of theoretical rotation of the combined planetesimals, were 90° apart. Our problem is merely to trace the progressive adjustment of the succession of axes to the successive stages of growth, as the planetesimals gathered into the core and the planet grew up.

The planetesimals carried more moment of momentum in their free state than after their fall, because some was lost in the assemblage. After infall, their momentum was divided between the *rotation* of the planet and the *revolution* of the planet. In the case of the earth, Moulton has computed that the part of momentum represented by the earth's rotation is 1/3,700,000 of that represented by its revolution. As the planetesimals before infall had still more momentum, it was only necessary that about 1/4,000,000 of the total momentum of the earth-forming planetesimals should be converted into rotation to give the total momentum of the adult rotation.

More than this: in strict analysis, the growth-creep was not a shift of an adult axis, but the creation of a series of new axes to fit the stages of the forming earth.

THE MODE OF EARTH-CREEP

Each planetesimal that joined the growing planet carried its own mass and momentum into it. The united mass thus formed required an axis adjusted to the new body. This new body was rarely concentric, in a strict sense, with the old mass. A new axis was required rather than a shift of the old axis. The only cases in which the old axis would be likely to be retained were those in which two or more planetesimals falling in at the same time exactly counterbalanced one another, a very rare case.

The new axis would, of course, be scarcely more than infinitesimally different from the preceding axis. The creep in any short period would be almost infinitesimally minute. But it was persistent through the hundreds of millions of years, or perhaps the billions of years, of growth. Its slowness in no way contravened its reality or its importance in the long secular sum total.

THE ACTUAL AMOUNTS OF AXIAL CREEP

Assuming that all the planetary axes originally lay in the planes of revolution of the respective adult planets, the axis of the earth crept $66\frac{1}{2}°$ during its growth; that of Mars crept between 66° and 67°; that of Jupiter, 87°; that of Saturn, 63°; that of Uranus, 8° (retrograde); that of Neptune, somewhat uncertain. Mercury and Venus are so exceptional in other respects that they may best be left for special discussion later (chaps. xxix and xxxii).

PROPORTION OF AXIAL CREEP TO RADIAL GROWTH

We have already called attention to the very ample competency of the infalling planetesimals to cause the creep of the planetary axes. In some respects this may be visualized more readily by a comparison between the radial growth and the axial creep. The average axial creep of the earth was only 1° for each 100 kilometers radial growth; that of Mars, about 1° for 54 kilometers growth; that of Jupiter, 1° for 800 kilometers growth; that of Saturn, 1° for 940 kilometers growth; and that of Uranus, 1° for 3,000 kilometers growth. It appears thus that the amount of axial change was small in proportion to the growth that caused it. The question of adequacy of cause seems to be met in a most ample way. Indeed, the question seems almost to be shifted to the other side. How could so much matter bearing so much momentum fall into a planet and not shift its axis more? The answer is close at hand. There was infall on both sides of the rotating planet, and both planet and planetesimals were moving in the same general direction. When planetesimals of equal momentum fell on opposite sides of the planet, they both tended to push the planet forward in its orbit. Thus the larger part of the momentum of planetesimals and planets alike became momenta of *revolution*. It was only the difference between the momenta of infall that tended to cause rotation. That which tended to cause revolution was so much the greater that its rotational part may be put at $\frac{1}{n \times 1{,}000{,}000}$ of the momentum of revolution.

REFERENCES

1. T. C. Chamberlin, "Secular Shift of the Axis," *Scientia*, XLII (1927), 17–18.

2. T. C. Chamberlin, "Synopsis," *Carnegie Institution of Washington, Year Book No. 26* (1926–27), pp. 340–41.

CHAPTER XXI

THE EVOLUTION OF THE MOON

The moon has long been held to form a class by itself. It is much larger relatively, and more distant from the planet mass that controls it, than any other satellite, though some of the satellites of the great planets Jupiter and Saturn equal and even surpass it in actual size. The orbit of the moon is inclined to the ecliptic only 5°8′; while the earth's equator, in or near which we might expect it to revolve, if it were a derivative satellite, is inclined $23\frac{1}{2}°$. The orbits of the satellites of Mars, Jupiter, and Saturn are, as a rule, much more closely co-ordinated with the equators of their primaries.

THE MOON REGARDED AS A PLANETOIDAL COMPANION OF THE EARTH

It is probably not entirely novel to regard the moon as a planetoid attending the earth, though the more common view is that the moon was derived from the earth. All the other satellites are here held to have had their origin in sub-whirls of the bolts of their primaries, these sub-whirls arising from convolutions characteristic of solar eruptions, as already described. The moon, however, seems to us more likely to have arisen as *a secondary eruption of the sun*, closely following the eruption which gave rise to the earth-bolt (see Fig. 30). Such an eruption is not regarded as altogether independent, but rather as a reaction from the prior eruption of the earth-bolt. Such an origin places the moon among the planetoids rather than the typical satellites.

A moon thus formed should have been less intimately

FIG. 30.—Photograph of an eruption of Colima, showing a primary and a secondary bolt. (Frederick Starr.)

dependent on its primary than satellites formed from sub-whirls of their primaries. In several respects the moon may be interpreted as showing independence of this kind and degree. It may have had a sphere of control of its own, at first, and some measure of individuality in its path and mode of growth. In its early stages, it may not have revolved within the sphere of control of the earth-bolt, but its path must have been very similar to that of the earth. As the moon and the earth grew, however, they were drawn toward one another by their mutually increasing gravity; and if the moon was not already within the sphere of control of the earth, it must have been drawn into it. Subsequently the moon must have circled spirally toward the earth until it had penetrated two-thirds of the depth of the earth's sphere of control and reached its present position. In all its later history, the moon quite certainly has served as a true satellite of the earth.

RELATIVE INFLUENCE OF GROWTH AND OF TIDES ON THE MOON'S POSITION

So long as the earth remained without an effective water-mantle, its tides were only those of its elastic body. As these lagged but little, they caused little retardation of the earth's rotation and little movement of the moon away from the earth by tidal reaction. During this stage, therefore, the tides offered little opposition to the drawing of the earth and moon toward one another by mutual growths.

When an effective water-tide came into action, there was a contest between the effects of the water-tide and the opposite effects of the growth. When the infall of planetesimals declined to insignificance, the tides had little opposition from growth. They must almost certainly have been opposed by occasional shrinkage of the earth which accelerated rotation. In very recent times, appeal has been made to ancient eclipses as affording evidences of a very slow secular retardation of the earth's rotation; but the determinations and the interpretations are attended by uncertainty and doubt—as has been well stated recently by Innes. The factor of growth, though actual, is now very small. Deformation of the earth is in spasmodic progress, as implied by earthquakes and other geologic data. The value of the inertia water-tide that inevitably springs from the rocking of the body-tide is wholly undetermined, and its algebraic effect on the estimates of the gravity water-tide is quite unknown. The tidal effects of the sun would continue even if those of the moon were reduced, by its retreat, to a negligible value—as pointed out by Moulton. Even if it were possible to make perfectly certain estimates of the value of present tidal retardation, it could not safely be projected backward very far, geologically speaking, without encountering contravening effects from both growth and shrinkage.

ONE FACE ONLY TURNED TOWARD THE EARTH

Aside from a little shift of face due to swifter or slower motion of the moon in its orbit, and aside from a very little wabbling, the moon always turns precisely the same face toward us. This means that it rotates *precisely* once in every revolution. If there were only a slight secular difference in any one direction, it would be cumulative and in time would give a notable change of face. This preciseness implies a positive agency always ready to act and competent to correct any influence that tends to change the moon's rotation relative to the earth. The presence of such an influence is therefore practically certain.

This peculiar relation of rotation to revolution is shared by one, or perhaps two, planets (Mercury and Venus) and by all the satellites of Jupiter and Saturn large enough and irregular enough to give evidence of their rotations. It is not, then, a peculiarity of the moon, or any single body, or of the satellites exclusively. It forms a dynamic genus by itself.

FAVORABLE CONDITIONS UNDER THE ADOPTED INTERPRETATION

If the moon took its origin, as suggested, from a secondary bolt closely following the earth-bolt, its original axis of rotation should have lain in the plane of its revolution which seems to have been near the ecliptic. To interpret its present position in harmony with this, it is merely necessary to suppose that the growth-creep of its axis was essentially ideal, as might well be in the case of a small body revolving in the feeding-ground of a large body. This attainment is assigned to the infall of planetesimals specially concentrated near the earth. At the same time, the impacts of these planetesimals on the opposite sides of the rotational axis of the moon brought about so close an approach to an equilibrium effect that the slow rotation left came under the control of the positive force whose nature we are seeking. These two classes of effects are assignable, for the reasons indicated, to other satellites and to the planets near the sun. The technical data are especially explicit in the case of the moon and are in full accord with this interpretation. The present axis of the moon's rotation is inclined only 6°41′ to the axis of its orbit, and only 1°32′ to the axis of the ecliptic. These imply that the way had been fully prepared for the action of the agency sought, first by growth-creep and secondly by an approximate balancing of the rotational effects of the planetesimal impacts on the opposite sides of the moon's axis. Some such preliminary preparation was prerequisite to successful action by the regulating agency, whatever it may be.

THE ONE-ROTATION-PER-ONE-REVOLUTION COMBINATION

In its broadest phases this is the commonest of common rotational phenomena. Every bird, every fish, not to say boulder, and every other body on the earth normally rotates once for every revolution of our planet. It not only holds good of every integer in the solid body of the earth but of all normal bodies floating freely in the fluids that surround the earth and are held to it by its gravity. It is a characteristic of bodies in a well-centered system. The basal question raised may take this form: Does the moon-earth relation constitute a *well-centered* combination? Is the moon dynamically a part of the more intimate system of action to which the high-flying bird, the balloon, and the flying-plane belong, or are its relations of a more foreign type?

There can be no question about the gravitative control of the moon by the earth, or of a similar control of the satellites of Jupiter and Saturn by their primaries, or of a similar control of Mercury by the sun. The other factors required are (1) a heavier end and a lighter end, as in the case of the bird, balloon, and airplane; and (2) a resisting medium sufficient to give the heavier end an advantage and cause it to take the position nearest the center of gravity and keep it.

The heights to which sounding-balloons rise and yet keep one face to the earth shows that the resisting medium may be quite tenuous. Is a resistance of this order, but still more tenuous at the height of the moon, sufficient to function in a similar way? The resistance may come from the combined action of the ultra-atmosphere, of the planetesimals, of the chondrulites (considered later), of the zodiacal particles, and of sporadic bodies. It must further be considered that the high speed at which the moon sweeps through this tenuous field has the effect of making it quasi-denser. By reason of its speed, the moon encounters great numbers of these at high velocities every revolution. When the enhanced resistance due to velocity of impact is duly taken into account, we incline to the view that the resistance was adequate. If so, the problem closes down to the question: Is one hemisphere of the moon heavier than the other?

THE DISTRIBUTION OF DENSITY IN THE MOON

It is a safe general proposition that a body which has grown up from planetesimal infall under the conditions already described would be more or less unsymmetrical in form and its hemispheres more or less unequal in density. We have already deduced (chap. xiv) a type of difference of this kind in the growth of the hemispheres of the earth. If the moon grew up as a companion planetoid, it is entirely consistent to assume that, like its companion, it became denser at one end than at the other, and that this led on to a heavy basin-hemisphere at one end and a lighter upland-hemisphere at the other. The evortical factor would be likely to be greater relative to the whole mass in the secondary bodies than in the more massive primary ones. But the main appeal must, of course, be to the concrete observable evidence. Does the face of the moon countenance this view?

THE CONCRETE EVIDENCE

Before we turn to the photographic evidence, let us recall that a normal full-face photograph of a globe of uniform reflecting surface is lightest at the center and grows duller toward the retreating borders. But if the borders are much relieved by mountains and other rugosities, these may throw back as much or more light than a smooth, flat portion of the surface in the center.

In the smaller, the dimmer, and the more generalized photographs of the full moon published in works on astronomy, one of the most notable features is the greater brightness of the rim and the duller aspect of the main central portions of the moon. This is precisely opposite to the normal effect of a uniformly smooth surface. It implies an upland surface on the border sufficiently rugged to throw back an unusual amount of light.

As the basis for a critical inspection, a photograph of the full moon selected as most suitable for this purpose from the entire collection at Yerkes Observatory by Director Frost and Professor Barrett, is here introduced

(Fig. 31). To assist in comparison, separate prints of the rim and of the main central portions, respectively, are added (Figs. 32 and 33). A comparison of these seems con-

FIG. 31.—Photograph of the full moon, selected as best fitted to show light (elevated) and dark (depressed) parts. Yerkes Observatory.

vincing in respect at least to the ruggedness of the rim. In his recent *Astronomy* (1926), Duncan says, "The highest lunar mountains, which rise to 25,000 feet or more, are situated in ranges near the limit of the visible side of the moon."

The darker portions are the "Maria" of Galileo and the older writers. They are extensive smooth basins and only seem to lack an adequate supply of salt water to be

FIG. 32.—Photograph of the rim of the full moon shown in Figure 31, to bring out the preponderance of light (elevated) areas over the dark (depressed) areas.

indeed "seas." The earlier view that these basins were actually seas still has the force of good testimony respecting their configuration and general relations. When it became clear that they could no longer be regarded as seas, they were generally interpreted as lava beds, which equally implies that they are basins. It seems quite possible, however, that they are only ash-plains formed by volcanic débris projected from surrounding craters (see the

FIG. 33.—Photograph of the central part of the moon, excluding the rim, to bring out the preponderance of dark (depressed) areas over the light (elevated) areas.

white lines). Explosion-débris, in the absence of air and of strong gravity, would be projected to great distances and would lodge in larger amounts on low, smooth tracts than on the steep faces of the high, rough tracts.

Olivier adds a consideration of obvious value:

We here desire to call attention to the effects of a minor cause which absolutely is known still to be going on, but which seems heretofore to have been overlooked. We know that about 20,000,000 visible meteors strike the earth's atmosphere daily. Making allowance for the extra attraction of the earth and the smaller area of the moon, still over one million must strike the satellite every day. Now the earth's atmosphere protects us from the direct striking action of these bodies, for even meteorites have lost most of their velocity before they reach our surface. On the moon there is no protection—and there is a continuous rain of these projectiles moving with velocities up to at least 44 miles per second, admitting only the parabolic limit and nothing higher. These strike the surface at every conceivable angle. Therefore there must be a continual effect, not unlike erosion, going on.

The worn rims of the older craters are better explained by this action than by exfoliation and volcanic blasts, which doubtless contributed to the same effect; while it also helps to explain the accumulations of débris in the craters and the basins.

The fewness and smallness of the craters in these basins, contrasted with the great numbers and sizes of the craters on the uplands and along the mountain tracts, is one of the specially significant features of the moon's face. We shall try presently to show that these are true volcanic craters of just the type the moon should produce. We cannot understand how such a singular distribution of craters as the moon shows could occur, if they were pits due to infall of meteorites or of any similar bodies. The distribution in that case should accord with the law of chance, whereas they are crowded thickly on the uplands and are few and small on the basins. The law of chance certainly ought to hold good where the number of craters reaches 30,000.

On the other hand, on the supposition that the basins were formed by the sinking of relatively heavy segments, the relative absence of craters in the basins is strictly in the line of sound theory. The relative abundance of craters on the elevated tracts and along the mountain ranges of the moon is equally true to theory.

The face of the moon seems, thus, to tell us that it is the outward expression of the heavy hemisphere of the moon, that it probably grew up from the stoss end of the core of the moon, and that natural selection of the heavier accretions brought this about in a manner similar to that which made the stoss end of the earth grow up into the basin-hemisphere of the earth.

If, then, it is the heavy basin-hemisphere of the moon that is constantly presented to us, and if the molecules of the ultra-atmosphere, the secondary planetesimals, and the meteors (mostly chondrulites with a few meteorites), acting together on the moon revolving swiftly through them, serve as a sufficient resisting medium, the problem of the moon's rotation falls into line with that of the bird and the balloon.

REFERENCES

1. F. R. Moulton, *An Introduction to Astronomy*, "Rotation," pp. 200–205 (1916); "Surface Features," p. 207; "Lunar Craters," p. 211; "Gilbert's View," p. 213.

2. J. C. Duncan, *Astronomy* (1926), "Rotation of the Moon," p. 121; "Lunar Topography," p. 124; "Citation," p. 125.

3. T. C. Chamberlin, "Synopsis," *Carnegie Institution of Washington, Year Book No. 26* (1926–27), p. 341.

4. C. P. Olivier, *Meteors* (1925), p. 254.

CHAPTER XXII

THE INTERPRETATION OF THE CRATERS OF THE MOON

Many of the craters of the moon surpass in breadth, depth, and sharpness of configuration the volcanic craters of the earth. While most of the lunar craters fall within the range of breadth and depth of those of the earth, some of them reach diameters of 50, 60, and even 100 miles and depths of 10,000 feet. Modern terrestrial craters do not often measure more than a fifth or a sixth of these dimensions, and ancient terrestrial volcanoes are not known to equal them. At first thought, it seems additionally strange that the smaller of two bodies close together should bear the larger craters.

These striking differences have given rise to the hypothesis that the lunar cavities are not volcanic craters at all, but explosion pits following the impacts of infalling bodies such as large meteorites or their equivalents. This alternative hypothesis has little or no *raison d'etre* beyond the supposed difficulty of the large size of the lunar craters.

THE ISSUE OF MAGNITUDE

But the difficulty of magnitude has two faces. Have the known infalling bodies any greater capacity to produce great pits than have the known volcanic agencies? This is the basal phase of the issue and is the first to be met. The test is right at hand. The earth and the moon are close

FIG. 34.—The craters of the moon, as photographed at Mount Wilson Observatory. Introduced here especially as a basis for the study of obliquity of infall. One-fourth of the impacts should fall at angles between tangent and 30°; one-half, between 30° and 60°; and one-fourth, between 60° and 90°. (Bartky.)

FIG. 35.—The smoother half of the moon, photographed at Mount Wilson Observatory. Introduced here for the study of the much smaller number of infalls per unit area, the scantness of oblique strokes on the plane surfaces, and the perfection of the relatively few crater rims.

companions, about equally distant from the center of the solar system and about equally exposed to infalling bodies; but there are some qualifications. The gravity of the earth is six times that of the moon, and infalls upon the earth should be more effective in proportion. The atmosphere of the earth intervenes and reduces the force of infall. As the issue rests mainly on craters 50–60 miles in diameter and 10,000 feet deep, small bolides are incompetent in any case, and only the restraint of the atmosphere on very great masses needs to be considered. On the earth, erosion must have cut away the rims of the craters and have filled the pits in much greater degree than on the moon. But still pits tens of miles across and thousands of feet deep should be readily detected by any respectable geological survey in any accessible formation in any era.

Making all due allowance for qualifying conditions, how stands the record? The most notable pit-forming effect assigned to infalling meteorites on the earth is Crater Butte (Coon Butte) in Arizona, where the explosion-pit is less than four-fifths of a mile in diameter. The total known meteoritic record ranges from this crater (almost too small to be recognized at the distance of the moon) down to insignificant holes in the soil. Even the pit at Crater Butte has been assigned, with a fair show of evidence, to a train of meteorites rather than a single large bolide, for no single large remnant was found by the extensive borings made expressly to find such a remnant. The filling and burial of such pits on the earth must of course be considered; but as already noted, if meteoric pits of the magnitude of the craters of the moon had been formed on the earth, even if distributed through all the terranes of the geologic column, they could scarcely have escaped very frequent detection. It is not to be overlooked that the greatest terrestrial example needs to be multiplied by 60–75 to give it standing as a witness of meteoric competency. The record of volcanic competency so far surpasses this that specific citation is needless. The testimony of the earth lends no support to the substitution of meteorites for volcanoes in an effort to explain the great magnitude of the lunar craters.

SPECIFIC CRITERIA

The craters of the moon are declaredly vertical and symmetrical. To a very notable degree their rims are complete and unmutilated except as they have been softened by age. All this is perfectly consonant with the view that they are volcanic craters formed on an atmosphereless body whose outer portion is largely made up of explosion débris. On the other hand, serious questions arise whether explosions produced by oblique infalls would be equally symmetrical. This has been much discussed with varying conclusions. So far as the high-angle infalls are concerned, it seems unprofitable to prolong it. The decisive criteria seem to me to lie in two other lines.

The circular rims of the lunar craters render the moon's face peculiarly susceptible to a decisive test. These circular rims form a stippled ground-plot, as it were, on which low-angle bodies would record themselves in unmistakable terms. It is hard to imagine anything better fitted for such a record than multitudes of sharp rims built of loose débris and standing forth from the surface in such a way that almost any mutilation by a bolide could not fail to reveal itself (see Figs. 34 and 35).

Of similar import are the facilities for a distinctive record afforded by the smooth, dry fragmental surfaces of the basins. (The white lines imply that these basins have débris upon their surfaces whatever may be their nature below.) Such wide smooth plains were specially susceptible of retaining characteristic furrows, troughs, slanting gouges, and ricochet-marks such as would inevitably be made by low-angle bolides on such surfaces. On the earth, in spite of its atmosphere and its relatively rapid erosion, meteoric bolides form definite records of a diminutive sort that bear no resemblance to deep vertical craters or explosion pits.

THE REQUIREMENTS OF THE CASE

The full force of the absence of these two classes of evidence can only be appreciated by giving due weight to the great number of the craters and to a normal distribution under natural laws. The distribution of the craters has already been mentioned. The distribution and the slant of the strokes is discriminative also.

It is stated authoritatively that 30,000 lunar craters have been mapped. The slants of so great a number of bolides falling by chance would distribute themselves closely according to the laws of chance. The 30,000 impacts may be grouped into three classes: (1) the high-angle impacts, from bolides falling at angles of 60°–90°; (2) the mid-slant impacts, from falls at 30°–60°; and (3) the low-angle strokes, from bolides striking at 0°–30°. Of the 30,000 chance infalls, according to the computations of Bartky, 7,500 should have come in as high infalls, 15,000 as mid-slant infalls, and 7,500 as low-angle strokes. Now with these great numbers in the low-angle class, it is not necessary to debate the explosive effects of the high-angle class or even the mid-slant class. The distinctive record that should have been made by the bolides that fell at angles ranging between a tangent and 30° should settle the question decisively. The absence of the appropriate record on the rims of the craters and on the plains of the Maria seems to me wholly fatal to the bolide theory.

It seems scarcely necessary to add the following:

VELOCITY OF INFALL

To produce pits 10,000 feet deep, the velocity of infall must have at least approached the parabolic velocity for the moon's solar distance. This is not far from the observed velocity of meteorites and makes them available if they were otherwise competent. But it excludes planetesimals, planetoids, satellites, and all bodies of the planetary system, for these move concurrently with the moon and could not overtake it at the requisite velocities.

At such high velocities, the attraction of the moon, one-sixth that of the earth, could have produced very little deflection of the bolides from their normal courses. What it did would probably have been more effective in drawing bolides that otherwise would have missed the moon into the low-angle class than in changing low-angle impacts into the mid-slant class, or from the latter into the high-angle class. The deflection of the bolides by the moon offers no escape from the force of the preceding arguments.

NO RECOGNITION OF LUNAR VULCANISM

An additional infelicity of the bolide theory, not often noticed, is that, by implication, it excludes vulcanism from the moon, since it does not recognize volcanic craters and distinguish them from bolide craters.

THE REQUISITE BOLIDES WANTING

To me the most radical objection to the impact theory lies in the fact that we nowhere find in the solar system any direct evidence of the existence of any class of bodies capable, by reason of their sizes, velocities, and directions of motion, of making pits 50–100 miles in diameter and 10,000 feet in depth, either directly or by explosive reaction. The competencies of planetesimals, planetoids, and satellites are of a distinctly different dynamic order; no meteorites of the requisite competency are known or probable, and no other class of bodies of the right order is known or reasonably assignable.

THE PECULIARITIES OF LUNAR VULCANISM

To appreciate the interpretation of the peculiarities of the craters of the moon, as here entertained, it is necessary to bear in mind that the concept of vulcanism under the planetesimal hypothesis departs widely from the familiar view inherited from the gaseo-molten theory of the origin of the earth. No universal liquefaction, no liquid interior, nor even any common liquid substratum from which ducts led lavas up to the surface, is postulated, or is even regarded as consistent with the specific evidences presented by volcanic phenomena as actually displayed. The growth of the moon was too slow and the infalls too gentle to develop general liquefaction. Small amounts of liquid may have been generated at certain times just where special impacts took place, but these must have cooled quickly and could not seriously affect the general solid state. Such small amounts of liquid rock as were developed in the interior of the moon are held to have arisen from chemical-physical reorganization brought about by increase of heat and local relief of pressure as the growth of the moon and its deformation proceeded. These local liquefactions are supposed merely to have constituted thin sheets, threads, or small pools *disseminated through the mixed solid material* of which the moon was mainly built.

It is held that, at first, the original accretions, as they fell upon the surface, formed a porous mantle. Later, as this became buried by further accessions, it was gradually compacted and began to form new combinations. These new combinations remained solid, in the main; but here and there some mutual solution took place. Not only did the larger part of the mixed mass remain solid, but it steadily became more and more solid by reorganization and by mechanical compacting. The disseminated liquid threads, sheets, and pools, responding to gravitative pressure, tidal kneading, and deformation, gradually wormed their individual ways toward the surface. They united more or less as they went, and so larger ducts were formed and perhaps considerable pools; but these were merely local concentrations. At a certain stage in its ascent, the liquid reached a place where its fluidal pressure overmatched the resistance of the porous overburden, and the remainder of the cover was blown off. Each particular duct found its own exit in its own time and way. Each duct followed what was the line of least resistance for it, quite without regard to other ducts. Hence the multitude and variety of the craters.

THE ARGUMENT OF MULTITUDE AND VARIETY

The process has thus been followed in detail to make clear why there are *so many craters*, why they are *so close together*, and why they are *so different in size*. If the ducts had been connected with any common stratum of liquid below, the lowest exit would have sufficed for all. There would have been outpours only in the basins. The upward individual creep of the liquid ducts explains why they blew out at such different heights. The fragmental condition of the outer material explains why the blow-outs were so deep and so vertical. The porosity and lightness of the outer cover material made great eruptions possible. These were aided by the low gravity of the moon. The fact that there was little local connection and no uniting substratum below makes it easier to see how there could have been 30,000 vents on the half-surface facing us. We see also why the craters, whether small or large, opened out on heights or on low-lands, as the local conditions favored. We see no signs of community of action, but the most abundant signs of individuality of action.

WHY THE LUNAR CRATERS DIFFER FROM THE TERRESTRIAL

We have noted that the lunar craters are more abundant on the uplands, ridges, and mountains of the moon than in the basins. In this particular, the volcanoes of the moon and of the earth are alike. But on the earth, about as fast as surface material becomes loose, it is washed away. What remains is more or less cemented. Almost everywhere, a water-table is formed not far below the surface; and the material above is usually water-soaked. There is, as a rule, an absence of a deep, dry, porous zone such as mantles the moon.

As the gravity on the earth's surface is six times that on the moon, the rise of self-compression with depth is markedly faster on the earth than on the moon. It is necessary to go much deeper into the body of the moon to find given degrees of compression and temperature such as promote reorganization and vulcanism. Reorganization is probably also delayed and restrained to greater depths by the dryness of the moon. Where there is an abundant supply of water from the atmosphere charged with gases, as on the earth, the chemical interchanges and the physical reorganizations that give rise to magmas must take place more readily than in a dry body like the moon.

Though the subsurface material of the earth is largely cemented, it is also fissured; the earth has suffered greater deformation than the moon. In the fissured zone, liquid rock finds relatively easy ways of escape and is less held back until explosive intensity has accumulated. It is only rarely that a terrestrial volcano blows off its cover violently. If, then, the level of liquefaction is nearer the surface and there is a fractured shell above it filled with water, and if there is no deep overburden of fragmented rock, why should not the disseminated liquids generated in the earth exude with relative ease; why should not the blow-outs of the moon surpass those of the earth in precisely the way and to the degree that the surface of the moon indicates?

THE MOON AN INDEX OF THE EARTH'S DIASTROPHIC COMPETENCY

If the earth and moon grew up in similar ways by accessions from the same belt of planetesimals, their relative degrees of density should give us at least some hint of the amount of compacting of the earth since it passed the lunar stage of growth. Taking 3.4, water standard, as the density of the moon, and 5.53 as that of the earth, we may safely assume that the difference is due to the greater compacting of the earth-matter due to its greater mass, for the earth could, and doubtless did, attract and hold lighter material than the moon. As a matter of fact, all the planets larger than the earth are lower in specific gravity.

To bring out the meaning hidden in the higher density of the earth, let us imagine the moon to have kept on growing with the density it now has until its mass was equal to that of the earth, and that it then shrank to the size of the earth. Its volume at the end of its supposed growth would have been 430,353,000,000 cubic miles. If it then shrank to the volume of the present earth, the shortening of its radius would have been 725 miles (1,160 kilometers). The actual shrinkage of the growing earth of course took place gradually, or at short intervals; but the result deduced from the supposed succession of growth and shrinkage of the moon gives a fair intimation of the order of magnitude of the actual shrinkage of the earth after it passed the size of the moon. This amount of shrinkage seems to fit the requirements of the great deformations recorded in the earlier terranes of the earth.

REFERENCES

For references see end of previous chapter.

CHAPTER XXIII

THE ORIGIN OF THE NORMAL SATELLITES

Of the twenty-six satellites the moon is the only one that bears evidence of a semi-independent origin; all the other twenty-five bear traits that link their histories more closely to those of the planets which control them. Their dynamic relations imply an intimate derivation from the planetary bolts that gave rise to their primaries. This similarity of origin is the more significant because they are attendants of five different planets, three of which have forward rotations, while the other two have retrograde rotation—and, what is more notable, two of the first class of planets have retrograde as well as forward satellites. There are thus three classes of satellite relations, and out of these arise some of the subtlest problems of the solar system.

The first class are attendants of planets of the middle section of the planetary series, where planetesimal overlaps and forward rotations prevail. They include the two satellites of Mars, the inner seven of Jupiter, and the inner eight of Saturn. These seventeen satellites include the largest and the smallest of the satellites; they thus form the greatest and most typical class.

The second class includes the two outermost satellites of Jupiter and the ninth, or outermost, satellite of Saturn. They are thus attendants on the two largest planets and are members of the two largest satellite families, but *they revolve in the opposite direction* from the other fifteen satellites of these families—the oddest freak, if freak it be, in the solar system.

The third class attend the outermost planets, whose rotations are retrograde; and they themselves revolve in the same direction. They include the four satellites of Uranus and the lone satellite of Neptune.

Notwithstanding these peculiar relations, all families of two or more satellites show a marked tendency toward adjustment to the equatorial planes of their primaries, however these may be inclined or may rotate. Even in the case of the lone satellite of Neptune, the orbit does not seem to be more than moderately removed from the poorly determined equator of the planet. This relationship to the equator involves the gathering of each satellite family into a disk. This must then surely be a distinctive feature of satellite evolution.

It is not strange, therefore, that the satellites were formerly supposed to have been "thrown off" from the equators of their primaries by centrifugal force. But this view is untenable, not only because none of the planets concerned have a rotation even remotely sufficient to discharge satellite material from their equators, or show any signs of ever having had such a rate of rotation, but also because the rotations of the outermost satellites of the two largest planets in directions opposite to the rotations of these planets is an outstanding objection of a formidable sort. Not only that, but Phobos, the little inner satellite of Mars, revolves around the planet about three times while Mars rotates once. In the same line of evidence,

Moulton has pointed out that the inner constituents of the inner ring of Saturn revolve about the planet much faster than the planet rotates. All attempts at the adjustment of these peculiarities to the theory that the satellites were "thrown off" from the planets meet with insuperable difficulties. This simple theory of the origin of the normal satellite seems, thus, altogether untenable.

This makes the formation of the satellite disks and their adjustment to the equatorial planes of their primaries a dynamic problem of the first order. This question will be the subject of the next chapter. It is foreshadowed here because the mode of origin of the satellites must be such as to lead on, by the mechanics of the case, to the idiosyncracies of the satellites as we actually find them.

THE ASSIGNED ORIGIN OF THE NORMAL SATELLITES

All these twenty-five satellites are held to have had their origins in eddies, whirls, or convolutions developed by the planetary bolts as they originally emerged from the sun, as already set forth in chapters xiii, xvii, xviii, and xix. To bring the essential state of things at this critical time to mind afresh, let us recall that in the emergence of the planetary bolts from the sun there was drag between the escaping bolt and the adjacent substance of the sun, and that this gave rise to convolutions in the contact zone, as already illustrated. A part of this turbulent matter was left quite behind and need not concern us here. But a part went with the bolts, and the bolts themselves were more or less deeply affected by the evortical motions that sprang from this junction drag. So much of this eddying, whirling, or evortical matter as kept within the spheres of control of the main planetary bolts—and perhaps even some that accompanied them outside their spheres of control—participated in the assorting process

FIG. 36.—An erupted solar knot followed by a train of sub-knots susceptible of becoming satellites if controlled by the primary projection. Yerkes Observatory.

that followed the emergence of the main bolts (chap. xiii). These sub-whirls would be likely to form secondary orbital systems (satellitesimals analogous to planetesimals, if we choose to carry distinction so far) and residual swarms of revolving accretions of their own, quite separate from the main residual swarm. These sub-swarms are held later to have formed cores which became centers of growth into satellites. These, of course, attended the planets that grew out of the main bolts. The normal satellites are in this sense held to be derivatives from the planetary *bolts* but not derivatives of the *planets* by fission in any form after the planets were formed.

Such eddies, whirls, or convolutions as were separated from the main bolts would revolve about them in divers directions, whereas the satellites now form disks. This disk-formation is our first problem. We must ultimately reach two satellite disks in which the outermost members revolve in directions opposite to the main family of satellites and the controlling planet. This is our second problem.

One step toward the final effects was common to all classes of satellites and may be added here.

THE GROWTH-CREEP OF THE SATELLITE ORBITS

Growth-creep has been sketched (chap. xx) as an inevitable effect of the infall of planetesimals on the cores of the growing planets. The infall must have had a similar effect on the formative swarms and cores of the satellites. This is the key to the peculiarities that distinguish the three classes of satellites that were ultimately formed. The revolutions of the satellites are essentially the same dynamically as the rotations of the planets. It is quite evident that planetesimals would plunge into the constituents of the satellite swarms quite as certainly as into the cores, and that the orbits of the growing satellites would be caused to creep to new positions and take on new forms quite as certainly as the cores of the planets. Next to this common action, the first problem is the assembling of the satellite orbits into disks and the adjustment of these disks to the equatorial planes of the controlling planets.

REFERENCES

1. F. R. Moulton, *An Introduction to Astronomy* (1916), pp. 273–74.
2. T. C. Chamberlin, "Synopsis," *Carnegie Institution of Washington, Year Book No. 26* (1926–27), pp. 241–42.

CHAPTER XXIV

THE GATHERING OF THE SATELLITE ORBITS INTO DISKS IN THE EQUATORIAL PLANES OF THEIR PRIMARIES

1. THE CONVERGING FUNCTION OF THE PLANET'S GRAVITY

It is to be noted at the outset that the satellite disks are never perfect and that they vary in approximation through a considerable range. In the large families of satellites, the inner members are much better adjusted than the outer ones. This difference is an argument against systematic centrifugal separation, and in favor of some such less rigorous agencies as those here assigned. These are three in number: (1) growth-creep, (2) the equatorial bulges of the planets, and (3) the vaulting molecules of the krenal ultra-atmospheres of the planets.

It is clear that if a planetesimal struck a satellite core and adhered to it, the combined mass would follow a new orbit combining the momenta of the two bodies. It is further obvious that growth-creeps of this kind would be of the same order as those of the planets they were attending. Our problem, then, is merely an inquiry into the specific way by which the satellite orbits were made to creep into disks adjusted to the equatorial planes of the planets.

For a representative case let us take one in which a growing planet, surrounded by growing satellites, is revolving in a normal planetesimal belt about the sun. Let the planetesimals be moving the faster and overtaking the planet and the satellites. The argument can be made just as well if the relative speeds are reversed. In either case the action is of the mild order.

The attraction of the planet may be pictured as a graded field of force, and its effect on the planetesimals

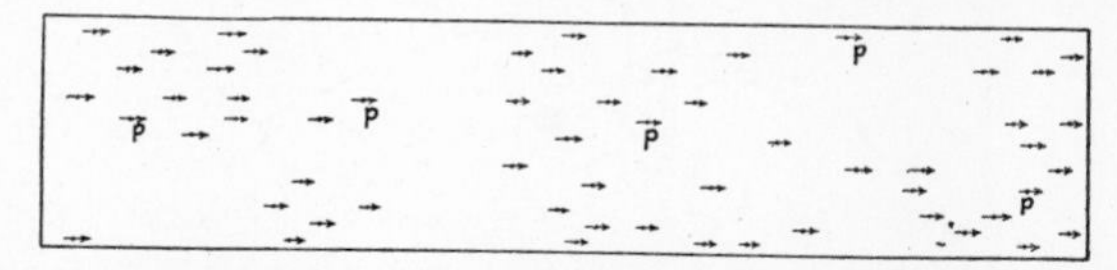

FIG. 37.—Diagram showing stream of planetesimals before action of planet.

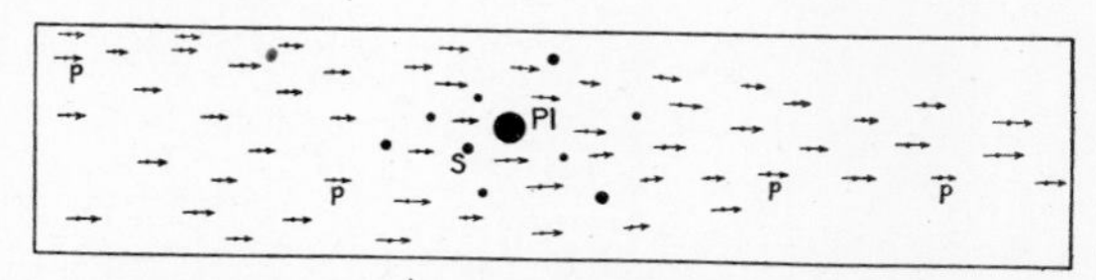

FIG. 38.—Diagram showing converging effect of the attraction of a planet (*Pl*) on the planetesimals (*p*, *p*, *p*) before the effect is felt on the satellites (*s*, *s*).

sweeping past it is somewhat analogous to that of a spherical lens converging the rays of light passing through it. The paths of the planetesimals will be bent toward the axis of the planet, as shown in Figures 37 and 38. This tends to form a cone of converging planetesimals, and these must obviously tend to push the satellites they encounter toward the axis of the cone in the lee of the planet.

If the growth-creep of the planet had brought its own axis of rotation into its normal relations to the stream of planetesimals, the cone of converging planetesimals would have its axis in or near the equatorial plane of the planet. In so far as the ideal relation of the planet's axis had not been reached, the cone would only point somewhere in the general direction of the equatorial plane, and only an approximate adjustment would be reached. But this would be remedied in some measure by the other agencies to be considered later.

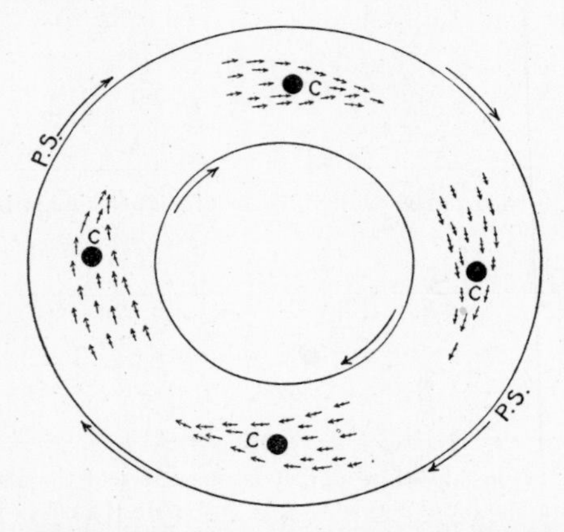

FIG. 39.—Diagram showing that in each revolution of the planet the converging cone (*c*, *c*, *c*, *c*) will describe a disk.

The converging cone thus formed represents only the effects of the planet's gravity on the planetesimals—and through them on the satellites—at a single point at any instant, but in the course of a revolution, the planet and the cone will have rotated and the cone will have described a disk (see Fig. 39). In a system in which the growth-creep has been fully developed, this disk would coincide with, or closely approximate, the equator of the planet.

If, at first thought, it appears that the effect of this

disk-forming tendency would be too small to be effective, it is to be observed that it is persistent and involves not only uncounted trillions of individual acts but hundreds of millions of revolutions under this converging influence. When not wholly adequate in itself, it would tend to bring the orbits of the growing satellites into the range of influence of the two other agencies which would add their aid in bringing the orbits into the disklike forms and the equatorial relations they actually occupy.

2. THE INFLUENCE OF THE EQUATORIAL BULGE

As the planets grew toward maturity they developed effective equatorial bulges as well as extensive envelopes of highly active molecules.

The equatorial bulges of the planets would have a precessional effect on all orbits near them. The shift of the orbits of the satellites arising from this would cause their nodes with the equatorial plane of the planet to move around the planet and so bring about new combining relations between the satellite cores and the converging planetesimals. The nodes were thus being perpetually shifted along the tract to which there was convergence from both sides of the equator, and this made it the best feeding environment of the planet.

3. THE INFLUENCE OF THE VAULTING MOLECULES OF THE PLANET'S ULTRA-ATMOSPHERE

As the planetary atmospheres increased, there should have been an increase of the vaulting molecules of the krenal ultra-atmosphere (see chap. ii). More of these vaulting molecules should reach the satellites in the equatorial tract than elsewhere. These vaulting molecules started from the rapidly rotating equatorial atmospheres of the planets which carried relatively high components of their momentum to the satellite cores. This added a very specific agency tending to cause the satellite cores to creep into rotational harmony with the planet. Even though the satellite cores did not hold these molecules, the collisions tended to drive the cores into the equatorial plane.

THE ADAPTABILITY OF THE DISK-FORMING COMBINATION

It is to be noted that the original drag effects presumably gave irregular results and that these disk-forming agencies were extremely adaptable, working in due proportion but not equally on satellite cores of all sizes and distances from the planetary center. They were not such as to imply rigid uniformity of effects or even such degree of rigid regularity as might be expected from a centrifugal or other mechanical cause arising from the planet's own mechanism. Inequalities of size, spacing, number, and order of occurrence were quite to be expected from the origin assigned, and, as a matter of fact, abound in the series of satellites actually presented.

There is also significance in the fact that the reduction of the satellites to disk form and to equatorial adjustment is far from uniform. In the large satellite families it is much more marked near the planets than at a distance from them. This is in full harmony with the fact that the gravitative effects of the planet on the passing planetesimals necessarily varied as the inverse squares of their distances from the planet. The inner satellites of

Jupiter and Saturn are assembled much more nearly in the equatorial planes of those planets than the outer satellites. While the outermost retrograde satellites of these two planets are less closely adjusted to the equatorial planes than the satellites next within them, they are still, in a broad sense, equatorial satellites. In the case of single satellites, as those of the earth and Neptune, the adjustment is less complete than in the larger satellite families.

REFERENCE

1. T. C. Chamberlin, *Carnegie Institution of Washington, Year Book No. 26* (1926–27), 342.

CHAPTER XXV

THE RETROGRADE SATELLITES OF JUPITER AND SATURN

That the two greatest planets of the solar system should each have large orderly satellite families revolving concurrently with their own rotations seems quite in the natural order of things. That it is also in the natural order of things in a planetesimal system that these satellites should be assembled into disks in the equatorial planes of their primaries we have endeavored to show in the last chapter. But that in each of these large, well-ordered families the outermost satellites should revolve contrary to all the rest is the strangest idiosyncracy in the whole solar system. But if we are prompted to look upon these as freaks, or as chance captures, or as overturns, or as accidents of any kind, we are faced with the extreme improbability that three chance events of the same strange kind should appear in the same relations in two orderly families and should at the same time be fairly conformable to the equatorial planes of the two families. However strange the combination of conformity and contrariety, it is clear that the retrograde satellites are not chance effects or stray captures. They bear too many evidences of systematic production, in spite of their apparent erraticisms. However much they may seem to be the "black sheep" of the two flocks, they are orderly members of the two flocks. They present a sharp insistent problem to be solved on the presumption that they too are in the natural order of things. As idiosyncracies, they are in the highest degree significant.

HOW CONTRARIETY GREW OUT OF CONCURRENCY

Concurrency is the keynote of the planetesimal method of planetary growth. Are these retrograde satellites "the exception that proves the rule?" Of the eighteen satellites that attend Jupiter and Saturn, fifteen revolve in a forward direction with the planets. All the large satellites are included in this number. The retrograde satellites are all small and far out. There are two good hints in this smallness and this distance from the crowd of satellites.

Let us call up afresh the picture of the Jovian and Saturnian systems just as they were commencing to pass from the nebular to the planetary stage. Two strong planetary cores were growing toward the adult planets, Jupiter and Saturn. A score or more of little cores surrounding these were growing toward satellites. All these cores were attended by their infantile feeding swarms. All the cores, large and little, were revolving together in the midst of the great planetesimal belts of Jupiter and Saturn. The general conditions, as we found in chapter xi, were favorable for forward rotations of the planets and forward revolutions of the satellites.

According to our interpretation, the little cores that were candidates for satellites had been formed from the small whirls that separated from the main planetary bolts as incidents of the tearing-out of the main bolts from the sun. Some of these should therefore have revolved about the main bolts in one direction and some in another. It was the function of the disk-forming process to work these by slow creep around into disks in the equatorial planes of the planets, as explained in the last chapter. But this growth-creep did not have the power of directly reversing revolutions. Particularly was this the case when the revolutions happened to be nearly in the equatorial plane already and far out from the planet.

Now let us note with care that all of these little cores, in whatever direction they were revolving about the planets, were moving during a part of the time *with* the stream of planetesimals that was building them up, and part of the time *against* the stream. The impacts in the one case represented the *difference* and in the other case the *sum* of the speeds of the planetesimals and the cores. There were, of course, intermediate types of impact, but for simplicity let us neglect these.

Now when the planetesimals and the cores came together concurrently and remained united, their joint speed was lower than the faster of the two. When the two met in contrary motions and happened to be elastic so that there was rebound, the smaller partner in the collision was likely to take on a higher speed than either had before, the other partner moving slower by way of compensation. If this swifter partner rebounded inward into the thicker assemblage of cores and planetesimals, it was liable to be caught and carried with the majority moving in a forward direction. But if its rebound were in the opposite direction, it would go out into the outer environment which had been thinned by the previous ingathering process. This would permit it to take a larger and freer orbit; it would also give it a better prospect of holding its course in its orbit.

Now, by the conditions of the case as above stated, *these swifter rebounds, hence these larger orbits, were retrograde.* They sprang from the backward-moving sides of the revolutions of the satellites, whirls, or cores. In a sense, this was the *retrograde* side of the revolving system. But it was only a part of the reactions from collisions on the retrograde side that were thrown into the outer, thinned zone where they had a chance to survive. Those that rebounded into the major crowd had ultimately to go with the crowd. Only a relatively small part of the satellite-forming material was thrown out into this outer, more open tract and into these larger retrograde orbits. This retrograde feature was merely a sub-phase of the regular satellite-forming process and was as normal mechanically as any other phase.

These considerations relate primarily to the feeding of the retrograde satellites, but similar considerations cover the case of the cores. Only a few of the originally few subwhirls that happened to have been given a retrograde motion were likely to survive the overpowering influence of the majority. The whole case is that of minority action, the survival of the little that kept out of the crowd and fed on the scant food of the relatively barren outskirts.

If the planets in these cases had not been powerful and the satellite material abundant, these exceptional lines of evolution might not have found enough retrograde material in the outer zones to build up so much as the small small satellites in question.

REFERENCES

1. F. R. Moulton, *An Introduction to Astronomy* (1916), "Retrograde Satellites of Jupiter," p. 289; "Retrograde Satellite of Saturn," pp. 298–99.

2. T. C. Chamberlin, "Synopsis," *Carnegie Institution of Washington, Year Book No. 26* (1926–27), p. 342.

CHAPTER XXVI

THE SATELLITES OF THE OUTERMOST PLANETS

The evolution of the satellites of Mars, Jupiter, and Saturn took place under the conditions that prevailed in the heart of the planetary system where there was almost certainly overlap of the planetesimal orbits. Neither the conditions near the sun nor those on the outer border of the system were quite the same. Obviously, the outermost zone was less affected by overlap. In the process of nebularization each planetary bolt is assumed to have developed a special planetesimal belt of its own, as well as a residual swarm of accretions which served as a feeder of the core. The planetesimal belts in the central portion of the system overlapped one another, or interpenetrated one another, more or less. Hence arose that type of perihelion-aphelion encounters described in chapter xi. But in the outer zone of the system these perihelion-aphelion encounters did not equally prevail, for obvious reasons. Neptune's orbit is nearly circular. There was a nearer approach to concentric motions, and the older concept of retrograde rotations was more applicable. The retrograde rotations of Uranus and Neptune and the retrograde revolutions of their satellites seem to find satisfactory explanation on this basis. There may have been, also, a retrograde rotation of the original planetary bolts, as postulated by the hypothesis that the passing star approached the sun from the southern heavens, as set forth in chapter xi.

The satellites of these outermost planets present two features of special interest: the symmetry and exceptional attitude of the Uranian system, and the divergence between the plane of Neptune's satellite and the planet's equator.

THE URANIAN SYSTEM NEAREST THE PRIMITIVE TYPE

Uranus has a family of four satellites of exceptional orderliness and symmetry. They revolve more nearly in the same plane, are better graded in size, and are spaced out into more orderly orbits than the other groups of satellites. Specifically, their distances from the planet are 120,000, 167,000, 273,000, and 365,000 miles, respectively; and their periods of revolution are 2.5, 4.1, 8.7, and 13.5 days, respectively. These short periods imply that dynamically the whole family is closely grouped about the planet and is under its full control. There are no appreciable signs of disturbance of the system from without or lack of working harmony within. While doubt has obtained respecting the position of the equator, the dynamic evidence implies that the plane of the planet's equator closely coincides with the plane of the satellite orbits, and that the planet's rotation is sufficiently rapid to give rise to an equatorial bulge large enough to influence the orbits of the satellites. This high degree of symmetry and orderly action is not only remarkable in itself but becomes singularly suggestive when it is noted that the satellites revolve about an axis that is inclined only 8° to the plane of the planet's revolution. By interpretation, *this plane is that of the axis of the original Uranian bolt.* This in turn seems to imply that the Uranian family—

much like the genus Lingula in biologic evolution—has lived throughout the planetary ages almost without change. Even more than that, it seems to carry the steadiness and orderliness of the family back to the very genesis of the system. The remarkable fact that the axis of the system has only crept 8° from its assigned attitude at the start very cogently supports the interpretation offered and almost gives us a concrete example of the axial and rotational conditions of all the planets and satellite systems at the outset.

This raises the question, why should the Uranian system have had this exceptionally steady evolution? In the first place, our tentative sub-hypothesis respecting the details of stellar approach and solar bolt-projection (chap. xvi), postulates that the bolt which formed Uranus was projected from a zone near the equatorial belt of the sun where the solar motions are more nearly balanced than farther away on either side. In the second place, Uranus lies near the border line between the forward-rotating planets of the middle group and the backward-rotating planets outside. There is the further fact that Saturn is 900 million miles away on one side and Neptune a billion miles away on the other, so that, while the whole Uranian system might be affected by its neighbors, they lacked differentiating power sufficient to affect its domestic development. This isolation left the Uranian family relatively free to develop on its own lines.

THE DISCORDANT EVOLUTION OF THE NEPTUNIAN SYSTEM

In the Uranian family we seem to have an example of conservatism in evolution and harmony in internal organization. In the smaller Neptunian family—only one planet and one satellite—discordance in internal evolution seems to have obtained in larger degree. The equator of the planet seems to be inclined about 20° to its orbit, while the orbit of its lone satellite is inclined about 20° more than this. In chapter xvii, we concluded that the creep of axis of a planet and that of its satellite attendants would be likely to differ from one another with time and change of conditions. Neptune seems to offer a confirmation of this. In the great satellite families of Jupiter and Saturn there is, as already noted, distinct concurrence between the orbits of the satellites and the equators of the planets, and we have been at some pains to explain this. We noted, however, that complete concurrence was not a necessary result. It does not obtain in the case of the earth-moon system, but that is peculiar in other respects. It is interesting, therefore, to find here, on the outskirts of the planetary system, so to speak, and under conditions of great isolation and presumptive freedom from external influence, a confirmation of our inference. We do not need to repeat the explanation. As Neptune and the earth are the only two planets that have but one satellite, perhaps those who feel so disposed may draw a preachment about the right size of a family.

REFERENCE

1. T. C. Chamberlin, *Carnegie Institution of Washington, Year Book No. 26* (1926–27), p. 342.

CHAPTER XXVII

THE PECULIARITIES OF MERCURY AND VENUS

Somewhat in the line of the famous trouble about seeing a forest, there is a difficulty in seeing the innermost planets because of the light. When their faces send the most light toward us, they are on the far side of the sun and its glare blinds us. When they are on our side of the sun, they turn their dark sides toward us. It is only when they are off on one swing of their orbits or the other, that there is any fair chance of seeing them, and then only as "phases." But these troubles are not subtle or masked; they are indeed unpleasantly obtrusive, but we need not be led astray by them.

But with these embarrassments from high intensity of light there come more subtle ones from high intensity of gravity and its inverse relations to space. We have considered this in chapter iv, but it has some special difficulties here. The same law, the law of the inverse square, determines the increases and the declines of solar light and of solar gravity; but the space relations are of a quite different type and are more tangible and impressive than the gravity-intensities, and so are liable to throw us off our balance. In diagrams of the planets we distort the distances of the outer and inner planets to bring them into any ordinary page. This is frankly done, and we try to make due mental allowances. But we are not equally alive to the distortion of the gravity-intensities in the opposite direction. The steps in gravity-intensity from Mercury to Venus and from Venus to the earth are much greater than those from Saturn to Uranus and from Uranus to Neptune. It is not easy to realize that the billion-mile space-step from Neptune to Uranus means very much less gravitatively than the 31-million-mile step from Venus to Mercury. But in reality, in planetary relations the spacially greatest is the least gravitationally, and the spacially least is gravitationally greatest. It is necessary to be on one's guard to maintain a balanced appreciation of values in the face of such seeming contrarieties as these. Yet they are perfectly consistent and altogether harmonious. Just here it happens to be the gravitational factor that counts.

THE MINIMIZED SPHERES OF CONTROL

Within the sun's domain the spheres of control of the individual planets are merely those areas within which the planets are able to take precedence of the sun in exercising certain gravitative influences. These areas are relatively greatest when the sun is farthest away, and smallest as it is approached; indeed, all such planetary spheres of control come to a vanishing-point before the sun's surface is reached. Naturally, Mercury, most of all, suffers from this sunward decline; and Venus suffers next. The radius of Mercury's sphere of control (using Moulton's computations as being based on later data than those of Laplace) is only 87,000 miles; that of Venus 419,000 miles. As these figures represent the distances from the centers of the planets beyond which satellites cannot permanently be held, only a very meager development of satellites was possible. It is not surprising to find none at all.

LIMITATIONS OF ATMOSPHERE

The conditions that limited the gathering of atmospheres about these planets were of a similar severe order. Atmospheres are dependent not only on spheres of control but on planetary temperatures and on the selective repellency of the sun. Besides, gases spontaneously enhance the velocities of a certain proportion of their molecules.

The non-technical reader may be glad to be advised that the parabolic velocity, or velocity of fall from infinity, is not the "critical velocity" of escape for the molecules of planetary atmosphere. It is a velocity that insures the escape, to be sure, but it is not the minimum or critical velocity of escape. All velocity above what is necessary to carry the molecule beyond the sphere of the planet's control and into the surrounding sphere of control of the sun, is superfluous so far as simple escape is concerned. To escape from the control of Mercury, a free molecule merely needs a velocity that will carry it a little beyond 87,000 miles, not to infinity.

But this is not all. By following its natural course through the vaulting and orbital ultra-atmospheres (see chap. ii), an atmospheric molecule may escape into the enveloping sphere of control of the sun at a velocity which is nearly 40 per cent below the parabolic velocity.

As already indicated, the several radiant influences emanating from the sun (of which radiation pressure is best known [see chaps. ii, iii, and iv]) sweep with special force through the spheres of control of Mercury and Venus. These agencies not only push molecules from the sun into the spheres of control of these planets but they push out some of the free molecules already in them. They thus play a part of their own in determining the holding or the escape of free molecules. The case is thus much less simple than it is usually made to appear in the literature of the subject.

THE ATMOSPHERE OF MERCURY

Mercury gives no direct observational evidence of any atmosphere. Theoretical considerations do not appear to permit, at the utmost, more than a thin layer of the heaviest of the inert atmospheric molecules, such as argon, zenon, krypton, and neon. At the high temperatures that prevail on the sunward side of the planet, chemical union has probably consumed all chemically active constituents. Even if such a thin inert atmosphere exists, it must lie so close to the planet's surface that it fails to manifest itself by the refraction of light passing by the edge of the planet. The absence of such refraction forbids more than such a mere semblance of an atmosphere.

THE ATMOSPHERE OF VENUS

There is no question but that Venus has gravitative power to hold an atmosphere of the terrestrial sort and that the planet actually has an atmosphere, but the recent observations of St. John and Nicholson, and of Slipher, raise a vital question relative to its nature, for they fail to detect any appreciable amount of oxygen or water vapor. Such an atmosphere is not improbable from the planetesimal point of view. It is quite clear from different lines of evidence that there is much more matter susceptible to oxidation and hydration in the solar system than there is oxygen and water to oxidize and hydrate it. Even in the exceptionally favorable case of the earth, on whose surface oxygen and water abound as perhaps nowhere else in the solar system, so far as we know, all investigators would probably agree that, if this surface oxygen and water were applied to the oxidation and hydration of the deep interior material, they would fall far short of adequacy. The seeming abundance of these vital elements is superficial—a product of the late history of our planet.

If Venus, throughout its late history, always presented one face to the sun—of which later—it would have had so high a temperature on the sunward side as probably to have promoted oxidation and hydration to a degree sufficient to have forestalled the accumulation of any substantial amount of free oxygen and water in its atmosphere. Irrespective of rotation, the insolation of Venus is now about twice that of the earth, and this alone might perhaps have promoted oxidation and hydration sufficiently to have consumed all available oxygen and water during its growth. Even if the consumption only went so far as to forestall the gathering of a water mantle, this would doubtless have led to the formation of a deep, dry, porous outer zone which would have permitted oxidation and hydration to have penetrated relatively more deeply than they do on the earth, for water itself and the cementation that arises through its agency are obstacles to oxidation and to hydration. Deoxidation and even dehydration are among the common processes that take place at moderate depths under a terrestrial mantle of water.

It seems, therefore, not at all improbable that with the higher temperature all the water vapor and free oxygen received by Venus penetrated deeply and entered into combinations with the abundant interior material susceptible of such combination. In this case the atmosphere would consist essentially of nitrogen, argon, and the rarer inert constituents. It would be *a very dry atmosphere.* It would have a very vigorous circulation, whatever its rotation, because of the unrestrained heating during the insolation period and the free radiation when insolation was cut off. As a consequence the atmosphere would become extremely dusty. It is difficult to overstress the trituration products that would fill the air, if perpetually dry and driven violently over the naked surface of the planet, since no vegetal mantle is assignable under the conditions. Such never-washed, dust-filled air would be swept constantly over the surface from the cold hemisphere toward the heated hemisphere, where it would rise and flow back as an upper return current enshrouding the planet in a mantle of extremely fine, highly reflecting débris. Such a mantle of finest possible dust would be much better fitted than a blanket of water-clouds to give the unbroken reflection which has so long thwarted efforts to fasten definite observations upon fixed points on the body of Venus.

This persistent difficulty of seeing the body of Venus is in itself a serious objection to the assumption that the brilliant reflecting-surface of Venus is one of water-clouds. The rising currents of a water-laden atmosphere are adiabatically cooled and become precipitant; but after the air has risen and discharged its moisture, it becomes very transparent and in its descent is adiabatically warmed and becomes relatively dry, cloudless, and singularly clear. The areas of cloudy ascent and of cloudless descent are approximately equal. The clear spots should be large enough to be visible at the distance of Venus. If Venus has a water-bearing atmosphere similar to that of the earth, about half of the body should be visible. The ancient geological picture of a universal envelope of cloud, on which we were once so fond of discoursing, was more rhetorical than logical.

THE ROTATIONS OF MERCURY AND VENUS

It was the natural assumption of the earlier astronomers that these planets rotated much as do the earth and Mars. This assumption has shown great tenacity; but a satisfactory demonstration, verifiable by all good observers, has always been lacking. The recent application of the Doppler-Fizeau method by St. John, Slipher, and others, reveals no rotation sufficient to be detectable by that method. The tenor of recent evidence trends decisively toward one rotation for each revolution in the case of Mercury; opinion is more reserved in the case of Venus, but still leans toward a rather slow rotation, if not strictly one rotation per revolution.

Perhaps the most significant of all the peculiarities of these two inner planets is the exceptional way in which their orbits are inclined to the invariable plane of the planets (inclined only $1^{\circ}35'$ to the ecliptic, which is more commonly used as a plane of reference). Lying as these little planets do between the sun and the majority of the planets, it might be expected that they would be aligned even more closely than most planets in the common planetary plane. But as a matter of fact, the orbit of Mercury is inclined 7° to the ecliptic, and that of Venus 3°24′. This suggests that some special influence, growth-creep perhaps, was felt by these planets that was not equally felt by the planets more distant from the sun. This is in harmony with the fact that the inclination of Mercury's orbit is about twice that of Venus, and also the fact that they are both under the specially intense force of the solar gravity, and with the further fact that they have always been closer within the range of the sun's projectiles than other planets. If Mercury and Venus have been subject to special bombardment by material shot from the sun, growth-creep of their orbits would have been inevitable. It is a matter of observation that the paths of Mercury and Venus lie through the thickest part of the disk of little bodies that reflect the zodiacal light. They must probably have been more or less affected by these bodies.

This suggestion and other questions raised by the peculiarities of Mercury and Venus may be left standing until the source of the zodiacal light shall be considered in chapter xxxii.

REFERENCES

1. "Rotation of Venus," *Carnegie Institution of Washington, Year Book No. 22* (1922–23); St. John and Nicholson, pp. 191–92; Slipher, p. 192.

2. T. C. Chamberlin, "Synopsis," *Carnegie Institution of Washington, Year Book No. 26* (1926–27), p. 341.

CHAPTER XXVIII

THE EVOLUTION OF THE PLANETOIDS

The planetoids form a numerous group of small solid bodies occupying a peculiar median place in the solar system. In the matter of dimensions and constitution, the old name "asteroids" is such a monstrosity that we cannot use it in the face of so appropriate a term as "planetoids." They are about as far as possible from being star-like bodies, and are much more in need of heat and light than capable of giving them. Their known number is more than a thousand. The largest of the few that can be measured are less than 500 miles in diameter. If the moon were hollow, sixty of the largest could be stowed inside it and leave room for rattling around. The group is strangely placed in the middle of the planetary series, with four great atmosphere-shrouded planets outside and four small, solid, nearly naked planets within. Coming in as they thus do, the planetoids make a declared break in the system. They do not really take the place of a planet. In spite of their number, their total mass is too small. Besides, they are widely and irregularly scattered. Their orbits give no support to the view that they were dispersed by explosion. Some of the sub-groups may, however, be related to a common ancestor in some way.

THE MEANING OF THE BREAK IN THE PLANETARY SYSTEM

The planetoids seem to us merely an incident marking the division of the planetary system. The real division is much more profound. They lie between strong contrasts. Mars, on one side, is next to the smallest planet; Jupiter, on the other side, is the largest, nearly three thousand times as massive as Mars. Four great planets, enshrouded in enormous atmospheres and very openly spaced, make a giant group on one side; four small solid planets, much nearer together, make a more compact group on the other side. This grouping seems to be even more significant than the break between the groups.

It was this declared grouping more than anything else that weighed in forming the sub-hypothesis of their genesis set forth in chapter xvi. A reference to Figure 28 will show the grouping in a suggestive light. Under this sub-hypothesis the planetoids may be regarded as the thin edge of the inner group of solid bodies. The great outer group may have a similar edge in the form of scattered bodies outside Neptune, of which there are some intimations.

It is a postulate of this sub-hypothesis that the great outer planets started from residual swarms massive enough to hold ordinary gases. But their present massiveness is not to be taken as wholly original. Their great distance from the sun weakens the relative strength of its gravity; the selective repellency of the sun's radiation is much reduced by distance and absorption; and the planets lie in a zone into which gases were driven from the more immediate environment of the sun—these patent conditions tended to build up these great planets. On the other hand, the smaller masses of the inner planets permitted the selective repellency of the sun largely to strip them of their gases and to drive these into the outer fields where the greater masses and the better conditions gave the great planets advantage in catching them. Jupiter had the first chance at these out-driven molecules; Saturn had the next; they seem to have realized upon their advantage. Their low densities are in accord with such special feeding on gas.

Thus a large assemblage of facts seem to sanction the interpretation of the planetoids as the scattered border of an inner group of diminutive and depleted planets from which they are themselves a gradation toward the still more diminutive.

This gradation downward to sizes too small to be measured leads straight to some of the most critical questions of planetary genesis. How did these diminutive bodies escape complete dispersion? What was their dynamic state as minute clouds or nebulae? What enabled them to live to form cores, and to live even in a little way, while other small assemblages failed, as will appear in the next chapter? There is no difficulty in understanding how such a mass as that of their next-door neighbor, Jupiter, could hold its substance together, even though it were riotous gas. It is easy to see why such a great planet should draw to itself more than its share of the planetary pabulum of the planetesimal field about it. But how these midgets could live and hold their places in the very heart of the system and next to the greedy giant of the family is really a question of decisive importance in the problem of planetary genesis.

However, we have already given answers under cover of more general themes.

(1) In the discussion of nebularization (chap. xvii),

we have shown how and why complete dispersion is forestalled within limits. (2) We there also found that the residue took on the form of a swarm in which each constituent revolved about the common center of gravity and kept within the common sphere of control. We pointed out that these individual motions were slow, and showed why and how they became slow by automatic selective action. (3) We may now add that the position of these little planetary mechanisms in the midst of the great planetesimal belts more than compensated for the dangers of great and greedy neighbors, for it placed the midgets in the common feeding ground. They were not left to their own meager planetesimal supplies but could poach on the common stock of planetary food between the legs of the giants, if you please. (4) The planetesimal movements were concurrent and suited for food even for weak bodies of their own species. (5) And then, perhaps most important of all, the midgets were born of evortical whirls and had even in their infantile constitutions a vital spark (mechanical, if you please) that made for a specific line of evolution. This in-running, out-running mechanism was akin to ingestion and evacuation and was especially fitted for selective appropriation and growth.

Besides, there is really a great gap between the smallest known planetoid and the largest known chondrule or meteorite.

THE SPECIFIC SOURCE ASSIGNED THE PLANETOIDS

It is thought that the passing star would only be effective in calling forth eruptions of the planetary order when it was directly over those parts of the sun that were already in a state of motion favorable to eruption. The four double eruptions that gave origin to the eight planets are assumed to have taken place when the star was passing over the main eruptive belts of the sun lying between 5° and 30° on each side of the sun's equator. Outside these belts there is turmoil, but it is more intricate and organized into smaller units. Such projectiles as could be called forth from this intimately twisted turmoil should be diminutive whirls disposed to separate and to evolve in their own diverse ways. The little whirls supposed to have grown into planetoids are assigned to diminutive eruptions from the higher latitudes of the sun next outside the great eruptive belts, as the star was approaching a vertical position over the latter and was about to call forth the large twin projectiles that were to form the planets.

PART III

THE GENESIS OF THE COMETARY FAMILY

It may seem idle to turn from the orderly ways of the planetary family to seek light on the genesis of our planet in the erratic behavior of the cometary family, but the wayward and the spectacular are often the best foil for the steady and the modest. The very orderliness of the planets and satellites requires that they should keep their distances, and that forestalls any close inspection. But the erraticisms of the cometary family bring its members, now and then, near us and give us a chance to pry into their secrets, if we have the wit to take advantage of our opportunities.

No other celestial bodies so persistently plunge into our upper atmosphere and give us all the light that is in them, as do the shooting-stars (chondrulites). No other celestial bodies so frequently drive through the whole atmosphere and reveal to us so certainly—in spite of external scorching—the nature of the matter that is moving through the environment of the earth, as do the meteorites. No other celestial assemblages teach so explicitly the mechanism of cosmic clouds of minute bodies as do the heads of comets. No other celestial phenomena carry such telling evidences of liability to depletion and disaggregation as do the periodic swings of the comets into and out of the inner environment of the sun. No schoolmaster's rod warns us so sharply that we have no call to litter up the inner domain of the sun with sophisticated confections of "gas" and "dust" as do the switches of the comets' tails.

These benefactions are only a fair compensation for the terror the comets inspired when our imaginations and our forebodings of the malevolent were more active than our observations and our loyalty to the cosmic administration. Looked at calmly and loyally, cometary manifestations throw cross-lights of immeasurable value into some of the shadowed corners of the planetary field.

At a mere glance, it is clear that the members of the cometic family are more diverse from one another than are the members of the planetary family. It appears also that these divergencies are of a different order. This difference gives us new lines of attack. It further appears that the cometary members are much more demonstrative and spectacular. This also should be to our advantage, if we are not dismayed or blinded by the spectacle. Furthermore, each member has its own way of making a great impression with a very little substance. The illusions of the comets are too familiar to need repetition. The little bodies that now and then come blazing through the atmosphere and dig into the earth's surface have probably given rise to more curiosity and speculation than any similar masses in the cosmos. They have passed themselves off as "little planets"; they have even been seriously regarded as the builders of the earth. The chondrulites, the merest midgets among midgets, burn themselves up to make a show; and for a time they passed themselves off as "falling stars." All three pass for more than they are. Even some of the supposedly sane descendants of the once terrified still clothe them with more or less of mystery.

Our first problem is to interpret their relations to one another. Which constitute the primitive units and which are derived?

CHAPTER XXIX

THE CONSTRUCTIVE UNIT OF THE COMETARY SYSTEM

A hint of what is primary and what is secondary in the genesis of the cometary family may be gathered from the outstanding characteristics of its three constituents—chondrulites, comets, and meteorites.

The chondrulites, interpreted as the source of shooting-stars, are very minute bodies (mean size of millet seed), exceedingly numerous (more than seven billion plunging into our atmosphere yearly), very widely distributed, very peculiar in make up, and very swift in motion, which take heterogeneous directions, and are very quickly volatilized on entering our atmosphere.

The comets are relatively rare swarm-like assemblages of small units in very open arrangement, devoid of refraction, shrinking and expanding with approach and retreat from the sun, and giving off minute particles and molecules under repellent action from the sun, forming spectacular tails. On the average, only about half a dozen come into sight yearly, and then promptly go out again.

The meteorites are peculiar composite masses ranging from ounces to tons in weight, made up in large part of chondrulites and chondrulite fragments. Like the chondrulites, they plunge swiftly into our atmosphere from various directions, but, unlike the chrondrulites, their masses are sufficient to withstand the volatilizing effects of atmospheric friction so that a residue reaches the surface of the earth. Instead of billions per year, however, less than half a dozen are actually seen to fall, though their

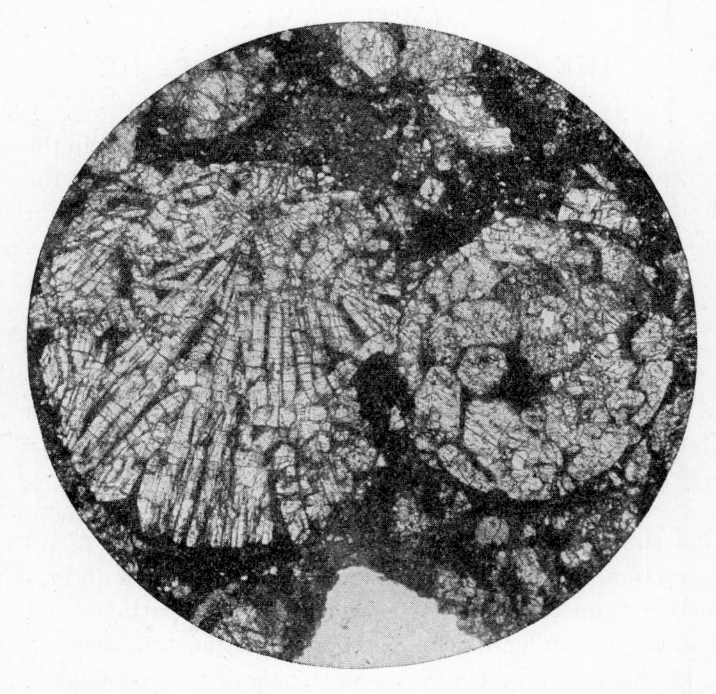

FIG. 40.—A microscopic section of the Parmalee meteorite, India, showing two chondrules, one having a radial structure developed from an eccentric point, while the other is porphyritic. (Merrill.)

total number may perhaps be one per day, or about one for every 20,000,000 chondrulites.

Such outstanding facts intimate that the multitudinous little bodies are more likely to be the primary units of construction than either the few larger bodies or the few swarms of little bodies. Let this serve merely as a hint of sufficient value to guide the order of our inquiry as we

FIG. 41.—An enlarged section of a chondrule from the Parmalee meteorite, showing irregular radial structure deployed eccentrically. (Merrill.)

seek more specific evidences. It implies that the chondrulites are entitled to first consideration.

CHONDRULES AND CHONDRULITES

These stately terms seem more formidable than they really are. "Chondrule" is merely Greek for *a little grain*.

It has been chosen as the technical name for a peculiar class of little accretions found only in meteorites. "Chondrulites" is merely a more general term here used to in-

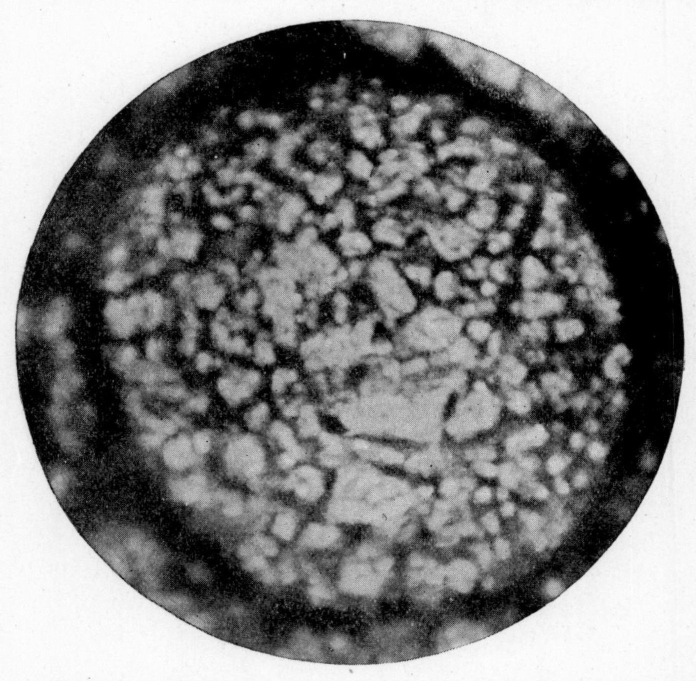

FIG. 42.—Enlarged microscopic section of a chondrule supposed to have undergone metamorphism after its original imbedment. (George P. Merrill, National Museum.)

clude not only chondrules but their débris and all such quasi-chondrulitic material as cannot strictly be called chondrules. It is here used for the primitive chondrulitic accretions, whether they develop into technical chondrules or not. As already noted, the mean size of these is commonly given as that of a millet seed. From this average size they range up to that of walnuts and down to a limit not yet satisfactorily determined. The most minute forms are sometimes described as "microscopic dust," but since dustlike particles (perhaps actually trituration dust) are driven out of comets' heads and away to unknown distances by solar repellencies of some sort, and since the chondrulites are not so driven away, it is a fair inference that chrondrules always have *sufficient mass to keep them under the control of gravity in spite of solar repellency.*

As already indicated, chondrules and chondrulite fragments make up the major part of the stony meteorites (90 per cent is Farrington's figure). There seem good reasons for believing that the metallic alloys—chiefly those of iron, nickel, and cobalt—arose from the same source as the stony chondrules and that the original accretions included practically all that now forms meteorites, whether stony or metallic, but that later changes separated them to the partial extent now observed. The evidence of this will gradually come out as we go on. There is abundant evidence of metamorphism, as urged by Merrill.

To reach the original state, our inquiry must be pushed as far back toward the genesis of the chondrules as possible. The mode of genesis, though merely inferential, is perhaps better suited to give a picture of the primitive state than is the metamorphosed state, for the formative influences seem to have been more environmental than mineralogic.

INTERNAL VERSUS ENVIRONMENTAL INFLUENCES

The general nature of isolated chondrules is shown, greatly enlarged, in Figures 40, 41, and 42, and their frag-

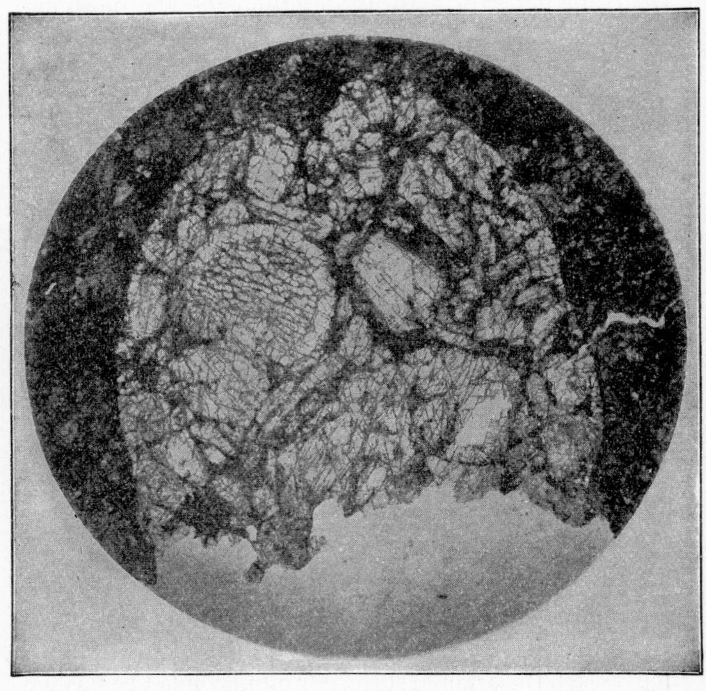

FIG. 43.—Enlarged section of the Dhurmsala meteorite, showing a large chondrule inclosing a smaller one of different structure. (After Tschermak. Engraving from Henry Holt and Company.)

mental condition in Figures 43 and 44. Ample descriptions may be found in the writings of Farrington, Merrill, and Olivier. Only those features that bear on their genesis and their cosmic relations can be cited here. In interpreting their origin and history, a distinction is to be observed between *ac*cretions, in which minute scattered matter of various kinds is merely gathered into spherules,

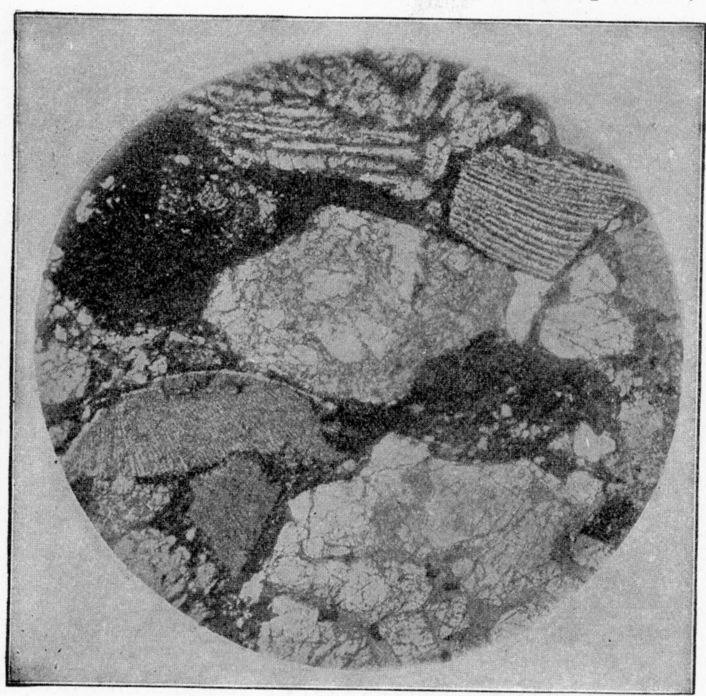

FIG. 44.—A microscopic section of the Mezo-Madaras meteorite, showing a heterogeneous mixture of chondrulitic fragments of various sorts. Portions of bronzite, chrysolite, and nickel-iron chondrulites can be recognized. (After Tschermak. Engraving from Henry Holt and Company.)

and *con*cretions, in which the constituent matter is also arranged in concentric form. These are not inconsistent with one another, and the first often leads to the second, and the second may show successive stages of development, one following the other; but *con*cretions do not usually evolve backward into mixed *ac*cretions.

Originally, all the chondrulites are believed to have been *ac*cretions from highly mixed, probably gaseous, matter, because they contain so many diverse substances in such small compass. If they were *merely* secondary assemblages, they should have had a simpler composition, as crystals and concretions usually do.

But there are also *con*cretions among the chondrules and some of these seem to have been formed originally as concretions, much as hailstones are. The radial chondrules in Figures 40 and 41 look as though they had grown up in free space while in motion, which made the growth eccentric.

But the concretional structure of many of the condrules was certainly formed later, for they inclose fragments of worn bits of chondrules and crystals that must have been earlier formed. It is quite clear that the chondrulitic state, as we now find it in meteorites, was the product of successive stages of fracture and reformation, often with trituration or some kind of wear between. The most typical and instructive forms appear to have had a varied history as chondrules before they and their débris were gathered into the meteorites. The evidence of this lies partly in the varied modes of accretion, partly in the fragmentation and wear after accretion, and partly in the heterogeneousness with which these fragments and worn bits were mixed into the meteorites.

The imperfect forms of many of the crystals inclosed in the chondrules seem to imply that even after the crystals were formed they suffered abrasion, fracture, and like experiences before they were brought into the concretional arrangement. In Figure 43 the inner chondrule seems first to have been well formed as a spherical granular concretion, then to have been broken, and after such breakage, assembled with many other fragments into the larger oval chondrule that occupies the center of the figure. There are many cases of such apparent successions of processes. They seem clearly to imply a rather long and changing formative history. The conditions that permitted this must, apparently, have been very peculiar and should therefore be quite distinctive.

It is of the same import that the chondrules are formed, not of some one susceptible mineral, but of a large variety of mineral species. These include not only crystalline and amorphous silicates but to some extent metallic alloys and compounds, and even glassy pellets. Such a mixed constitution counterindicates simple mineralogic or petrologic action as the characteristic agency in their formation. Of course, such mineralogic and petrologic agencies were important participants in the complex of formative processes.

We seem forced, therefore, to conclude that the formation of the chondrulites, in all their varieties and phases, was due to a prolonged process in which the environmental factor was more essential in the causation of the *distinctive* features than the mineralogical and petrological factors.

THE ORIGIN OF THE CHONDRULITES

The foregoing characteristics of the chondrules, and the associated bodies of their kind included under the broader term "chondrulites," seem to afford conclusive evidences that they were formed prior to the meteorites into which we find them agglomerated in a more or less metamorphosed condition. The characteristics of comets, cited in the next chapter, seem equally to show that the chondrulites were formed prior to their assemblage into cometic swarms.

To enter into the composition of meteorites and at the same time into the formation of cometic swarms seems to imply that the chondrulites were formed from dispersed matter in free motion in open space. These conditions are fundamentally similar to those in which the planetesimals were formed, except that the latter had the help of a passing star. As already noted once, and again to enforce the distinction, the passing star drew the planetesimals into a single disk of concurrently revolving accretions and thus distinguished them dynamically from chondrulites and meteorites which move in heterogeneous orbits. With the previous description of the origin of the planetesimals in mind, the postulated origin of the chondrulites is easily grasped.

From time to time, as is well known, there occur specially vigorous eruptions from the sun. As cited and illustrated in chapter xiii, Pettit has shown that the calcium elements in some of these eruptions received additional impulses *after they left the sun.* The projected calcium matter was flying outward faster at the time it disappeared—doubtless by dispersion and cooling—than when it left the sun.

Whoever looks at Figure 45 cannot fail to be impressed with the vigor of the propulsion that pervades it, however it may be interpreted. The top of this prominence reached an altitude higher by more than 60,000 miles than that from which the tail of the great comet of 1843 is said to have started when that comet was nearest

FIG. 45.—An illustration of vigorous eruption and propulsion 140,000 miles high, photographed at Mount Wilson Observatory, July 9, 1917. The little white disk in the lower right-hand corner shows the relative size of the earth.

the sun. Here, then, is an overlap of two leading kinds of evidence of solar repellency, the eruptive and propulsative actuation of the prominences and the driving off of comets' tails. That this repellency is only selective is made manifest by the fact that the comet head itself continued to pursue its elliptical orbit under the force of the sun's gravity. Comets thus show that one part of their substances, that which forms their permanent heads, follows the laws of gravity without sensible deviation under the repellency of the sun; while another part, the selected matter that forms their tails, is driven off by influences that emanate from the sun and are effective in spite of the sun's gravity.

In the vigorous solar eruptions the material projected and propelled from the sun is at first hot and gaseous; but by reason of its divergent projection, its intrinsic expansion, and its radiation, as it sweeps out into interplanetary space, it is rapidly cooled below the volatile temperatures of the main materials that make up the chondrulites. These are thereby forced to form precipitates, and these in turn naturally aggregate as they are forced against one another by the agitation in the projected mass. The minute accretions thus first formed are interpreted as the primitive chondrulites. They are supposed to have embraced practically all kinds of matter precipitated. As these were formed in open space under high motion and actuated by inheritances from the collisional action of the solar gases, the chondrulites were themselves subject to sharp collisions. These interpretations seem fully to explain the fragmental and triturated conditions that prevail. The scattered and mixed states of the fragments is clear evidence that the chondrulites were not formed in place.

REFERENCES

1. O. C. Farrington, *Meteorites, Their Structures, Compositions and Terrestrial Relations* (1915).

2. George P. Merrill, *Metamorphosis of Meteorites*, XXXII (1921), 385; author of many original descriptions of meteorites.

3. C. P. Olivier, *Meteors* (1925), "Classified Number of Meteorite Falls," p. 240; "Citation 254—Origin of Meteorites," pp. 255–72.

4. T. C. Chamberlin, "Brief Early Statement of the Chondrulite Theory of the Origin of Meteors, Meteorites and Comets," *Carnegie Institution of Washington, Year Book No. 19* (1920), p. 380.

5. T. C. Chamberlin, "Diastrophism and the Formation Processes. XIII. The Bearing of the Size and Rate of Infall of Planetesimals on the Molten or Solid State of the Earth," *Journal of Geology*, XXIII (1920), 696–701.

6. T. C. Chamberlin, "The Cometary System," *Carnegie Institution of Washington, Year Book No. 26* (1926–27), pp. 342–44.

CHAPTER XXX

THE ORIGIN AND CONSTITUTION OF COMETS

In the early stages of the projection and propulsion of the hot solar gases that were to form chondrulites, the conditions were highly dispersive, as in the formation of planetesimals. But the active dispersive influences were soon exhausted, and further dispersion depended on the courses which each unit had attained previously and on the new influences that arose within the outer zones into which the chondrulites were propelled. There was no passing star to pull the projectiles back after they had passed it and to switch them into orbits. We seem, therefore, only to be following the logic of the case and the evidence of the comets' tails, in supposing that they sped out into the outer zones of the solar domain (chap. iv), far beyond the zone of the great planets.

Meanwhile, the propulsatory influences of solar radiation—and probably allied propulsatory influences—had been suffering reduction on account of absorption by intervening matter. On the other hand, the backward pull of gravity had been increasing relatively by reason of this same intervening matter. Thus the ratio of these opposing influences had been constantly changing in favor of gravity. It is a logical inference that the chondrulites soon came to lose speed and that when they reached the outermost zone of the sun's domain, as defined in chapter iv, their outward flights were gradually slackened until most of them, or at least many of them, were stopped altogether and turned about toward the sun. At the same

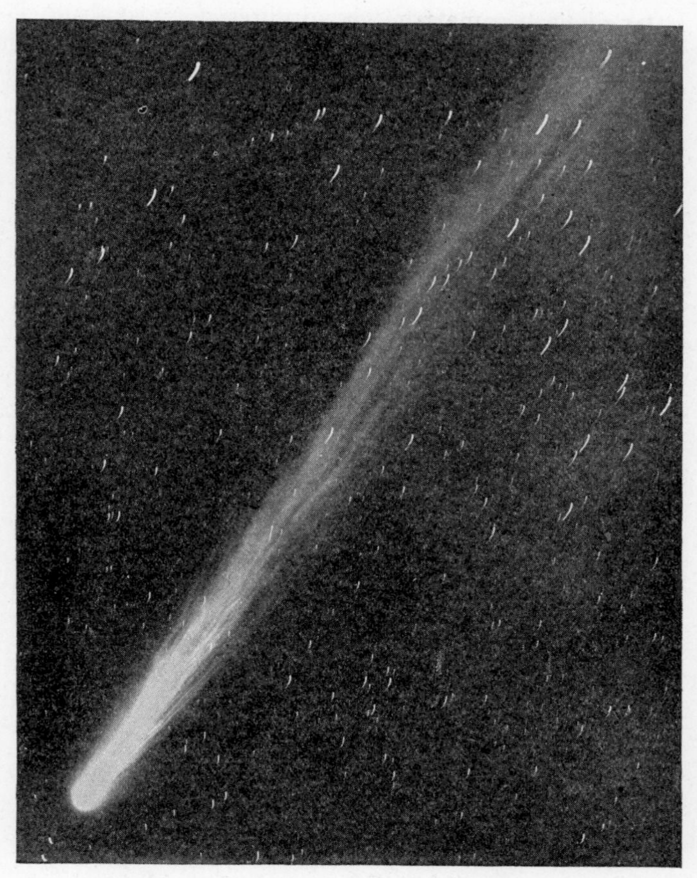

FIG. 46.—Morehouse Comet, 1908. Photograph by E. E. Barnard, furnished by E. B. Frost, director of Yerkes Observatory.

time, the accretions had been growing, and some of them had passed from the smaller sizes subject to solar repellency to the larger sizes subject to gravity instead. These latter alone became true chondrulites, for chondrulites fall toward the sun in spite of solar repellency. The chondrulites were thus a product of selection, as was the case of planetesimals; but they would only become such by growth as they were projected from the sun and grew by accretion.

As soon, therefore, as any given accretion reached a certain stage of growth, it began to be pulled back by the solar attraction in spite of the enfeebled repellency that continued to act on it.

We have, then, from this time on, only to deal with such accretions as had become subject to solar gravity. These slowed down gradually in the outer zones, practically to zero; turned about; and started sunward, at first very slowly.

In addition to the effects of absorption and growth, the counterpush of the radiation from the stars outside set in, as previously shown (chap. iv), before the sun's gravitation was overmatched by stellar pull. This radial counterpush was constantly increasing and played a part in restricting the number of even the smallest accretions that might otherwise have escaped from the sun's control.

RELATIVE INCREASE OF THE CHONDRULITIC ATTRACTIONS

Another and rather subtle factor entered the combination of forces in this outermost zone. In addition to the fact that the inertia of the chondrulites had become almost zero by the slowing down of their motions, the attraction of the sun in this zone had become relatively very feeble, because the sun was so far away; while the attraction of the chondrulites for one another was relatively great because of nearness to one another. They could assemble in this zone more freely than when they were in high motion and under strong solar pull in the inner zones.

THE FORMATION OF SWARMS OF CHONDRULITES

Under these conditions it seems inevitable that swarms of chondrulites should gather by mutual attraction whenever their slow motions were mutually concurrent, but not as a rule, when their motions were opposite or transverse. The swarms would thus be a selective product: they would include only a part of the chondrulites. Those that had mutually antagonistic or transverse motions would mainly remain independent and follow individual orbits of their own. These independent chondrulites encountering our atmosphere would form our everyday sporadic shooting-stars.

CHONDRULITE SWARMS EQUAL COMET HEADS

Those chondrulites that did assemble into swarms would form a mechanism in every way suited for functioning as heads of comets. These would be open assemblages in which each chondrulite would follow its own path about the center of gravity of the assemblage, while the assemblage as a whole responded to the gravity of the sun. Such a mechanism originating in such a situation seems to elucidate in the happiest way the peculiar behavior of comets.

THE CHARACTERISTICS AND BEHAVIOR OF COMETS

That comets' heads have a very open structure is implied by their strangely small masses; the visibility of stars through many thousand miles of cometary matter; and the absence of refraction, which shows that they are not gaseous, as does also the driving off of the tails. That the component bodies are very small is implied by the meteor showers that arise from their residue when disintegrated, of which we shall hear more presently.

There is commonly a concentration of the comet toward the center, which, when present, is called a nucleus. This is perhaps the part which remains persistently under the mutual control of the swarm, while the thinner and vaguer part outside may be the overflow described later and known as the coma. A nucleus is not always present, and the whole comet head is not infrequently broken up and separated when near the sun. The whole comet is liable to be dispersed, if forced to sweep about the sun for a long period in short orbits, as is the case of some of the comets subjugated by Jupiter and the other great planets.

But here, as in so many cases, the dynamic factor carries the most decisive evidence. The comets usually shrink as they approach the sun, and expand again as they retire from it. This is so peculiar and distinctive a phenomenon as practically to demonstrate that the head is formed of small bodies in very slow revolution about their mutual center of gravity. The attraction of the sun acts as though its mass were concentrated at its center, and hence the lines of attraction issuing from this point to the individual constituents of the cometic swarm *have small components directed toward the center of the swarm* (see Fig.

47). These special centripetal components are additional to the centripetal components of the mutual attractions

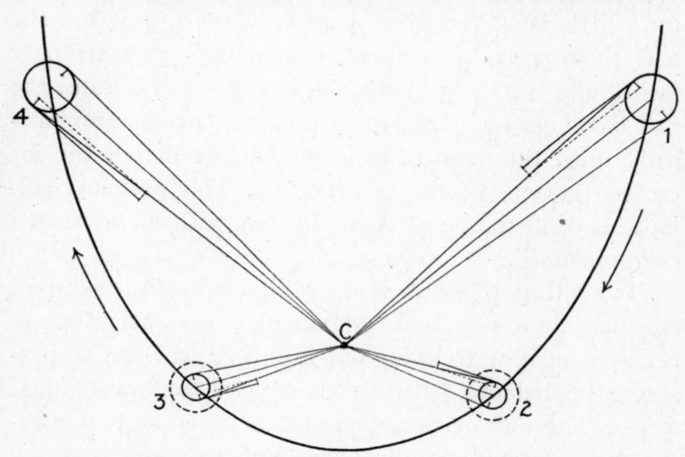

FIG. 47.—Diagram illustrating the shrinking of the head of a comet on approaching the sun, and its restoration on retreat from the sun, made on the assumption that the comet head is a swarm of chondrulites revolving about their common center of gravity. *C* represents the center of the sun, from which its attraction may be regarded as proceeding as from a point. The four circles, 1, 2, 3, and 4, represent four positions of the comet's head during its perihelion loop. The lines radiating from *C* represent the directions of solar gravity. As the comet approaches the sun, there is a small component of the outer lines of solar attractions that is directed toward the center of the comet's head, as represented at position 1 by the parallelogram of forces. At position 2 this is represented as having caused the shrinkage from the outer to the inner circle. This shrinkage has caused an acceleration of the motion of the chondrulites. This accelerated motion restores the comet's head to its former size, theoretically, for the inward component of the sun's attraction declines as the comet gets farther and farther away.

of the constituents. The very slow revolutions of the constituents develop slight centrifugal forces so adjusted automatically to the centripetal components (mutual attraction) as to balance them and keep the constituents deployed, as they are seen to be at any given instant, save for a little lag. As a given comet swarm approaches the sun, these special centripetal components grow stronger (see Fig. 47), the head shrinks in consequence, and the rate of revolution of the constituents increases automatically until their centrifugal components match the increased gravity of the constituents. This prevents collapse beyond the point of equilibrium with the increased components.

In retiring, the centerward component of the sun-pull declines; the centrifugal component of revolution causes each chondrulite to swing out into a larger orbit to preserve the balance between centripetal and centrifugal forces. This automatic adjustment between mutual gravity and solar pull by shrinkage and expansion, as the comet follows its orbit, seems scarcely less than a specific confirmation of the dynamic mechanism assigned the heads of comets.

OVERFLOW OF THE COMETARY SPHERES OF CONTROL

The spheres of control of the comets over their own constituents, as against the sun, not only shrink as the sun is approached, and expand again as the comet retires, but they shrink and expand faster than do the swarms, for the spheres of control reach zero before the sun is reached. If, therefore, the head of a comet just filled its sphere of control when most distant from the sun, the border of control will shrink within the outer part of the swarm. This outside part is no longer controlled by the cometic mass but each constituent proceeds on an independent course under the direct control of the sun.

This state of overflow appears to be a common condition of comets' heads in the inner environment of the sun where we see them. Many of them seem to be too large to be controlled by the gravity of the assemblage alone.

Such shrinkages of the spheres of control within the limits of the comets' comas make clear the liability of comets to lose part of their constituents while making close approaches to the sun.

THE ORBITS OF COMETS

It is important to distinguish between the normal primary orbits of comets and such secondary orbits as may be imposed upon them by the great planets. When not otherwise specified, the former are to be understood in this discussion. These primitive orbits are all very narrow and all very long, while all their perihelia, so far as known, are relatively close to the sun. They are either all very elongated ellipses or depart from ellipses only slightly in being parabolic or hyperbolic. Such departures are probably only temporary deviations due to the attraction of the planets. It is very significant that *radical* departures from elliptical orbits are not known. If comets came from without the solar system, their orbits should not only be hyperbolic but very diversely so; and they should often be very highly hyperbolic. As such orbits are either absent or extremely rare, the assignment of comets to an outside origin is definitely counterindicated. The *slightness* of the modification of the highly elliptical orbits in the direction of parabolic and hyperbolic orbits is really a *criterion*. It points to *the zone of origin* of the comets. The zone could not have been outside the outer reaches of the solar domain without giving more distinctly hyperbolic orbits, as a rule. It could not have been inside these zones without revealing its inability to give the observed high velocities toward the sun. It therefore could scarcely have been elsewhere than in the outer zones of the sun's domain.

THE SHORT AXES OF THE COMETARY ORBITS

For a complete explanation of normal cometic orbits, it is necessary to show how the short transverse axes arose. This leads to the recognition of a new phase of the method of dynamic encounter without bodily contact, in addition to, and different from, that which is made the basis of the planetesimal hypothesis of the origin of the planets. This phase is distinctly novel, and it is not strange that it was not detected sooner.

The propulsion of chondrulites into the outermost zones of the sun's domain gave them a position from which not only the great lengths of their elliptical orbits could be derived but also the potential energy of position necessary to give rise to the observed velocities of fall toward the sun. But if no other influence had come into action, the chondrulites would have fallen straight back into the sun and no orbits at all would have been formed. It seems inevitable, however, that during the long period occupied by the chondrulites in slowing down, stopping, and getting under way on the return, they would have been drawn sidewise by some inequality in the attractions of the stars outside whose distribution and motions are known to be irregular. This transverse deviation may have arisen from individual stars or from adjacent star clusters, or the inequalities of the galaxy, or, as is not improbable, from combinations of these. By reason of such transverse deviations they would, on return, have missed the sun by some small measure and would have swung into very narrow elliptical orbits about it. This applies alike to isolated and to assembled chondrulites. The great comet of 1843 is said to have missed the sun by about 78,000 miles only in a fall of many billions of miles. It serves to show how little relative side-pull was necessary to throw the comet into an elliptical orbit in lieu of plunging directly into the sun. Many other great comets have missed the sun by similar short distances. No comets are known to have very distant perihelia. When the long time taken by the chondrulites in making their outer turns is duly considered, this interpretation does not seem to lay any strain on the deviating possibilities of outside inequalities of attraction. It seems rather that the side-pulls might well have been greater, and perhaps they were greater, for there may be comets whose perihelia are so far away from the sun that we never see them.

Both in the matter of potential energy of fall and in that of lateral deviation, the interpretation closely fits the requirements of the case. It is but another application of the principle of dynamic influence without bodily contact.

THE COMETIC SWING BETWEEN FRIENDLY AND HOSTILE REGIONS

During their long sojourn in the outer zones of the sun's domain, comets creep through a vast cold realm in which gases and other substances are inert to the last degree, and they are specially subject to absorption, adsorption, and other forms of coherence by contact. Most of the motions in this region must be very slow, the collisions very gentle, so that the conditions are friendly to such organizations as are favored by condensation. Sterile as the region seems to us, it may well be good feeding ground for comets. They should there have loaded up themselves with gases to an extent they could not retain under the hot conditions near the sun. They may well also have attached to themselves fine solid particles (trituration dust, perhaps) which they could not hold near the sun. Electric charges may have played some notable part in aggregation in this supremely dry cold region. These charges may later have played an important part in the dispersion of gases and dust in the region of the sun.

Moving slowly out of this zone of darkness and inertness, the comets gradually gain speed and at length plunge swiftly into the increasing heat and light of the sun's immediate environment. Their absorbed and adsorbed gases are then driven out; their trituration dust shaken off; new dust may be made by the unwonted agitation of the constituent chondrulites in this inner zone. The dynamic bonds that held the chondrulites together as a swarm are there weakened and sometimes wholly destroyed. In this enfeebled state, the comets are subjected to adverse pulls by the planets and to selective repellencies emanating from the sun—conditions very strongly contrasted with those of the extreme outer ends of their orbits.

The whole history of a comet is thus a seesaw between conditions favorable to accessions and conditions that forced discharge of the most minutely divided matter and even the dispersion of the cometary swarm itself.

Whenever a comet, in approaching the sun, comes within the effective attraction of a planet, its speed is almost sure to be increased at first by forward pull, and to be retarded later by backward pull. The comet's path is thus almost certain to be changed. It may become parabolic or hyperbolic in some small degree and for a time, on the one hand, or it may become a shortened and broadened ellipse on the other. Jupiter is credited with having shortened the orbits of quite a little family of comets; their aphelia now have about the same distance from the sun as its own orbit. Comets thus subjugated and forced to swing round and round within the hostile solar region suffer seriously in the loss of tail-producing power and in a tendency toward disintegration. The chief source of this appears to be the shrinkage of the comet's sphere of control every time it closely approaches the sun, leaving some of the chondrulites outside the limits of control. Such shrinkage of the sphere of control may go so far as to leave a large part, or even the whole head, outside. The constituents are then pulled out into a train. The subjugated comets are soon seen to lose their tails and to diminish gradually until they finally disappear as comets. After this they are traceable only by the meteor showers to which they give rise when the earth crosses the trains formed by their scattered constituents. Disintegration of this sort seems to be the natural course of comets after they are compelled to revolve persistently in the hostile inner environment of the sun. Those that are permitted to return to their native feeding field probably reorganize and reload themselves and have longer lives.

THE TESTIMONY OF THE DISINTEGRATED RESIDUE OF COMETS

The products of their disintegration give decisive testimony as to the constitution of comets' heads. As already noted, the trains into which the disintegrated comets pass give rise to "meteor showers." These have been watched with more than ordinary interest for a century. In all that time it does not appear that a single bolide has been seen to come from among the multitudes of shooting-stars and survive the vaporization of atmospheric friction until it reaches the ground, thus to demonstrate decisively that meteorites are among the constituents of comets' heads. This is not a demonstration that there are none there, but it does seem to imply that they are too few to have any important function in the constitution of comets.

THE TALE OF THE TAIL

Is it a lingering residue of former frightfulness that has bereft us of the wit to see the plainest of plain imports brought to us year after year by the tails of the comets? Nothing could be plainer, and few things more spectacular, than the story they tell of the hostility of the great inner zone about the sun to free molecules and trituration dust. Free molecules and fine particles are forced out from the comets' heads and driven directly away from the sun at high velocities. The free molecules include at least carbon monoxide, cyanogen, sodium, and iron, whose molecular weights are high enough to indicate notable range and power of repellency. The paths of the comets have traversed all essential parts of the inner of the four zones defined in chapter iv. While we certainly would like to know just what the mechanism of this repellency is, that is not so material as the fact that repellency of this order affects thus decisively these minute substances in the zone to which the terrestrial planets belong.

The demonstration is twofold. Gases and fine dust do not loiter in this inner field. They are only held there by adequate counterforce, such as the gravity of the earth and of Venus, and feebly the gravity of Mars, but not the gravity of the moon or of Mercury. On the other hand, the comet tails do show that molecules and very fine particles are driven freely across the space between the sun and the inner planets. The overlap of the tail-traversed zone and the zone of solar eruption and propulsion covers the whole inner environment of the sun. The tale of the tail is thus a sweeping story, literally and figuratively.

REFERENCES

1. F. R. Moulton, *An Introduction to Astronomy* (1916), "Comets," pp. 313–22, 442.

2. J. C. Duncan, *Astronomy* (1926), pp. 258–65.

3. T. C. Chamberlin, "The Cometary System," *Carnegie Institution of Washington, Year Book No. 26* (1926–27), pp. 342–44.

CHAPTER XXXI

THE PLACE OF METEORITES IN THE COMETARY FAMILY

In any discussion of serious genetic import, it is necessary to distinguish three classes of small bodies that habitually swing around the sun in planetary space: first, those that revolve concurrently in a narrow disk and are thereby fitted to collect into planets—the planetesimals; second, those that follow heterogeneous courses and are thereby unfitted to form planets, though they may gather into bodies of smaller size and of discordant dynamics—the chondrulites, the assigned source of shooting-stars; and third, those bolides which plunge through our atmosphere and subject themselves to intimate study—the meteorites. In this discussion I shall eschew the indiscriminate use of the term "meteorite" and confine it to the well-known and fully described class of bodies whose place and functions now become a definite question.

METEORITES MERELY AGGLOMERATES OF CHONDRULITES

The relations of meteorites to chondrulites have already been implied in the main by the citation of the simple fact that the stony meteorites, and presumably the metallic meteorites, are largely made up of chondrules, chondrule fragments, and allied units embraced in the broad term "chondrulites." This in itself indicates that

meteorites are agglomerates of chondrulites. That the latter had a peculiar history of fracture and recementation, attended by gain and loss, and by chemical and physical metamorphism, is also implied. As already cited, the chondrules bear decisive evidence that they underwent a series of changes in the process of their formation. They were not only broken, but in reformation, instead of simple recementation of the original fragments in place, there was also an assemblage of alien fragments (Figs. 40–44), showing both loss and gain between breakage and recementation.

A similar history of change, presumably in free open conditions, seems to have run without break into the processes of aggregation that formed the meteorites. They show, as do the chondrulites, successive breakages and separation, with loss and gain and mixture. This seems to imply the same open conditions attended by sharp collisions, with subsequent reaggregation and recementation. The materials are often brecciated, carry veins, are slickensided, and bear other indication of a varied and peculiar diastrophic history.

The question of their relative importance in the cometary family and the solar system is not, however, settled by these evidences of the mode of their formation. If all or most of the chondrulites had been gathered into meteorites these might have had a commanding place in their family and perhaps even in the solar system.

THE RELATIVE UNIMPORTANCE OF METEORITES

There are three lines of evidence bearing specifically on the relative importance of meteorites: the testimony of disintegrated comets; the relative fewness of meteoritic falls compared with shooting-stars; and the absence of individual bodies *of meteoritic dynamics* large enough to be seen outside the earth's domain, even telescopically.

THE NEGATIVE EVIDENCES OF METEOR SHOWERS

There is now no reason to doubt that comets disintegrate and that the disintegrated constituents give rise to meteor showers. The units of these showers present all the characteristics of shooting-stars. The short-lived streaks of the shooting-stars are such as would be formed by bodies of the chondrulite order plunging into the upper zone of our atmosphere and suffering vaporization almost in an instant. The only peculiarity of the "showers" is the frequency of the streaks and their radiation from some point in the orbit of the disintegrated comet. These showers have already been cited as evidence that comets' heads are swarms of chondrulites, not of meteorites in the strict sense.

Now, as already urged, it is a remarkable fact that although these showers have been under close observation for about a century, they are not known to have demonstrated the presence of a single bolide large enough to function as a meteorite, and massive enough to endure the vaporization of the atmosphere and bring a residue to the earth's surface. And yet such a demonstration has been an expected result and still remains so, the presumption being that in time a true meteorite will show itself and prove that it was once a constituent of a cometary swarm. But the negative testimony of the meteor showers seems to imply decisively that large agglomerations of chondrulites do not take place frequently under the conditions that prevail at the assembling of the comets' heads.

In certain respects the conditions that prevailed at the formation of comets' heads, as here interpreted, were distinctly favorable for chondrulitic agglomeration. The motions assigned the chondrulites in the outer zones of the solar domain were relatively slow and their mutual attractions relatively great. In the comets' heads when formed, the motions were measurably concordant and favorable to aggregation.

On the other hand, all the chondrulites, whatever their compositions, were extremely cold while in the outer zones, and hence more brittle and elastic than they were when near the sun. Hence, rebound and fragmentation may well have been the order of the day in this frigid outer zone, while welding may have been very limited, though gaseous absorption may have been enhanced by the low temperature.

THE PROPORTIONS OF METEORITES TO CHONDRULITES IN THE TERRESTRIAL REGION

Bearing in mind that the position of the earth is relatively close to the sun, we may catch a logical hint by comparing the proportions of meteorites to chondrulites in this region, as shown by their plunges into our atmosphere. Olivier gives the number of meteorites *seen* to fall in the twelve decades from 1800 to 1920. The falls seen during the first three decades of the nineteenth century are relatively few, doubtless because the number of recording observers was few and because their distribution covered only a small part of the earth. But combining the remaining nine decades from 1830 on, the average number of meteorites seen to fall per year was only 3.7. In the last sixty years it was 4.2 per year. Olivier thinks that when full allowance is made for the uninhabited areas of ocean, desert, forest and the polar regions, the real number of falls may reach 1 a day. The standard estimate of shooting-stars is 20,000,000 per day. The chondrulites are much smaller than the meteorites, but, as we have urged, not indefinitely smaller, since the chondrulites are governed by gravity and not by solar repellency. Present data are insufficient for any final conclusion as to the relative masses of chondrulites and meteorites that enter our atmosphere in any given period. They seem, however, to make it clear that *the ratio of meteorites to chondrulites is much greater in the environs of the earth than in the heads of comets.*

This leads to the view that, while chondrulites are highly dominant in comets' heads, meteorites are *relatively* more abundant near the sun, however sparse in reality.

The first suggestion that arises from this is that meteorites are relatively concentrated toward the sun. This is inherently probable from their density and collisional habits. But meteorites must have been *formed* before they could be concentrated, and so the second suggestion is that the meteorites were mainly aggregated in the close environment of the sun. The aid of a formative process seems to be required. This is close at hand when the suggestion is once made.

If the extreme cold of the outer region explains the paucity of meteorites in comets' heads because of the greater fragility and non-coherence of the chondrulites there, why should not the opposite effects of softening and viscousness due to heating near the sun explain the agglutination of chondrulitic material into meteorites at the inner ends of their long orbits? Does not this also offer a plausible explanation of the segregation of the nickel-iron into considerable masses, because welding would take place more freely with metallic masses than with stony material? Let us follow up this hint.

By the chondrulitic hypothesis of the genesis of the cometary family, all its members—chondrulites, comets, and meteorites—had orbits of the same extremely elliptical type at the outset. They were subject to the same modifications by the planets later. At first, then, all had perihelia close to the sun. This had two effects, high heating and relatively frequent collision, for chondrulites and meteorites alike were concentrated near the sun at the inner end of their orbits but very widely deployed at the outer ends. The vapors of sodium have been detected in some comets when near the sun. It may therefore be assumed that at each perihelial passage the material of the chondrulites was softened and that the metallic elements in particular became quite susceptible of adhesion when they collided. This helped on the agglomerative process by which the meteorites as a class were formed, and was especially effective in segregating the alloys into metallic meteorites. There must have been a graduation of temperature conditions from the hot regions of the sun to the frigid outer regions, and so all kinds of effects between the hot softness of one end and the rigidity of the other end should appear in the broad record of the genus.

Figures 48 and 49 show how intimate the relations of

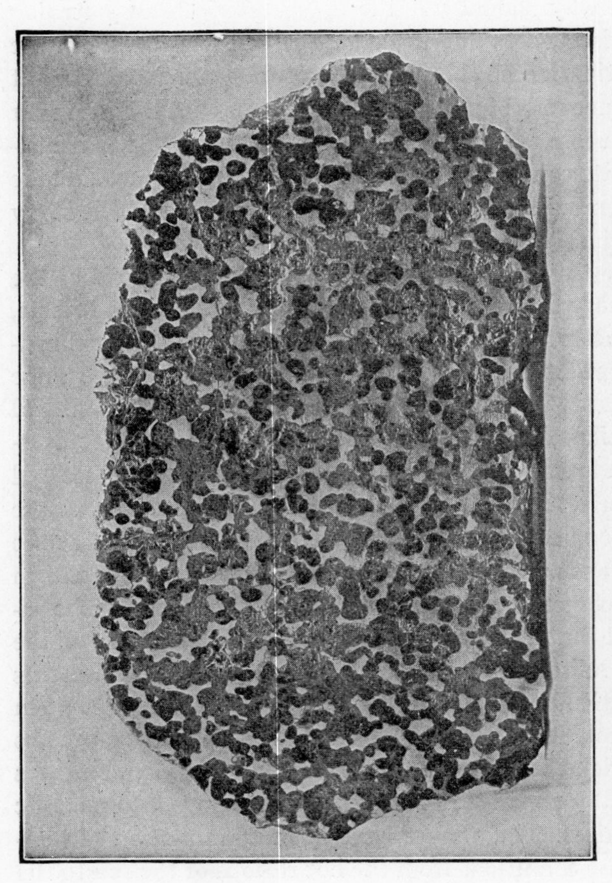

FIG. 48.—A section of the Brenham, Kansas, meteorite, showing an intimate mixture of nickel-iron (the light-colored portion) and silicate compounds (the dark-colored portion). (Ward-Coonley Collection. Engraving from Henry Holt and Company.)

FIG. 49.—A section of a part of the Brenham, Kansas, meteorite, showing, in close relations, a coarse crystallization of nickel-iron and an intersegregation of metallic and non-metallic material, implying that the same general conditions affected both kinds of segregation. (Ward-Coonley Collection. Engraving from Henry Holt and Company.)

the metallic and stony constituents sometimes are and how difficult it is to suppose that the metallic element had any other origin than the stony part.

FIG. 50.—A section of the Mount Joy meteorite formed of nickel-iron lumps, giving the mass a brecciated or semi-conglomeratic appearance. The lumps have, however, been interpreted as crystalline segregates. (By courtesy of O. C. Farrington.)

Figure 49 is especially instructive by showing that intimate mixture is closely associated with almost complete segregation of the metallic part.

Figure 50 seems on its face to show that agglomeration of small metallic lumps really takes place, but Farrington finds that there is common orientation between some of these apparently separate lumps and infers that the appearance of an agglomerate arose from crystalline segregation. The specimen has not yet been put to the crucial test of separate analyses of the lumps.

During their whole lives the chondrulites and meteorites were swinging from the hot ends to the cold ends of their orbits and from the cold ends to the hot ends of their orbits. Probably, also, they rotated more or less and thus suffered rather rapid changes of temperature from the sun's action. It is thus easy to picture a meteorite growing up amid gains and losses, among which the coherence of the metallic alloys was greater than that of the stony material.

As this long and complicated process was an alternation of gain and loss, with only a mere preponderance toward permanent aggregation, it is not strange that the admixtures should be highly various and that there should have arisen stony meteorites (aerolites), mixed metallic and stony meteorites (siderolites), and metallic meteorites (siderites), and that these should have graded intimately and intricately into one another.

THEIR DESTINY

The chondrulites and meteorites are, of course, affected by the repellent agencies that emanate from the sun. The chondrulites are affected more than the meteorites because of the higher ratio of their surfaces to their substances. But the inward velocities of chondrulites and meteorites show that both are dominated by solar gravity. As already noted, the chondrulites are therefore not indefinitely small. If their motions relative to one another were concurrent, they might unite with little loss of energy and so build themselves up to large sizes and maintain their places in the solar system. But as their motions are heterogeneous, with a large antagonistic factor, their mutual collisions cause loss of revolutional energy and gradual approach to the sun whence they arose and to which they ultimately seem destined to return. In this the meteorites no doubt take precedence because they are relatively less restrained by solar repellency.

A return of what was earlier shot forth does not imply any gain to the thermal resources of the solar system, but incidentally some loss through the radiation involved. There was some gain, however, from the transverse pull of the stars that gave them the transverse factor of their orbits.

The third argument against the importance of meteorites in the solar system lies in the absence of any large permanent progeny. If bodies of a planetary size, or even of a planetoidal or satellite size, grew from the meteorites, they would have the combined energies and momenta of the constituents that formed them, and these would betray their origin. No such body in the whole vast solar domain has thus far been discovered, even with the advantages of modern telescopes and photography. Until such a product of meteoritic aggregation is discovered, we may well strike meteorites out of the list of planet-producers. But we must credit both meteorites and chondrulites with small additions to the substance of the planets, and this may have more importance as a minute addition to planetary soils than has heretofore been recognized.

CHAPTER XXXII

SECONDARY OR CHONDRULITIC PLANETESIMALS

It is generally believed that the soft glows known as the zodiacal light and the gegenschein, or counterglow, are reflections from a disk of scattered matter lying in or near the plane of the planetary disk and extending outward from the sun to an undetermined distance beyond the earth. Its discoidal form and planetary position give it a planetesimal aspect; but it does not seem sufficient to class it simply as a planetesimal residue, even if one is inclined to think that a residue of the original planetesimal disk remains. We have just seen that solar repellency is a declared force that must be reckoned with. The particles that reflect the zodiacal light must clearly have better staying qualities than the free molecules and dust driven away from comets. This, however, of itself does not exclude planetesimals, chondrulites, or meteorites. But neither chondrulites nor meteorites, of themselves, should be assembled in the plane of the planets, nor have a special relation to the earth, such as that of the counterglow, always directly opposite the sun. At best, the zodiacal light is only a faint glow, usually unnoticed except under favorable conditions; while only a few people have eyes good enough to see the gegenschein. The glow deepens toward the sun and this gives the section we see a wedge-like form, 20° or 30° wide near the sun but only 3° or 4° wide where it passes the earth. The greater distinctness of the glow near the sun seems to imply that it has some rather definite relation to the sun. The planetary system has its greatest mass at the distance of Jupiter and tapers toward the sun, ending in a quite attenuated edge at Mercury. So, too, the gegenschein, an oval patch of faint glow always directly opposite from the sun, seems to imply that the distribution of the material that reflects the glow is in some way dependent on the earth. It thus appears that though the scattered matter has a definite planetary relationship, it does not have the same distribution as the original planetesimals.

Moulton's interpretation of the gegenschein, which we accept, makes it an eddy or whirlpool of planetesimal-like particles caused by the joint influence of the sun and the earth. By similar action there should be similar eddies opposite Mercury and Venus; as also, opposite Mars and the outer planets, if the zodiacal disk reaches so far.

If we extend the whirlpool effect to Venus and Mercury, we must also consider whether the disk-forming process (to which we have assigned the assembling of satellite disks about the equators of Jupiter, Saturn, and Uranus [chap. xxiv]) would not also come into function here. It seems altogether logical to conclude that, if the zodiacal particles revolve about the sun in planetary fashion, as they seem to do, they should be assembled into disks attending the earth, Venus, and Mercury. This, at least, may serve as a working hypothesis to open up the dynamic questions that seem to lie back of the zodiacal glow. These postulated disks would be so superposed in the line of our vision as to have escaped detection thus far, but perhaps they may not be beyond detection by more refined scrutiny directed to that end.

If we thus satisfy what seem to be the requirements of the mechanics of the case by postulating three subdisks, centered respectively on the orbital planes of the earth, Venus, and Mercury, with an eddy back of each planet, we must face the question: How should such disks arise in the natural evolution of the planetary and cometary systems as now interpreted?

ASSIGNED ORIGIN OF THE ZODIACAL PARTICLES

It is unnecessary to consider seriously any notion that the zodiacal matter is formed of gas or free molecules, for the testimony of the comets' tails stands sharply opposed to any such view. In this close inner environment of the sun, the only tenable hypothesis seems to be that these particles are accretions of the chondrulitic or planetesimal type, massive and dense enough to withstand the repelling influences that emanate from the sun.

We do not need to build up any new hypothesis. We have already urged that chondrulites are formed by cooling and accretion from occasional solar eruptions and propulsions, and that this has been the mode of their formation during the whole history of the cometary system. We have now merely to add that certain of these chondrulites were shot near enough to Mercury, Venus, and the earth to be caught by their attractions and swung into special orbits related to these planets individually, just as comets have been caught and swung into orbits related to Jupiter and other large planets (see Fig. 51). The essential feature of these new orbits is that their aphelia are near the orbit of the planet that captures them. In this case the earth, Venus, and Mercury should each capture and assemble a multitude of chondrulites whose aphelia are near the orbits of these planets and whose perihelia are nearer the sun and of course on the opposite side.

Such captured and subjugated chondrulites would thus take on the dynamic characters of planetesimals of

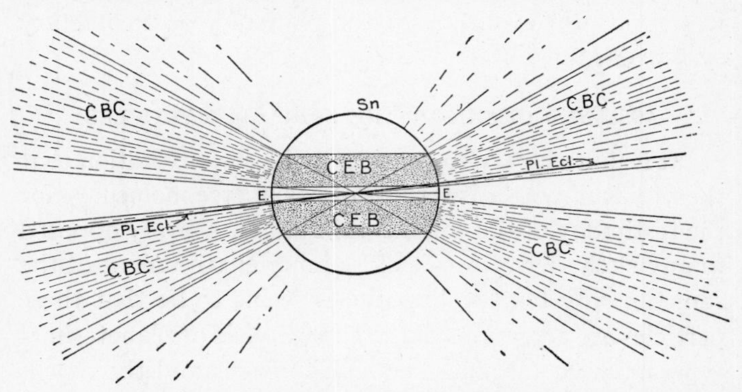

FIG. 51.—Diagram illustrating the probable distribution of chondrulites. *CEB*, chief eruptive belt of the sun. *CBC*, chief belt of chondrulites.

a rather special order, that is, *planetesimals made such by planets previously formed.* These would really be planetesimal children of the planets, the other parentage being chondrulitic. It will suffice to distinguish them from the original planetesimals called forth by the passing star if we call them simply *secondary* or chondrulitic *planetesimals*.

If formed in this way, they were thrown into sets by the very process of capture. A somewhat disklike assemblage was thus attained at the outset. All that remained to be done was a fuller organization by the inevitable workings of the disk-forming process set forth in chapter xxiv.

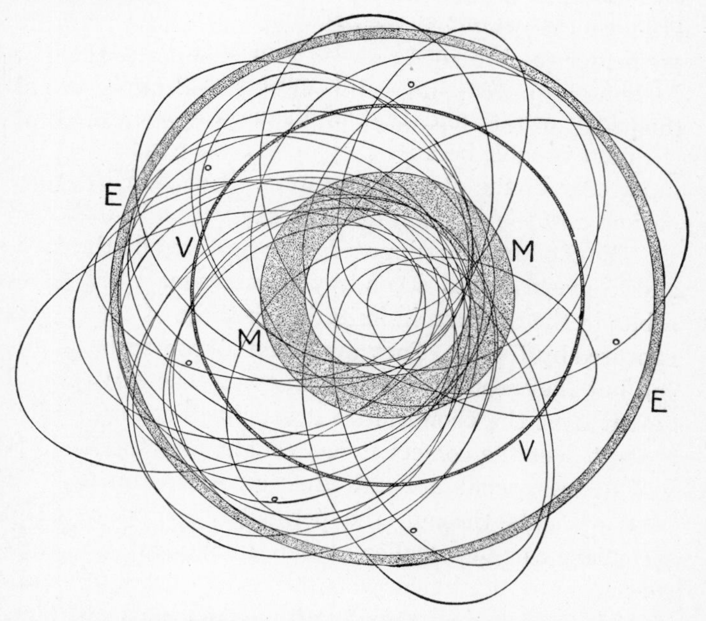

FIG. 52.—Diagram illustrating the hypothetical effect of chondrulitic planetesimals on the orbits of Venus and Mercury.

We may safely assume that the earth as the largest of these inner planets was at least one of the most effective in building up a family of secondary or chondrulitic planetesimals, and that it is best suited to illustrate the results in diagrammatic form. We have attempted this in Figure 52. As each planet may act as a chondrulite catcher in any part of its orbit, and in any stage of precession, *orbit-tracts* are used in the diagram instead of mere orbital lines. These tracts cover the range from the perihelion to the aphelion of each planet. This brings out into clear vision one of the peculiarities of the two innermost planets, the sharp contrast of their eccentricities. The orbit of Mercury is the most eccentric of all the planetary orbits; and that of Venus, the least. This is the more notable because they lie so close together on the inner edge of the planetary system. It challenges explanation, and the diagram makes a suggestion in that line.

The chondrulites supposed to be captured by the earth and converted into secondary planetesimals are given orbits in the diagram in imitation of those of the comets captured by Jupiter. They would not, of course, be identical, but they would be similar in type. The earth would lord it over the chondrulites it caught, much as Jupiter lords it over the comets it has caught and subdued. It will be seen what a swath the eccentric orbit-tract of Mercury cuts through the perihelial portion of these secondary earth-controlled planetesimal orbits. It is further to be noticed that whensoever an encounter takes place between one of these earth planetesimals and Mercury, the planetesimals are almost invariably moving faster than Mercury. This may be seen to be so by the trend of the orbits at the point of encounter, as explained in chapter xi.

But if the orbit tract of Venus be inspected in the same way, the velocities will be found to be much more equable. May we not then build on this the tentative working hypothesis that the terrestrial chondrulitic planetesimals were one of the agencies, perhaps the decisive agency, in giving Mercury a very eccentric orbit and Venus a very circular orbit? Similar secondary planetesimals would be assembled by Venus and Mercury, but their orbital effects would be less.

If one of these earth-converted chondrulitic planetesimals plunges into Mercury, it makes a small contribution to all the qualities of Mercury's motions, growth-creep, inclination, precession, and all. While almost infinitesimal in any single encounter, the action was recurrent and served as a nearly steady secular force. This opens a new line of inquiry into the possible causes of the outstanding peculiarities of Mercury, as also of Venus, and to some extent of the earth. At the same time, it raises the question whether any solution of the idiosyncracies of these planets can be even presumed to be complete, at least in minute and delicate matters, that does not seriously consider the effects of the zodiacal planetesimal throng in which they have been moving for an unknown era?

This is perhaps as far as it is wise to press this matter on the basis of a naturalistic analysis, until the ground shall be traversed by experts in celestial mechanics. But we are entitled to observe that here, as in many another problem of the natural world, the first and most important function of research is *the disclosure of the actual problem* in its full realities and in all its complexities, for the correct solution of the wrong problem may be the greatest of mistakes.

REFERENCES

1. F. R. Moulton, *An Introduction to Astronomy* (1916), "The Zodiacal Light and Gegenschein," pp. 262–64.

2. T. C. Chamberlin, "The Secondary Planetesimal System, *Carnegie Institution of Washington, Year Book No. 26* (1926–27), p. 345.

CHAPTER XXXIII

THE SUN'S CHILDREN

I

We have thus found that the two solar families were similar in origin but different in development. Both sprang from solar propulsativity acting in co-operation with outside attractions. The co-operation was purely dynamic; there was no material contact in either case; but the co-operation was different in kind and in degree.

II

The planetary family was called into being by a single effective attraction, taken to be a passing star, whose field of force encountered that of the sun merely by their mutual approach. This definite dynamic encounter gave rise to eruptions of large rotating solar bolts propelled in opposite directions from the sun toward and from the star. These were drawn into subcircular orbits by the mutual swing and pull of the sun and the star, as they swept curvingly past one another.

III

The ulterior source of the eruptions that were the first step in the formation of the cometary family is obscure. No stellar stimulus is clearly indicated. But occasional great solar eruptions are matters of observation. Stellar co-operation in the cometary genesis only appeared when the ejected matter reached the outer zones of the sun's domain, and even then it was only just enough to cause the backward-falling matter to miss the sun and swing into very narrow elliptical orbits. This little deviation varied from event to event, and so not only the planes of the orbits but the direction of motion in the planes varied correspondingly. The cometary family is thus not a brood—in the full sense that this is true of the planetary family—but an unrelated succession of independent births.

IV

The passing star exerted a restraining, as well as stimulating, influence. On the one hand, its distortional pull on the sun called forth bolts that became planets. It held them back, on the other hand, from shooting out indefinitely, and pulled them into subcircular orbits about the sun, imparting to them a portion of its own kinetic energy by virtue of which the bolts—and the planets into which they grew—have continued ever since to circle about the sun, and give promise of still doing so for an indefinite eon to come.

V

The solar projectiles that were destined to form comets, instead of being restrained and swinging into orbits in the inner zones of the sun's domain, were permitted to shoot out into the outer reaches of the sun's sphere of control, where the counterpush of light from the stars overmatched the pressure from the sun and aided the solar gravity in restraining further flight and furnishing conditions for the formation of cometary swarms of chondrules, thus giving rise to the breeding zone of the comets.

Restraint thus aided in the formation of the comets, but the method and place, as well as the results, were quite different from the restraint that ended in the formation of the planets.

VI

The planetary bolts, on emerging from the sun, were deployed by selective action into planetesimals in great orbits about the sun and into residual swarms of heavy accretions revolving in open fashion about their common center of gravity. Later both of these assorted products were slowly gathered into planets, planetoids, and satellites. These, evolving concurrently, formed the orderly planetary family.

VII

In an analogous way, the projectiles that were to form the cometary family were assorted into swarms and isolated chondrulites, of which the former later functioned as comet heads and the latter as the source of "shooting stars" and of meteorites. But here, again, the mode of actions followed lines quite other than those that led to the planets.

VIII

The residual swarms of the planetary bolts were relatively massive, moved in a well-adjusted disk in concurrence with one another, and lent aid and supplies to one another and were thus enabled to form solid cores which grew into relatively permanent bodies.

IX

The cometary swarms were less massive, followed isolated courses at variance from one another, were subject to great extremes in passing from one end of their orbits to the other, and suffered much from the adverse pulls of the planets in doing so; and as a result they seem never to have been able to form a permanent growing core.

X

The chondrulites followed very diverse, highly elliptical orbits and were widely separated in the outer reaches of their courses, where they were very cold and brittle and liable to fragmentation if they collided; but in their inner courses near the sun, they were more concentrated, were warmer and softer, more liable to collide and more likely to cohere when in collision. It is held that the hot zone about the sun was the chief place of agglomeration of chondrulites into meteorites.

XI

The marked superiority of the planetary mechanism lay primarily in the endowment of kinetic energy received from the passing star. This was effectively abetted by the concurrent action of the members of the family that arose from the unity of their origin. The planetary family is the type of celestial harmony and orderliness and this insures its internal stability and presumptive longevity.

XII

The weakness of the cometary family lay in the lack of unity in the stellar co-operations and in its feebleness in each particular case. The principle of *unum sed leonem* did not obtain. Instead of one great birth, there were an unknown number of little births. It was most unpromising for each litter of chondrulites that it took its own course and often traversed the paths of the mightier planets as well as those of its own family. They thus worked at cross-purposes both within and without the family. This as surely led to destruction as the harmonies in the planetary family led to construction, and to its great prospective future.

XIII

The cometary mode of evolution is the more general as also the more prolific; the planetary mode of evolution is the more limited and the more effective. The cometary evolution from the sun probably began as soon as the sun became effectively eruptive and propulsatory; it probably has been in function ever since and probably will continue in action for an unknown eon in the future. Its products, for the most part, probably find their final resting place in the sun whence they came.

XIV

The genesis of a planetary family is a much rarer event. Its genetic conditions are very special; its results are correspondingly unique so far as our vision goes; probably they are not at all unique in reality. Rarity of such a nativity is a great asset. A second planetary evolution from a given star would necessarily destroy the previous family. The small likelihood of another star approaching our sun short of an almost unthinkable period is a fundamental factor in a rational prognosis of our planetary future. The symmetry and harmony of our planetary system is specific evidence that no star has come within a seriously disturbing distance since our planetary system was formed. A scrutiny of the heavens shows no impending threat from collision or disruptive approach. Supplementing this fundamental basis for future endurance, the superior massiveness of the system, its vast hidden stores of energy, its conservatism in the expenditure of its energies, and its orderly, harmonious habits combine to give our planetary family an outlook for the future far surpassing that of the current stage of the cometary family. The mechanism of the latter calls for continual renewal.

XIII

It is to the credit of the planetesimal hypothesis that it should have led to the kindred chondrulitic hypothesis of the origin of the cometary kin of the planets. It is to the credit of the chondrulitic hypothesis that it pays back the debt by showing that similar principles, acting under different conditions, elucidate strangely diverse and once terrifying phenomena.

INDEX

INDEX

PRINTED IN U·S·A·